W9-BQT-767

CONSTRUCTING A WORLD

Constructing

A

World

Shakespeare's

England and the

New Historical

Fiction

Martha Tuck Rozett

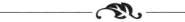

STATE UNIVERSITY OF NEW YORK PRESS

Published by
State University of New York Press, Albany

For information, address State University of New York Press,
90 State Street, Suite 700, Albany, NY 12207

Production by Marilyn P. Semerad
Marketing by Michael Campochiaro

PR
888
H5
R69
2003

Library of Congress Cataloging-in-Publication Data

Rozett, Martha Tuck, 1946–
    Constructing a world : Shakespeare's England and the new historical fiction / Martha
Tuck Rozett.
        p. cm.
    Includes bibliographical references and index.
    ISBN 0–7914–5551–3 (acid-free paper) — ISBN 0–7914–5552–1 (pbk. : acid-free paper)
        1. Historical fiction, English—History and criticism. 2. Great
Britain—History—Elizabeth, 1558–1603—Historiography. 3. Elizabeth I, Queen of
England, 1533–1603—In literature. 4. American fiction—20th century—History and
criticism. 5. English fiction—20th century—History and criticism. 6. Historical fiction,
American—History and criticism. 7. Shakespeare, William, 1564–1616—In literature. 8.
Shakespeare, William, 1564–1616—Adaptations. 9. England—In literature. I. Title.

PR888.H5 R69 2002
823'.0810903—dc21
                                                                                    2002024049

                    10 9 8 7 6 5 4 3 2 1

In Memoriam: Eugene Tuck 1909–2000

Contents

Acknowledgments

arts of chapters 1 and 2 originally appeared as "Constructing a World: How the Postmodern Historical Fiction Reimagines the Past" in *Clio: A Journal of Literature, History and the Philosophy of History* (25.2, Winter 1996); part of chapter 7 originally appeared as "Creating a Context for Shakespeare with Historical Fiction" in *Shakespeare Quarterly* (46.2, Summer 1995); and the Marlowe Society of America kindly invited me to present part of chapter 4 at the meeting of the Modern Language Association in December 2000. I would like to thank the many friends and students who have talked with me about historical fiction over the years and referred me to books and articles I might not otherwise have encountered. I am especially grateful to Cynthia Mahamdi, Candace Murray, Jeffrey Gibson, Carey Cummings, Monica Bishop, David Birch, and Helene Scheck. I would also like to thank the novelists George Garrett and Barry Unsworth for their willingness to discuss the historical novelist's craft. My friends and colleagues Judith Barlow, Randall Craig, and Jennifer Fleischner, and my brother, Jonathan Tuck, read early drafts of the manuscript or parts thereof; I have tried to follow their wise counsel. The staff at the State University of New York Press provided invaluable editorial assistance and, as always, my husband John Rozett was a generous and forbearing resource on technical matters.

Chapter 1

Introduction
Historical Fiction Old and New

*I*n the early 1980s, just as the New Historicists, with their invocation of "the historicity of texts and the textuality of history" were transforming the way readers understood literature, Umberto Eco's novel *The Name of the Rose* became both a critical success and a bestseller. Widely celebrated as a postmodern historical novel, this dazzling mixture of "thick" historical research and popular detective fiction elements invited its readers to view historical fiction as an academically respectable genre, and a vehicle for recovering and reimagining the past in unconventional ways. A few years later, Eco responded to published commentary on his novel in an eclectic text called *Postscript to The Name of the Rose*.[1]

Originally published as an eighty-page mixture of short, fragmentary chapters, photographs, and illustrations of medieval architecture and manuscripts, the *Postscript* is partly a "poetics" designed to "help us understand how to solve the technical problem which is the production of a work" (Eco, *Name of the Rose* 508). Eco explains how the historical fiction writer must become immersed in historical evidence: to tell a story, "you must first of all construct a world, furnished as much as possible, down to the slightest detail" (512). In his case, this required committing himself to a specific date, reading architectural plans and registers of the holdings of medieval libraries, and even counting the steps in a fourteenth-century stairway. Eco's *Postscript* is also a manifesto proclaiming the authority to which serious historical fiction can lay claim: the characters in a historical novel may not appear in

1

encyclopedias, he notes, but everything they do could only occur in that time and place. Made-up events and characters tell us things "that history books have never told us so clearly," so as "to make history, what happened, more comprehensible." By reimagining the past, the novelist thus performs the analytical role of the historian, by "not only identify[ing] in the past the causes of what came later, but also trac[ing] the process through which those causes began slowly to produce their effects" (534). In constructing a world, the novelist also "constructs a reader," for one important difference between serious and formulaic historical fiction, Eco says, is that innovative historical fiction like *The Name of the Rose* "seeks to produce a new reader" whereas formulaic fiction "tries to fulfill the wishes of the readers already to be found in the street" (522–23).

In the years since Eco's novel appeared, a number of contemporary novelists, most of whom are not exclusively or even principally known as writers of historical fiction, have been similarly immersing themselves in the language, the texts, and the material culture of the past, and have produced some remarkable works of fiction. What they share with the New Historicists—and what distinguishes their novels from traditional or "classic" historical fictions and allies them with postmodern fictions—are a resistance to old certainties about what happened and why; a recognition of the subjectivity, the uncertainty, the multiplicity of "truths" inherent in any account of past events; and a disjunctive, self-conscious narrative, frequently produced by eccentric and/or multiple narrating voices. Postmodern fictions frequently play genres off against one another, making fluid the boundaries between novel and autobiography, novel and history, novel and biography, and combining different "registers of discourse," to use Linda Hutcheon's term (such as the mix of literary-historical, theological-philosophical, and popular-detective-fiction discourses in *The Name of the Rose*). At times, Hutcheon adds, such fictions are "formally parodic" in their "critical or ironic re-reading of the past," but as historical fictions, they are nevertheless "modelled on historiography to the extent that [they are] motivated and made operative by a notion of history as a shaping force" (4, 9–10, 23, 113).

Historical fiction as a genre has always borrowed freely from other genres. It shares some characteristics with each of the mass-culture genres—the romance, the western, fantasy, detective fiction—but generally lacks the pronounced formulas and predictable conventions of those genres. Often, historical fictions have masqueraded as exemplars of other literary forms, such as the memoir, the biography, the autobiography, the epistolary novel. In contrast to those historical novelists who employ the conventions of the panoramic realistic novel, with its large cast of characters and detailed descriptions of place and the accoutrements of daily life, the more innovative writers tend to blur the boundaries between "research" and imaginative extrapolation to produce fantastic and disorienting transformations of the past. The playing out of alternative scenarios associated with counterfactual science fiction is another recurring strain in nontraditional historical fiction, reflecting both the writer's and the reader's desire to return to and change the past, to challenge the finality of accomplished action, to question the authority of history as we know it.

In 1971 Avrom Fleishman sensed that the genre of historical fiction was evolving. He noted that "with the passing of the sense not only of progress but even of comprehensible relationships among historical events" plot becomes more difficult and artificial. He predicted that historical novels would either join the ranks of experimental fiction or "retire from the province of serious literature" (207, 255). Many of the most interesting novels published since *The English Historical Novel* appeared implicitly acknowledge the indeterminacy that qualifies and undermines any effort to locate the "comprehensible" causal relationships on which conventional historical narrative relies. Their authors resort to experimental fictional strategies in order to reimagine those relationships, and so offer readers a more disrupted, fragmented version of "history," requiring them—us—to work harder. Readers of innovative historical fiction often find themselves going back through the novel to fit the pieces together and reconstruct chronology, while confronted with arcane vocabulary, unfamiliar diction, and allusions to period texts—generally without the footnotes or glossaries that accompany editions of past literatures. In effect, they participate in constructing the fictional world, bringing their own knowledge of history to the process. These are the "new readers" of whom Eco spoke in his *Postscript*, and they are responsible for the critical and commercial success of what I will be calling the New Historical Fiction.

The distinction between "new" and "old" historical fiction is hardly as absolute as these antithetical labels suggest, however. Contemporary genre theorists acknowledge that genres are more like families than like classes, families in which the members are related in a variety of ways without sharing any necessary or defining single feature. And because they are constantly changing, the critical language for identifying and describing genres is similarly imprecise and in flux. In *Kinds of Literature*, Alistair Fowler asks, "How can traditional genre theory have anything to say about forms so new and so various as those of 'the novel'?" In principle, he continues, "any form that can be invented can be identified, just as any definition of it can be disproved by subsequent literature. No doubt most fictional genres have still to be identified." By identifying "new," or innovative and experimental, historical fiction as a subgenre which shares characteristics generally (though not always, or always in the same way) absent from "old," or conventional, historical fiction—itself a fluid and imprecise category—I am following Fowler's injunction "to explore new groupings" that "have taken their departure from earlier groupings" (33–35).

Let us begin with the kind of history innovative historical writers have chosen to reconstruct and reinterpret. Whereas much traditional historical fiction is based upon political, military, and dynastic history, the New Historical Fiction has moved on (just as recent historical scholarship has done) to less familar aspects of the past. For example, the technology of making watches and other elaborate mechanical constructions during the Enlightenment, along with that period's passion for collecting, is the subject of Allen Kurzweil's *A Case of Curiosities* (1992), while Andrew Miller's *Ingenious Pain* (1997) is based on extensive research into eighteenth-century surgical and medical practices. Both are highly original first novels that combine magic realist strategies with esoteric detail. So does Umberto Eco's *The Island of the Day Before* (1994), a very densely written novel set in 1643 in which the charting of longitudes is the principal character's obsession; the seventeenth-century vocabulary of shipbuilding, seiges, and fortifications posed a particular challenge to Eco's translator, William Weaver (Weaver 17).[2] In each case, the precision associated with science and mechanics is juxtaposed with a contrasting freedom from the rules of conventional fiction.

Like *The Name of the Rose*, these "difficult" and atypical novels are reaching surprisingly large audiences; witness Patrick Suskind's bestseller *Perfume* (1985), a grotesque excursion into the world of scent manufacturing in eighteenth-century France, and Steven Millhauser's Pulitzer Prize-winning *Martin Dressler* (1997), a surreal fantasy about a self-made entrepreneur who builds impossibly elaborate luxury hotels in turn-of-the-century New York. *Angels and Insects* (1992), a pair of novellas by A. S. Byatt that brings together nineteenth-century parapsychology with Darwinian science, was the basis for a film of the same name. These and other recent historical fictions employ unconventional narrative strategies; one particularly interesting example is the Canadian novelist John Steffler's *The Afterlife of George Cartwright* (1993), which is based on an actual journal kept by a gentleman explorer at one of the first fishing and trapping stations on the coast of Labrador. Steffler imagines Cartwright trapped eternally in time on the day of his death, May 19, 1819, reliving his past in recollections adapted from the journal along with letters and other narratives. Time progresses, however, so that the novel's setting is simultaneously the "past" of Cartwright's earlier life, the moment of his death, and the 170 years that follow. All of these novels stretch the limits of fictional realism, while at the same time they initiate the reader into the material, scientific, and technological cultures of the past from oblique perspectives.

When Frances Sherwood sent her first novel, *Vindication*, to Jonathan Galassi at Farrar Straus and Giroux in 1992, he immediately recognized its appeal and planned a large first edition of thirty thousand copies. This "passionate and surprising vision of life and love," as the jacket copy describes it, reinvents Mary Wollstonecraft with, as Sherwood's author's note acknowledges, "many deviations . . . from the actual history of the eighteenth-century

author of 'Vindication of the Rights of Women' and her contemporaries"
(n.p.). Galassi identified Sherwood with "a new breed of historical novelists
whose work is unapologetically suffused with twentieth-century attitudes,
even as it delights in the foreign textures of everyday life in the past" (Talbot
19). Publishers are seeking out New Historical Fictions because of their ability to attract readings. *Girl with a Pearl Earring*, by Tracy Chevalier (2001)
was a *New York Times* bestseller; its popularity coincided with major exhibits
of the seventeenth-century Dutch artist Johannes Vermeer's works. Another
recent historical fiction that takes its title from a Vermeer painting, *Girl in
Hyacinth Blue* by Susan Vreeland (1999), approaches the past longitudinally;
like Adam Thorpe's *Ulverton* (1992) or Eva Figes's *The Seven Ages* (1986),
Vreeland's novel leads the reader through successive moments in history, as
the painting is passed from one owner to the next. This approach to historical fiction writing, popularized by Edward Rutherfurd's bestselling *Sarum*
and *London*, charts the topographical, sociological, and linguistic changes a
culture undergoes through a series of linked episodes.

Although the success of *The Name of the Rose* in the early 1980s brought
the New Historical Fiction to the attention of a large reading public, it was
certainly not the first historical novel to begin transforming the genre.
William Golding and John Banville both anticipated some of Eco's fictional
strategies in the way they constructed the worlds of fourteenth-century architecture and sixteenth-century science. Golding's *The Spire* (1964), a strange
and disturbing novel that chronicles the building of the spire atop Salisbury
Cathedral, never mentions Salisbury Cathedral by name or provides explanatory historical details to orient the reader, as most conventional historical fiction does. This is the kind of novel that sends you to the history books, since
much of its suspense turns on whether the foundations of the cathedral will
in fact support the unprecedented four hundred–foot spire.[3] *The Spire* evokes
the enormous faith that sustains Jocelin, the dean of the cathedral, in the face
of his fellow clerics' resistance, the townspeople's fears, and the skepticism of
the masterbuilder Roger Mason. Like other historical fictions about medieval
church architecture, such as Edith Pargeter's *The Heaven Tree* (1960) and
Henri Vincenot's *The Prophet of Compostela* (1982), *The Spire* translates spa-
tial, mathematical, and visual concepts into complex imaginative language.
Moreover, all three novels dramatize the relationship between building and
theology, religious mysticism and stonemasonry, while drawing the reader
into a narrative that is shaped by the linear process of construction. *The Spire*
also looks forward to other New Historical Fictions I will be discussing (as
well as backward to modernist novels) in its use of diction and syntax to
reflect abnormal states of mind. As the novel draws to a close, the increasing
madness of the two central characters infects the narration and culminates in
Jocelin's vivid hallucinations just before his death.

John Banville's *Doctor Copernicus* (1976) is the first of three novels inspired by Arthur Koestler's *The Sleepwalkers: A History of Man's Changing Vision of the Universe* (1959), itself a rethinking of the way early modern science developed. In an essay on the novel, the historian Wini Warren observes that Banville sought "to provide a psychological explanation of Copernicus's . . . penchant for secretiveness," a question that has "plagued historians for centuries" (388). She argues that Banville's novel is in many ways more "true" to Copernicus's life than the accounts of historians who mythologize him as the progenitor of the new science, imposing on his life both their own need to see him as a devoted astronomer and a "presentism" that views scientists as dedicated professionals (397, 394). Banville evokes Copernicus's cantankerous personality through shifting narration, as when Rheticus, the historical figure who published an account of some of Copernicus's ideas during his lifetime, is introduced as the speaker of the long third section of the novel. Rheticus may or may not be a reliable narrator: as he proceeds to defend himself against Copernicus's accusations in his testimony, the reader begins to wonder how much to credit his depiction of the aging Copernicus as crafty and sinister, living in sin with his housekeeper and resisting publication of *De Revolutionibus Orbum Mundi*. When the point of view shifts for the last twenty-two pages, in a mix of first- and third-person narration culminating in an interior dialogue between Copernicus and his brother Andreas, Banville evokes the experience of reviewing one's life just before death, slipping in and out of lucidity, much as Golding had done in *The Spire*. Resisting the "philosophy of happy ignorance" voiced by the ghost-Andreas, the dying Copernicus wants desperately to believe that "we can *know*" (239). Like many other New Historical Fictions set in the Middle Ages and Renaissance, this one dramatizes the perplexities surrounding faith, and the radical doubts and skepticism that beset so many in those eras.

The New Historical Fiction published throughout Britain, North and South America, and Europe during the 1980s and 1990s complemented a corresponding development in historical writing. As the distinguished historian John Demos (an early practitioner of the new social history) observes, it had become evident by 1990 that "there were two trends approaching convergence: that of novelists drawn to historical fiction and that of scholars attempting a seminovelistic brand of history." After confessing his initial resistance to the notion that historical fiction could provide a way into the past, Demos says he found that fiction writers were paying

> scrupulously close attention to significant human detail. [Margaret] Atwood's Bronfman Lecture describes her experience of "wrestling not only with who said what about Grace Marks [in *Alias Grace*], but also with how to clean a chamber pot, what footgear would have been worn in winter, the origins of quilt pattern names, and how to store parsnips."

To a man and woman, the historical novelists have addressed precisely this challenge, and their "wrestling" process has taken them into the tiniest minutiae of evidence. (Another novel to mention, after all: Charles Frazier's acclaimed *Cold Mountain*, in which the minutiae are so dense as to become almost suffocating. Still, to follow Frazier's central character on his journey home from Civil War soldiering is to know the life of that time and place in a wholly immediate way.) (1528–29)

The "tiny minutiae of evidence" Demos speaks of is uncovered by a new kind of research on the part of the novelist; whereas the "old" historical fiction often includes large chunks of textbook history presented in a transparently didactic way, the New Historical Fiction constructs the world of the past through little-known, sometimes bizarre details drawn from unlikely historical sources.

Just as novelists were increasing their use of the research methods of historians, so historians discovered that "a focus on the story is both intellectually innovative *and* rhetorically appealing," in the words of Sara Maza. Maza's wide-ranging 1996 review essay in the *American Historical Review* charts the "turn to 'narrativity'" and the attendant use of fictional strategies in "the new cultural history" and related fields like anthropology and legal studies (1494–95). This "turn" is both new and old. Until the early nineteenth century historiography was regarded as a literary art, a point made repeatedly by the philosopher of history Hayden White, who observed that the great historians of the past both recognized and accepted "the inevitability of a recourse to fictive techniques" in the writing of history (123). White's work on historiography in the 1970s coincided with other theoretical developments in the overlapping fields of linguistics, anthropology, cultural history, and literary theory. Building on the work of Claude Lévi-Strauss, he argued that "[o]ur *explanations* of historical structures and processes are thus determined more by what we leave out of our representations than by what we put in" (90). Hence historical narratives are "not only models of past events and processes, but also metaphorical statements which suggest a relation of similitude between such events and processes and the story types that we conventionally use to endow the events of our lives with culturally sanctioned meanings" (88). For White, the similarities between histories and novels are in many ways greater than their differences; history, he proclaimed, "is no less a form of fiction than the novel is a form of historical representation" (122).[4]

By the early 1990s, a new generation of cultural historians had emerged who employed strategies very similar to those of New Historicists like Stephen Greenblatt. As Dale H. Porter notes, these historians

argue that historical documents are, in their own ways, prose texts created in response to historical circumstances. They represent human experience, which is not determined *a priori* by circumstances but "constructed" by each of us, applying models and meanings available in our locality. The cultural historians "interrogate" or "deconstruct" particular texts, using a single document or a unique collection as an entry into a particular cultural milieu or *mentalité*. (334–35)

Porter wonders whether such works have crossed the line between nonfiction and fiction. The answer, he suggests, is that "hybrids" are appearing in both realms, and he offers examples of fiction-histories like Alex Haley's *Roots* which deal with "groups of people whose historical experience was not typically recorded in standard public documents" (343). These accounts contrast with the traditionally accepted "'guaranteed' past—like the gold in Fort Knox—that people could depend on" (342).

This book will address some of the ways in which the New Historical Fiction has unsettled the assumptions of conventional literary history—the gold in Fort Knox, if you will—that have been cherished by so many devotees of Shakespeare's England. The phrase "Shakespeare's England" encompasses not only the life and times and contemporaries of that most written-about of playwrights, but also of the characters who appear in the English history plays. This period is a frequent subject of popular formula-fiction romances due to its distinctive, easily replicated "atmosphere," but it has also inspired much serious, traditional historical fiction and fiction-biography, as well. The recent flourishing of the New Historical Fiction has, not surprisingly, produced some remarkable revisioning of Shakespeare's England. Novelists have sought out this period in history, possibly for the same reasons the New Historicists have, because it offers instances of divided and destabilized societies, characterized by political and religious tensions, high ambitions, and rapid social and cultural change. Adjacent stretches of English history will make occasional appearances in this book as well.

The novels I discuss are frequently metafictional and metahistorical in the questions they implicitly or explicitly raise about the nature of history and the relationship between what we call history and fiction. As Brenda Marshall observes in *Teaching the Postmodern*, the reader of such novels becomes an active participant:

We not only watch the postmodern narrator-author write; we are also made aware that the writer is writing quite consciously for us. The narrator-author challenges the reader to participate in creating the picture. And the reader must comply, if only in the attempt to make sense of the text. (153)

In a discussion that invokes such contemporary theorists as Foucault and Lyotard, Marshall adds that postmodern historical fiction "fragments what was thought unified" (169). This skewing, rearranging, and falsifying of historical details reveals the "caprice of recorded history" and inculcates "an incredulity toward metanarratives" (170, 175). The novelist "teaches" the past by dismantling conventional historical truths, while the reader, in turn, "learns" to think in terms of multiple, contradictory histories rather than a single internally coherent one.

Although *The Name of the Rose* and the year 1980 serve as a logical starting point for discussing the New Historical Fiction, some notably innovative historical novels were way ahead of their time. John Barth's *The Sot-Weed Factor* (1960) seemed a curiosity when it first appeared, but it in fact anticipated later developments in historical fiction with its remarkably authentic-looking mock seventeenth-century orthography. Demos calls this "an early masterwork of the historical fiction genre" and regards Barth as "simply too far ahead of things to get the credit he surely deserves" (1527). Several years later, in an essay "about Aboutness," Barth acknowledges that his comical treatment of early colonial Maryland is, "not finally about tidewater Maryland and its history" just as Dickens's *A Tale of Two Cities* is "not about the French Revolution in the way that Carlyle's *History of the French Revolution*" is, for "great literature is almost always about itself" (181, 188, 191).

Not surprisingly, the novelists themselves recognize and celebrate their innovative predecessors: in a new edition of Ford Maddox Ford's long-neglected trilogy *The Fifth Queen* (which was originally published in 1908 and which takes its title from Henry VIII's fifth wife, Katherine Howard), A. S. Byatt praises Ford's "highly visual, scrupulous rendering of the Tudor world." William Gass describes *The Fifth Queen* as

> slow, intense, pictorial, and operatic. Plot is both its subject and its method. Execution is its upshot and its art. *The Fifth Queen* is like Verdi's *Otello*: made of miscalculation, mismaneuver, and mistake. Motive is a metaphor with its meaning sheathed like a dagger. It is one of Shakespeare's doubtful mystery plays. . . . For prose, it is the recovery of poetry itself. (27)

Mary Renault, preëminent chronicler of the ancient world in historical novels of enduring popularity among scholars and general readers alike, pays homage to Rose Macaulay's *They Were Defeated* (1932), a novel, she says, "whose smell of authenticity goes quite to one's head." Set in Cambridge in 1640 with fictional renderings of Herrick, Cleveland, Milton, and Cowley, *They Were Defeated* proves that "the actual speech" of that day can indeed be made understandable without resorting to "phony archaism" (Renault 86). The avid reader of serious historical fiction can no doubt think of other novels about other periods in history that anticipated many of the fictional strategies I will be discussing in the following chapters.

George Garrett's *Death of the Fox* (1971) is a more recent harbinger of the New Historical Fiction. It is an encyclopedic novel reminiscent of nineteenth-century fiction in its enormous scope. In an essay published shortly before *Death of the Fox* appeared, Garrett explains that he began his research in the 1950s, intending to write a biography of Sir Walter Raleigh; he gradually shifted direction in the 1960s, partly because so many biographies of Raleigh were appearing. Struck by the "blank spaces and mysteries in Raleigh's life," he realized that "where the biographer and historian must go on tiptoes," the traditional historical novelist would choose "to fill in these blank spaces with imagined detail, to stand boldly, attributing one motive or another for the seemingly inexplicable action, siding, then, with one historian or another by turning his careful surmise into a definite stance." (*Dreaming With Adam* 26) Garrett found himself resisting this time-honored method, however, "because the blank spaces and the dark corners seemed so much a part of [Raleigh] and his character." (26) So he chose to "accept them as inherent mysteries and . . . find another way of using them in fiction." (26) The "mysteries" that Garrett wanted to evoke fictionally transcended the known and unknown facts of Raleigh's life; hence Garrett's project became nothing less than getting at the "essential mystery" that was "larger than the man," belonging as it did to the age—what Garrett calls "the renaissance imagination" (27). The new historical novelist's role, paradoxically, is "not to *understand* a piece of history and to make it live again," as a traditional historical fiction writer might claim to do, but rather, to "imagine" the lives of other human beings "without assaulting their essential and, anyway, ineffable mystery" (33–34). In other words, the past must remain a foreign country even when the reader's journey has been completed.

Garrett's vision of historical fiction writing anticipates Linda Hutcheon's description of historiographic metafiction in *A Poetics of Postmodernism*: this self-reflexive postmodern form of historical fiction, she observes, "does not mirror reality; nor does it reproduce it. It cannot. There is no pretense of simplistic mimesis in historiographic metafiction. Instead, fiction is offered as another of the discourses by which we construct our versions of reality . . . " (40). Or, as Patricia Waugh explains, "Any text that draws the reader's attention to its process of construction by frustrating his or her conventional expectations of meaning and closure" is metafictional in the way it "problematizes . . . the ways in which narrative codes—whether 'literary' or 'social'—artificially construct apparently 'real' and imaginary worlds . . . " (22). The history that emerges from contemporary metafiction is provisional: "no longer a world of eternal verities but a series of constructions, artifices, impermanent structures"(7).

Because I have tried to limit myself more or less to Shakespeare's England, much of the innovative historical fiction that has been published since 1980 can be mentioned only in passing. Here are some novels set in other times and places from which my inferences about the generic characteristics of the New Historical Fiction are derived; most of them deal with British or European history from the medieval period to the eighteenth century. For lack of a better organizing principle, I list them in order of original publication except where two novels by the same author are included: Frederick Buechner, *Godric* (1980); John Banville, *Kepler* (1981); Peter Ackroyd, *Hawksmoor* (1985) and *Chatterton* (1987); Homer Aridjis, *1492* (1985) and *The Lord of the Last Days* (1994); Jeanette Winterson, *The Passion* (1987); Sebastian Vassalli, *The Chimera* (1990); Evan S. Connell, *The Alchymist's Journal* (1991); Sebastien Japrisot, *A Very Long Engagement* (1991); Thomas Norfolk, *Lempriere's Dictionary* (1991); Susan Sontag, *The Volcano Lover* (1992); Adam Thorpe, *Ulverton* (1992); Barry Unsworth, *Sacred Hunger* (1992); Frances Sherwood, *Vindication* (1993); Andrzej Szczypiorski, *Mass for Arras* (1993); Louis de Bernieres, *Corelli's Mandolin* (1994); Jill Paton Walsh, *Knowledge of Angels* (1994); Madison Smartt Bell, *All Souls' Rising* (1995); Penelope Fitzgerald, *The Blue Flower* (1995); Douglas Glover, *The Life and Times of Captain N.* (1995); Kathryn Harrison, *Poison* (1995); Michael Pye, *The Drowning Room* (1995); Robert Begiebing, *The Strange Death of Mistress Coffin* (1996) and *The Adventures of Allegra Fullerton* (1999); Sheri Holman, *A Stolen Tongue* (1997) and *The Dress Lodger* (2000); Iain Pears, *An Instance of the Fingerpost* (1998); and A. S. Byatt, *The Biographer's Tale* (2000). A longer list would include some earlier, relatively unknown novels that exhibit certain characteristics of the New Historical Fiction, like Sylvia Townsend Warner's *The Corner That Held Them* (1948) and the Dutch novelist Hella S. Haasse's *In a Dark Wood Wandering* (1949), *The Scarlet City* (1954); and *Threshold of Fire* (1964).

Some of the novelists on my list (and others I have not included) appear on the lists of other scholars who see common characteristics among innovative historical novels. For example, Susan Onega is particularly interested in novelists for whom

> the attempt to recreate a concrete historical period in traditional terms is only a pretext for a much more interesting and disturbing aim, which is to enter the tunnel of time in order to recover the other, suppressed, half of Western civilization and history: the mythical, esoteric, gnostic and cabalistic elements which once formed an inextricable unity with reason

and logic, and which have been progressively repressed and muffled since the Middle Ages by the mainstream of rationalism. (57)

Monika Fludernik's essay on history and metafiction contains a list that includes novels about nineteenth- and twentieth-century American history, conspicuously absent from my list. She notes that recent historical novels

> straddle the fiction/history boundary in triple and quadruple manner, radicalizing the hybridization which was already the keynote of the historical novel and gleefully subverting any genre features of traditional fiction or historiography.

In contrast to the satirical metafiction of the 1960s and 1970s, Fludernik observed that we are seeing "a new, more serious mode of historiographic metafiction . . . one that is less playful, more specifically concerned with 'history' (in different ways) and less simplistically and dichotomously mythological. . . . " She ends by saying that we can call this evolving genre "the new historical novel" (101).

In her collection of essays *On Histories and Stories*, A. S. Byatt speculates about why the past is the subject of so much modern fiction. When she began writing novels in the 1960s, Byatt recounts, "we were being lectured by C. P. Snow and Kingsley Amis about how good fiction *ought* to describe the serious social concerns of contemporary society. It seemed perfectly adequate to dismiss historical fiction as 'escapism'. . . . " Now, however, historical fiction is being written "for complex aesthetic and intellectual reasons. Some of it is sober and some of it is fantastic, some of it is knowing and postmodernist, some of it is feminist or post-colonial rewritings of official history, some of it is past prehistory, some of it is very recent" (93). Her list includes authors whose work I will be discussing, such as Anthony Burgess, Jeanette Winterson, and Barry Unsworth, along with others like Julian Barnes, Graham Swift, Angela Carter, Marina Warner, Caryl Phillips, and J. M. Coetzee. The many forms of current historical fiction, she observes, include "parodic and pastiche forms, forms which fake documents or incorporate real ones, mixtures of past and present, hauntings and ventriloquism, historical versions of genre fictions. . . . " The writers' purposes are similarly various: "incantatory, analytic, romantic, or stylistic. Or playful, or extravagant, or allegorical . . . [but] even the ones apparently innocently realist . . . do not choose realism unthinkingly, but almost as an act of shocking rebellion against current orthodoxies" (38–39). Byatt speculates that postmodern writers are returning to historical fiction because they are attracted to the idea that there is no such thing as "an organic, discoverable single self. We are perhaps no more than a series of disjunct sense-impressions, remembered incidents, shifting bits of knowledge, opinion, ideology and stock responses"

(31). Speaking of her own most well-known novel, *Possession*, she recalls playing

> serious games with the variety of possible forms of narrating the past—
> the detective story, the biography, the mediaeval verse Romance, the
> modern romantic novel, and Hawthorne's fantastic historical Romance
> in between, the campus novel, the Victorian third-person narration, the
> epistolary novel, the forged manuscript novel, and the primitive fairy tale
> of the three women, filtered through Freud's account of the theme in his
> paper on the Three Caskets. (48)

Some of the generic traits Byatt mentions in passing appear in Seymour
Menton's study of recent Latin American fiction. Menton attempts to
describe the postmodern historical novel through a sample of 367 novels
divided into mostly post-1979 "New Historical Novels" and more traditional
"Not-So-New Historical Novels 1949–1992" that are useful for contrast. He
identifies six characteristics of New Historical Novels, not all of which can be
found in each novel:

1. The subordination . . . of the mimetic recreation of a given historical
   period to the illustration of three historical ideas . . . (*a*) the impossibility of ascertaining the true nature of reality or history; (*b*) the
   cyclical nature of history; and (*c*) the unpredictability of history. . . .
2. The conscious distortion of history through omissions, exaggerations, and anachronisms.
3. The utilization of famous historical characters as protagonists, which
   differs markedly from the Walter Scott formula . . . of fictitious protagonists.
4. *Metafiction*, or the narrator's referring to the creative process of his
   own text [and] questioning of his own discourse. . . .
5. *Intertextuality*: "any text is constructed as a mosaic of quotations; any
   text is the absorption and transformation of another" [Menton is
   quoting Julia Kristeva].
6. The Bakhtinian concepts of the *dialogic*, the *carnivalesque*, parody,
   and *heteroglossia*. [The dialogic] contain[s] two or more often conflicting presentations of events, characters, and world views . . .
   [while the carnivalesque employs] humorous exaggerations and . . .
   emphasis on bodily functions . . . [and heteroglossia is] the multiplicity of discourses, or the conscious use of different types of speech.
   (22–25)

To these characteristics Menton adds six "modalities" that distinguish the
New Historical Novel from the traditional romantic historical novel. They
are "the fanciful and pseudo-historical . . . and totally apocryphal"; "the alter-
nation between two rather widely separated time periods"; "unabashed

anachronism"; the way "the representation of the past masks comments on the present"; "historical detective stories"; and "apocryphal autobiographical novels" (25). Every novel I will be discussing in the following chapters displays several of the characteristics Menton lists. As his typology suggests, the New Historical Fiction exhibits the most interesting developments in contemporary fiction.

When scholars like Fludernik and Menton use the term "the New Historical Novel" they may not realize that the term is actually over a century old. In *The Historical Novel from Scott to Sabatini*, Harold Orel notes that the historical novel's popularity waned after the enormous success of Walter Scott's fiction in the early nineteenth century, but revived in the 1880s, so much so that "within thirty years more than five hundred such novels were issued by publishers," and the phenomenon "came to be known by the phrase 'The New Historical Novel'" (1). The vogue of historical fiction had a "long run," but within months after the end of the First World War, its moment had passed (15).

Apart from some scholarly studies of Scott's fiction, remarkably little has been written about the historical novel as a genre, considering its longevity, popularity, and variety. The PN 3400 section on genre in a typical large university library contains dozens of books on science fiction, romance, and detective fiction, but only a bare half-dozen on historical fiction. While it is not my intent to survey the existing critical literature on historical fiction here, a few texts deserve mention, if only because of the way they articulate the contradictions and perceived shortcomings that have been repeatedly associated with the genre. Two European treatises on the historical novel have been recently reissued by the University of Nebraska Press, a sign, perhaps, of renewed critical interest: Georg Lukacs's *The Historical Novel* (1955), and Alessandro Manzoni's *On the Historical Novel* (begun in 1828 but not published until 1850). The latter has been newly translated by Sandra Bermann, with a long introduction putting the two works in perspective; both, she notes, were influenced by continental philosophy and in different ways were concerned with the ethical and didactic function of fiction (58). Despite the fact that their books were written a century apart, Bermann adds, "both Lukacs and Manzoni view the novel itself as a form that is peculiarly split, dichotomous, and therefore problematic" (54).

Although he was ostensibly defending the historical novel against critics whose arguments he paraphrases in *On the Historical Novel*, Manzoni reluctantly concluded that

> the historical novel is a work in which the necessary turns out to be
> impossible, and in which two essential conditions cannot be reconciled,

or even one fulfilled. It inevitably calls for a combination that is contrary to its subject matter and a division contrary to its form. Though we know it is a work in which history and fable must figure, we cannot determine or even estimate their proper measure or relation. (72)

Manzoni's resistance to the hybrid nature of historical fiction was in effect a rejection of his earlier novel *I Promessi Sposi (The Betrothed)*, written between 1821 and 1827. Eco praised this novel in his *Postscript to The Name of the Rose* for its departure from nineteenth-century historical fiction conventions: instead of

a celebration of Italian glories from a period when Italy was a land of the strong . . . [Manzoni] chooses the seventeenth century, a period of servitude [and] tells of no battles, and dares to weigh his story down with documents and proclamations. (523–24).

As a recent study of innovative Italian historical fiction points out, the revisionist "critical historical novels" written by Eco and others transcend the generic boundaries understood by Manzoni, with his "prescriptive and censoring" paradigm (Coletta 14). Contemporary novelists acknowledge, rather than try to conceal, the confrontation between fiction and history as they seek to interpret the past, although they also follow Manzoni's example in "tell[ing] the stories of those who did not have a voice in the historical world" (Coletta 15). Looking ahead from Manzoni to the historical fiction of the present, Bermann articulates one difference between the old historical fiction and the new:

How could Manzoni know that a reader might eventually become less interested in the reaffirmation of positive facts than in a demonstration of man's conscious—or even unconscious—fictional transformation of them? (59)

Lukacs takes a Marxist view of the historical novel, seeing the fiction of Scott and his successors as "a perfect coincidence between the short career of the historical novel and the early nineteenth century, a period of alliance between the bourgeoisie and the proletariat" (Bermann 55). Although he arrives at his conclusions differently from Manzoni, he likewise has doubts about the future of the historical novel due to the difficulties inherent in fusing empirical history and imaginative fiction.

Manzoni's and Lukacs's skepticism about historical fiction as an enduring and multifaceted genre reflects a larger anxiety about the pitfalls that confront the historian. In *The Use and Abuse of History* Nietzsche inveighs against the "'monumental' contemplation of the past" that causes "the individuality of the past [to be] forced into a general formula and all the sharp angles broken off for the sake of correspondence." As long as the past is principally used as a model for imitation, it is always in danger of being a little altered and touched up and brought nearer to fiction. Sometimes there is no possible distinction between a "monumental" past and a mythical romance. . . . (15)

In a sentence that anticipates the New Historicists, Nietzsche proclaims: "For the things of the past are never viewed in their true perspective or receive their just value; but value and perspective change with the individual or the nation that is looking back on its past" (19).

Much of the New Historical Fiction serves as a corrective to what Nietzsche calls "monumental history" by creating oblique, revisionist micro-histories from overlooked historical archives. Mario Vargas Llosa, the Peruvian novelist whose fiction belongs to the Latin American "boom" in magic-realist historical fiction, explains that

> The reconstruction of the past in literature is almost always false in terms of historical objectivity. Literary truth is one thing, historical truth another. But although it is full of lies—rather, because of this fact—literature recounts the history that the history written by the historians would not know how, or be able, to write, because the deceptions, tricks, and exaggerations of narrative literature are used to express profound and unsettling truths which can only see the light of day in this oblique way." (Parini B4–B5)[5]

Peter Ackroyd addresses this conundrum in *Chatterton* (1987), a novel about the poet Thomas Chatterton, who died mysteriously at the age of eighteen in 1770. Ackroyd juxtaposes his subject's brief life, Henry Wallis's painting *The Death of Chatterton*, (for which the nineteenth-century poet George Meredith posed as the poet), and the researches of a fictional twentieth-century character named Charles Wychwood in an elaborately layered postmodern fiction. Adapting detective fiction conventions, he uses Wychwood's discovery of a portrait and papers to trigger some ingenious speculation regarding Chatterton's life and death. One of the documents Wychwood discovers contains an observation that sounds very like Nietzsche's, recast in remarkably convincing period diction and orthography:

> I reproduc'd the Past and filled it with such Details that it was as if I were observing it in front of me: so the Language of ancient Dayes awoke the Reality itself for, tho' I knew that it was I who composed these Histories, I knew also that they were true ones. (85)

Here Chatterton is speaking of his poetry, which was inspired by Shakespeare and other sixteenth-century poets. Ackroyd plays with the idea, developed throughout the novel, that an invented history can be "true" to the time it recreates even if it is methodologically "false." Reading the biographies of Chatterton, each of which "described a different poet . . . so that nothing seemed certain," Wychwood concludes that "If there were no truth, everything was true" (127). Or, as Meredith asks Wallis, "so the greatest realism is also the greatest fakery?" (139).

The resistance to distinctions between the "true" and the "false" in historical fiction can be alarming to writers of nonfiction. The biographer Margaret Forster offers another perspective on this and other instances of the new historical fiction in the *New York Times Book Review*. Forster begins her review of Sherwood's *Vindication* with the pronouncement:

> Novels based on the lives of real people, even long dead people, are always dangerous enterprises. Dangerous because they tamper with received truth, dangerous because their avowed aim is to lie, all in the name of satisfying unsatisfied curiosity. Is this sort of distortion right, is it fair?

She goes on to ask whether the "many deviations" Sherwood acknowledges in the author's note are "important are not?" Her answer, clearly, is yes, as she describes the "distinct queasiness" she felt when confronted with invented episodes "that never happened and that are alien to the spirit of Wollstonecraft." She ends her review by urging the reader to seek out the "necessary corrective" of a standard biography immediately after finishing the novel (21). Three weeks later, the *Book Review* published a long letter from novelist Russell Banks. The letter chides Forster—who, after all, is the biographer of Daphne du Maurier, an historian and historical novelist. Forster "ought to know," says Banks, that

> Whereas a novelist is primarily concerned with creating in language a morally coherent universe, a biographer or historian seems to be concerned instead with establishing Ms. Forster's "received truth"—a dignified and valuable task, to be sure, but no more the job of a novelist than that of a poet, painter, film maker or musician.

He concludes, aphoristically, that "Novels are not versions of history; they are visions of life" (27).

Many readers would argue that historical novels *are* versions of history, although not in the same way that biographies are. If fiction writers can be accused of filling in the gaps in "history," they do so because biographers allow those gaps to occur when they decide what to include and what to omit. Both fiction writers and biographers are also guilty of imposing a shape, or narrative, on the disparate events of a life, as they seek for explanatory structures of cause and effect.[6] "Every inclusion is also an exclusion, every temporal structure, however minutely described, remains a generalization," observes Richard Humphrey in *The Historical Novel as Philosophy of History*. But the historical novel, he argues, fleshes out generalizations, replacing the "generalization[s] characteristic of narrative history with [a] more discriminating kind of generalization" (18).

In one of the best contemporary essays about historical fiction, Cleo Kearns approaches the genre's paradoxical nature from a somewhat different perspective, using as her starting point the "dubious pleasures" of reading the novels of Dorothy Dunnett (a very popular and prolific contemporary British writer). Kearns perceives an uneasiness at the heart of historical fiction due to its "essentially hybrid nature, dependent for power on a destabilising of the boundaries both between 'reality' and 'fiction' and 'high' and 'popular' cultures" (38). This uneasiness, she continues, is deeply unsettling [to] certain bourgeois and scientisic modes of thought. In its respect for convention and historicity, however, it can be deeply consolidating of these modes as well" (39). Historical fiction is an inherently postmodern form, says Kearns:

> Instead of tackling history's power straight on, it subverts it from within. While these other forms, narrative history, the realist novel, the documentary, etc., are busy constructing the reality effect, the historical novel is busy deconstructing it, though not without, in classic deconstructive fashion, first establishing a certain complicity with its task. The historical novel, in other words, is saying something like "let us *imagine* that *this happened*, let us fill in the gaps that discomfit the historians, but fill them in so convincingly that *our* reality effect, based as it were on nothing but air, will seem more substantial than *their* reality effect which claims the security of 'fact.'" (40)

The power Kearns ascribes to "history" is in many instances a patriarchal power, the power an essentially conservative tradition appropriates to uphold a particular version of the past. And yet, as Kearns points out at the beginning of her essay, reading historical fiction is a typically female activity. So is writing historical fiction: women writers have long been laying claim to the gaps in recorded history, often by choosing women as their subjects.

In *The House of Desdemona*, the historical novelist Lion Feuchtwanger offers an explanation for women's prominence as creators and consumers of historical fiction, although he does so in language that would infuriate contemporary readers. Feuchtwanger begins from the assumption that "the author is not re-creating history for its own sake but uses the costume or disguise of history as the simplest stylistic means for achieving the illusion of reality" (14). By "removing himself from his own time and by regarding it as something foreign," the author can "make the audience or reader feel the peculiar and the essential quality of his own time" (140–41). *The House of Desdemona* was left unfinished at the author's death in 1958; it breaks off just at the point at which Feuchtwanger was starting to address the "extent of the participation of women in the production of historical narrative, both the genuine and the trash varieties" (194). He takes a long look back through history, starting with attributions of biblical narratives and the *Odyssey* to women writers, and on into the eighteenth and nineteenth centuries.

Generalizing freely, Feuchtwanger observes that "women take more seriously than men the preliminary work requisite to writing an historical novel," a process that takes "much diligence and patience . . . [for] one must wade through many long historiographical studies in the hope of discovering some small utilizable fact. . . . "(195). Although his depiction of the *Hausfrau* novelist engaged in "the same tiring work . . . over and over again" to produce "neat and shining results" (196) makes us cringe (remember that this was, after all, an unfinished draft!), he was in fact writing during a period in which women writers were producing an abundance of historical fictions, some of them about women who had been overlooked or misconstrued by male historians.[7] As the following chapters will demonstrate, some of the most innovative and some of the most conventional historical novels continue to be written by and about women.

Perhaps the subversive power Kearns speaks of explains why so much that has been written about historical fiction dwells upon its shortcomings. In retrospect, Manzoni's assessment of historical fiction as "a work impossible to achieve satisfactorily because its premises are inherently contradictory" (72) sounds quite contemporary; it brings to mind deconstruction's appropriation of the rhetorical term "aporia" to signify a point of impasse at which the text's self-contradictory meanings can no longer be resolved (Baldick 15). This note has been sounded again and again as the genre's perceived contradictions, often called "problems," persist in troubling critics.

For example, an early essay on the genre written in 1897 by Brander Matthews infers from novels like Thackeray's *Vanity Fair* and *Henry Esmond* that "fidelity [is] simply impossible to the story-teller who deals with the past . . . the more he labors, the less life is there likely to be in the tale he is telling: humanity is choked by archeology" (21). Of the "ordinary historical novel" (what Feuchtwanger calls "trash"), he declares:

> it provides the drug [readers seeking escape] desire, while they can salve their conscience during this dissipation with the belief that they are, at the same time, improving their minds. The historical novel is aureoled with a psuedosanctity, in that it purports to be more instructive than a mere story; it claims—or at least the claim is made in its behalf—that it is teaching history. There are those who think that it thus adds hypocrisy to its other faults. (26)

And, he adds in the next paragraph, the historical novel also falsifies the past, representing it inaccurately as a "better" world than the reader's own (27).[8]

Three decades later, Ernest Bernbaum attempted to explain why the historical novel had fallen into disrepute among critics. This, he says, is a genre "without its Aristotle" to provide "an explicit statement of its real

nature, a defense of its being" (428). Created "in an age which presupposed
an idealistic aesthetics, the historical novel had flourished in peace." But with
the rise of empiricism in the second half of the nineteenth century, the "past"
became "an objectively existing reality which scientific historians could copy"
(429). "Predictions of the death of the genre," Bernbaum concludes, "have
been made at least once a decade for a hundred years," (439) and yet the historical novel continues to be a remarkable anomaly: "a genre flourishing in
the world of literary experience, and despised in the world of literary
thought" (440).

When the more recent "world of literary thought" does turn its attention to historical fiction, the discussions again revert to the "problems" associated with the genre. Harry E. Shaw begins his book *The Forms of Historical
Fiction: Sir Walter Scott and His Successors* by observing that historical fiction
is a form that "suffers from neglect, even contempt" (9). Later, in a section
entitled "The Problem with Historical Novels," he notes that "standard," or
mainstream historical novels "cannot enact all levels of human experience
with equal success"; that is, they cannot be analytical and descriptive and at
the same time "particularize" through "imaginative excursions into groups
and individuals" (48). Another "problem" is that when "characters become
translucent to allow historical processes to shine through them more clearly
they also tend to become thinner as representations of 'inwardly complex'
human beings" (48).

Mary Lascelles identifies still another "problem" confronting the historical novelist, "the two-fold necessity of involving his fictitious characters with
the persons and events of history at the outset, and extricating them at the
close" (41). Edith Pargeter, the author of *The Heaven Tree Trilogy* and other
historical novels and historical detective fiction (under the name of Ellis
Peters), addresses a variant of this concern when she explains that

> when writing history, even in the form of fiction, every documented and
> ascertainable fact must be respected, and an effort made to present
> events and locations as truly as possible . . . the castle that never existed I
> could place where I chose, provided I took care to account for its absence
> at the end. (Peters and Morgan 160)

Many writers of the New Historical Fiction ignore these "problems"; or,
in characteristically postmodern fashion, they invest their fictional worlds
with the impossibilities and contradictions that earlier novelists sought to
avoid. In a 1979 essay that offers a classification of the kinds of historical fiction, Joseph W. Turner reflects the shift to a postmodern sensibility when he
suggests that the "conflicting commitments" the novelist makes to history
and fiction can "never be simply (nor even finally) resolved" (342). An
inevitable "tension exist[s] within the terms of the genre" and in the case of

the "documented historical novel . . . the conventional distinction between history and fiction threatens to collapse." (341) Echoing White, he concludes that "to argue that documented historical novels are or are not valuable because they do or do not stick to the 'facts' amounts to something of a false problem" (342).[9]

The best defenders and explicators of the historical novel have been the novelists themselves. From the time of Walter Scott onward, some of the most influential historical novels have been accompanied by critical essays, like Eco's *Postscript to The Name of the Rose*, Marguerite Yourcenar's "Reflections on the Composition of *Memoirs of Hadrian*," or the essays in Christa Wolf's *Cassandra: A Novel and Four Essays*. The latter is a retelling of the story of the fall of Troy from Cassandra's point of view, accompanied by four essays on the "Conditions of a Narrative." The essays take the forms of travel narratives, a work diary, and a letter to a reader identified only as "A" to whom Wolf recounts the reading, thinking, and questioning that preceded the writing of the novel, repeatedly returning to the question: "Who was Cassandra before anyone wrote about her?" (273). Eco, Yourcenar, and Wolf all write in an informal, conversational style, and in diary-like speculative fragments, quite unlike the structure and diction of conventional literary criticism. In each case we see the mind of the novelist at work, considering and rejecting possible approaches, using the past to reflect on the present, discovering clues, making hypotheses.

An especially eloquent commentator on her craft is Marguerite Yourcenar, who wrote her magnificent portrait of the emperor Hadrian over a period of twenty years or more. Puzzling out issues of narration, she remarks, "Another thing virtually impossible, to take a feminine character as a central figure, to make Plotina, for example, rather than Hadrian, the axis of my narrative. Women's lives are much too limited, or else too secret" ("Reflections" 327). About the genre she has chosen, Yourcenar observes, "In our day, when introspection tends to dominate literary forms, the historical novel, or what may for convenience's sake be called by that name, must take the plunge into time recaptured, and must fully establish itself within some inner world" (329). Her essay "Tone and Language in the Historical Novel" (first published in 1972) takes as its subject the "enormous stumbling block" posed by the challenge of recreating the speech patterns and tones of the past in the absence of recordings or transcripts (28). "Happily," she observes, "there are sub-literary documents . . . which haven't undergone the filtering or rearranging literature entails"; these include legal documents and decrees, letters, and graffiti, "voices out of the past, some of them practically in their raw state" and hence able to provide "those inflections, those quarter tones, those articulated half smiles which yet can change everything" (31).

Yourcenar explains that she told Hadrian's story as a memoir, "half narrative, half meditative, but always essentially *written*" so as to avoid falling "into error, into melodrama or pastiche, or both" that direct dramatization through dialogue would have entailed ("Tone and Language" 32-33). She adds that she used a completely different approach for her novel set in sixteenth-century Europe, *The Abyss*: "Life reconsidered by Hadrian from the perspective of memory gave way to life experienced from day to day at a level very close to the level of spoken language." (37) In her search for "the lively tone of verbal exchanges in the sixteenth century" she relied on Shakespeare and "his Elizabethan emulators," for

> some of the lyrical soliloquies of Lear or Hamlet, which audibly belong to the world of the theater, nonetheless tell us something about the language for emotions violently felt by certain especially strong or thoughtful people. They shed a light on the thinking, feeling men at the end of that century which we don't have again in the same intensity for any other era before our own. (38)

Here is Yourcenar describing her method of composition:

> At the risk of creating the impression of excessive meticulousness, I confess to having turned to dictionaries for every doubtful word—that is, for each word which I suspected had entered the language after the sixteenth century or, at most, after the beginning of the seventeenth; and those words I ruthlessly suppressed because they carried with them ideas that my characters could not have had in that form. (40)

Yourcenar's method distinguishes her fiction from the kind of popular novel in which characters from the past sound very much like us. But her self-imposed mandate extends farther: she also attempted to avoid words that had ceased to be used after the sixteenth century. Her essay points to a common feature in more conventional historical fiction; the mingling of contemporary dictions and sentiments with deliberate archaisms like "Mayhap," "Aye," or "wilt thou."[10]

Such scrupulous attention to the nuances of language, more than anything else, distinguishes the very best historical fiction from its more conventional counterparts. Describing the composition of *The King Must Die* and her approach to the issue of diction which so preoccupied Yourcenar, Mary Renault said this in *Afterword*:

> You cannot step twice into the same river, said Herakleitos. People in the past were not just like us; to pretend so is an evasion and a betrayal, turning our back on them so as to be easy among familiar things. This is why the matter of dialogue is so crucial. No word in our language comes

to us sterile and aseptic, free of associations. If it was coined yesterday, it tastes of that, and a single sentence of modern-colloquial slang, a turn of phrase which evokes specifically our own society, can destroy for me, at any rate, the whole suspension of disbelief. (85)

Both Yourcenar and Renault belong to an earlier generation of novelists than most of the writers I will be discussing. Their detailed reconstruction of period language is shared by their successors, although the New Historical Fiction writers also experiment with verbal strategies that call attention to the juxtaposition of past and present.

Few novelists write at length about their methods or compose bibliographical essays as detailed and scholarly as Yourcenar's fifteen-page author's note at the end of *Memoirs of Hadrian*; however, most writers of the New Historical Fiction do provide intriguing glimpses into the composition process thorough author's notes, annotated bibliographies, or afterwords. Through these texts the novelists delineate "fact" from "fiction," reveal their sources to the reader who might wish to retrace their steps, and provide glimpses of their methods of composition. The page entitled "About the Author" at the end of Cynthia Morgan's *Court of Shadows*, for example, informs the reader that

> during the several years [the author] worked on the novel she read hundreds of books about the period as well as scholars' facsimiles of Elizabethan writings about fencing and the London underworld. She also read Elizabethan plays, especially Shakespeare's, almost every day. (n.p.)

There are certain conventions novelists observe in these author's notes, similar to the conventions that recur in the prefaces and acknowledgments at the beginnings of fiction and nonfiction books alike. At the end of *Poison*, Kathryn Harrison confesses to an intentional distortion, "and it was that first lie which encouraged many more untruths." She goes on to discuss historical speculations regarding the cause of Queen Maria Louisa's 1689 death in Spain (316). Sometimes the author's note simply finishes the story, by telling us what happened to the characters after the novel's stopping point. At the end of *The Blue Flower* Penelope Fitzgerald provides a few pages of history, with brief quotes from letters written by her subject, the poet Novalis, followed by a list of marriage and death dates. Madison Smartt Bell provides a detailed year-by-year chronology of events for his account of an uprising led by the African slave Toussaint L'Ouverture in Haiti just prior to the French Revolution, along with a glossary of unfamiliar words entitled "Another Devil's Dictionary."

Like historians, some writers of historical fiction are scrupulous about acknowledging their sources. Sheri Holman's author's note in *A Stolen Tongue* reveals that her bizarre account of a fifteenth-century quest for the

stolen body parts of St. Katherine is based on her narrator's twelve-volume
Latin work and an 1896 translation of part of it; she gives credit to the translator for the places where her narrator Felix "speaks for himself in this novel"
(341). Judith Tarr's *Pillar of Fire*, a conventional historical fiction in respect
to its diction, characterization, and treatment of sexuality, is nevertheless
unconventional in the way it challenges received biblical history. Tarr's
author's note explains that she followed the "outrageous" theory set forth by
Ahmed Osman in *Moses: Pharoah of Egypt*:

> By tweaking and fiddling with the chronology of the Exodus, selecting
> carefully from the archeological record, and citing not only the
> Pentateuch but the Koran, Osman manages to construct the thesis that
> Moses was not simply the pupil of Akhenaten but was in fact the exiled
> and discredited pharaoh. His thesis requires a great deal of stretching
> and adjustment of the historical and scriptural evidence— but from the
> novelist's perspective it is pure gold. (657)

Sometimes the author's note is a brief manifesto about the nature of
historical fiction; Jill Paton Walsh's, which comes at the beginning of *A
Knowledge of Angels*, states that

> This story is based very remotely on the true story of the Maid of
> Chalons— *vide* Rousseau, *Epitre II sur l'Homme.*
> It is set on an island somewhat like Mallorca, but not Mallorca, at a
> time somewhat like 1450, but not 1450. A fiction is always, however
> obliquely, about the time and place in which it was written. (x)

The Drowning Room's end note draws attention to nonverbal sources; speaking of his recreation of the "notorious" Dutch woman Gretje Reyniers who
arrived in New Amsterdam in 1642 and is referred to in early court records,
Michael Pye declares that "the most important source has been pictures and
prints, mostly in the collections of the Amsterdam Rijksmuseum and the
Amsterdam Historical Museum. . . . " He concludes, most provocatively,
with these words: "I have invented her in this book, which is dangerous. If
she isn't satisfied with the flesh I've found for her, I know I'll hear" (252). In
both of these instances, the novelist seems to be speaking in a quasi-fictional
voice, constructing herself or himself as "the author" with an intuitive access
to the past and understanding of the present.

However brief or incomplete, an author's note enters into a kind of
dialogue with the novel, reminding the reader that the novelist has reimagined and in a sense rewritten "history" as it existed before the novel came
into being. The novelists whose reinventions of Shakespeare's England I
will be discussing have altered my understanding of the past in countless

ways, and their fictions mingle with Shakespeare's fictions in my teaching. The final chapter of this book grows out of my own teaching experiences over the years and addresses the way historical fiction can serve to bring Shakespeare's England to life for undergraduate and graduate students. To do so is to transport students into another time and place more fully than any textbook can, for as Gore Vidal, himself the author of many historical fictions observes,

> the past is another country, and to bring it to some sort of dramatic life takes a capacity for which there is no English word. It was not until the eighteenth century that a German, J. G. Herder, coined *Einfuhlen*—the act of feeling one's way into the past not by holding up a mirror but by stepping *through* the mirror into the alien world. (115)

Readers of detective fiction are swept along on the tide of narrative by a desire to find out how the crime occurred and how the solution was reached. For readers of historical fiction something analogous occurs. How much is invented and how much is history, we find ourselves wanting to know. How much history did the writer need to assimilate to make invention possible? At what point, and in what way, did the history get transformed into fiction? And what kind of history is this—would it look naive and unscholarly to a professional historian, or to adherents of particular schools or approaches? The fact that so much serious, well-researched historical fiction—both old and new—attracts readers raises still other questions. Does blurring the line between history and fiction run the risk of trivializing what "actually" happened? While as readers we may not be troubled by the liberties taken in fictional transformations of Shakespeare's England, we may feel otherwise about the Holocaust, another frequent subject of both historical fiction and revisionist history. When witnesses to the historical events are still living, when we have access to documentation far more extensive than the records that survive from the sixteenth and seventeenth centuries, does this make a difference?

Finally, who decides where the dividing line lies between history and fiction? *The New York Times* reports that the historical novel *Artemisia* by Alexandra Lapierre, whose title character was one of Europe's first significant women artists and which contains the extensive notes and documentation of nonfiction, was published as a narrative biography in England but as a novel in the United States (Bricklebank 23). Consider also the case of *Dead Certainties (Unwarranted Speculations)*, a fascinating pair of linked historical novellas by the well-known cultural historian Simon Schama, whose scholarship has hitherto fallen squarely in the category of nonfiction. *Dead Certainties* was given a Library of Congress "F" classification for history rather than a "PS" for American fiction, despite the fact that Schama calls his text "a work of imagination, not scholarship." One of the novellas consists of several fragmentary stories about the way General James Wolfe's death during the French and Indian War has been constructed, inspired by Benjamin West's epic painting *The Death of General Wolfe*. Much as Foucault, Stephen Greenblatt, and Schama himself have done, historical novelists view paintings as nonverbal artifacts from which the past can be reconstructed.[11] Schama concludes his book with an afterword and a note on sources in which he quotes from Henry James's *The Sense of the Past*, a fiction about a historian who wants "evidence of a sort for which there had never been documents enough." (Schama 320). Commenting on his own postmodern method, Schama speaks of "the self-disrupting nature of the narratives," with their "abrupt interventions—like windows suddenly opened—" (321). Schama's simile, with its inadvertent allusion to computer software, is wonderfully suggestive. When the windows of fiction and history—not to mention cultural anthropology, art history, literary theory, and detective fiction—can be opened and shut at will, who is to say what new hybrids will fly in and out of them?

Chapter 2

Of Narrators; or How the Teller Tells the Tale

$\mathcal{T}$he title of this chapter is modeled on several recent historical novelists' mimicry of the chapter headings or titles used by earlier writers. Bacon, Montaigne, and other sixteenth-century essayists used the "Of ___" formula to organize their essays around a topic or concept; eighteenth-century novelists used the "In which___" formula or variants thereof (for example, "In Which Our Travellers Meet With A Very Extraordinary Adventure," the tenth chapter of Joseph Fielding's *Tom Jones*); and similar chapter titles can be found in many other medieval and early modern texts. In *Godric*, Frederick Buechner begins his chapters with titles beginning with "of" or "how" to approximate the tone and episodic narrative design of a medieval saint's life. Eco's chapter headings in *The Name of the Rose* follow the "In which ___" pattern, with more than a hint of irony, as for example in the opening chapter, "In which the foot of the abbey is reached, and William demonstrates his great acumen." John Mortimer's wildly satirical *Will Shakespeare: The Untold Story* nearly always uses titles beginning with "of" for its forty chapters. They are not so much descriptive as they are provocative: for instance, chapter 17 is titled "Of Breeches Parts, Petticoat Parts And The Sin Of Self Love," and chapter 36 promises to tell "Of A Printing Which Brought A Great Embarrassment, And Of How A New Prince Hal Forgot An Old Friend." Chapter headings such as these are an aspect of the novelist's narrative strategy, for not only do they cue the reader

27

regarding the text's structure and contents, but they also set the tone for what follows. The creator of the chapter headings is not simply a transparent narrator; he or she is also a presence who is communicating something by dividing and labeling segments of the story in this manner.

All of the novels I discuss in this chapter use some form of first-person narration. The narrators in New Historical Fiction can be self-reflexive and self-mocking, at times using pompous or satirical chapter headings as a sly wink to the reader regarding their roles as storytellers. At other times they are elusive and cryptic, changeable and inconsistent, deceptive and self-deceiving, didactic, clairvoyant, prolix, self-indulgent. Vocabulary, orthography, shifts in diction, metafictional digressions, and a range of vocal registers all contribute to the creation of a speaking voice that is at once modern and centuries-old. Third-person omniscient narrators are less likely to capture the sounds of the past than first-person ones, for they are not as convincingly rooted in the novel's time and place; this may explain the recurrence of first-person narration in the New Historical Fiction.

Most of the novels I have chosen were published during the decade between 1989 and 1998, a particularly fertile and experimental period for serious historical fiction. Their authors write in a mix of forms, including nonhistorical fiction, historical mysteries, essays, plays, and criticism. All of them offer unsettling and provocative reimaginings of sixteenth- and seventeenth-century England, while exhibiting a variety of narrative strategies that have come to characterize the genre of postmodern historical fiction.

In his Elizabethan trilogy, written over a period of twenty-five years (see chapter 3), George Garrett recreates Shakespeare's England in more painstaking detail than any other novelist currently writing. *Entered from the Sun*, the third novel in the trilogy, is ostensibly about the mysterious gaps in our collective knowledge concerning the death of Christopher Marlowe, one of literary history's most celebrated unsolved cases. Marlowe is not a character in the novel, however, for *Entered from the Sun* is more concerned with fictional characters who become involved in two independent searches for the "truth." Two residents of London, Joseph Hunnyman, an out-of-work player, and Captain Barfoot, a secret Catholic and scarred veteran of foreign wars, are separately approached in 1597 by agents of mysterious, unnamed patrons to investigate Marlowe's death four years after it occurred. Marlowe's death has been so prominently fictionalized, starting immediately after it occurred, that it provides an ideal subject for an historiographic metafiction, one that reflects our uncertainty about the boundaries between history and fiction and the way in which these discourses "textualize" and "archeologize" the past, to use Linda Hutcheon's terms (93).

The narrator of *Entered from the Sun* gradually reveals his presence in what might otherwise appear to be a rather conversational third-person narration by the "author" who addresses the reader in an "author's greeting" that precedes the first chapter. A few paragraphs into the second chapter, it becomes clear that the speaking voice is a character who belongs to the late sixteenth-century world of the novel. He calls attention to himself through a parenthetical aside: "(and, believe me, there are many thoughtful persons who in their wisdom profess to believe that this world will end with this self-same century and with the reign of the old Queen). . . . " (15). A few pages later, he speaks directly to the reader about himself:

> As for myself.
> Why, that's nothing to concern yourself about. I am here present as a voice only, a voice from the dark. Hoping by the power of words and words alone (though they may sometimes cast real shadows like sudden wings) to permit you to see and judge for yourself.
> Otherwise think nothing of me. For this is in no way my story. I insist on that. (29)

The novel's most conspicuous postmodern disruption comes about halfway through the text. The mysterious narrator who claimed not to be part of his tale confesses to having misled the reader: "I confess I have played you false," he says, by witholding "some little truth" (164). He eventually identifes himself as "Paul Cartwright," the man who hired Barfoot to investigate Marlowe's death on behalf of his master (who turns out to be none other than Sir Walter Raleigh). But he is also a seemingly unrelated character, a frustrated, aspiring poet infatuated with Hunnyman's mistress Alysoun.

With characteristic postmodern self-reflexivity, the narrator comments on his narration, warning us that it is biased, since his failure as a poet and playwright have made him bitter: "Be wary," he tells the reader. "Trust me no more than I trust you" (172). Bitterness, for him, is a hallmark of the age, and perhaps ours as well, he suggests: "I am thinking of those of us (may I include yourself?) who once upon a time eagerly swallowed the sweet wine of the world. And have lived to taste the dregs of it, bitter at the bottom of the cup." (171). Were Garrett to offer his own sweeping generalizations about Elizabethan England, he would be guilty of old-historicist tactics; instead, he lets this not-very-reliable fictional voice proclaim bitterness and high ambition to be "the two great ills of our times" (171).

The elusive ghost-narrator of *Entered from the Sun*, it turns out, is also "a scribbler" like Marlowe, one who once "aspired (O sadly foolish!) to become an uncommon and honored poet," and he speaks of Marlowe elegiacally as a writer "whose plays are charged with more explosive ambition and aspiration than I allowed myself to imagine" (282). The narrator portrays Marlowe as a Faust-like playwright who sold his soul to the devil, "otherwise (I ask you!) how could he ever have achieved the undeniable glory and shining of his words?" (283). In a rare burst of emotion, he exclaims:

I swear to you that I would gladly have changed lives and places with him, Marlowe, I mean, even knowing *in advance* that Ingram Frizer would thrust knife blade hilt-deep into my brain, in payment for having enjoyed a modest portion of Marlowe's gifts and good fortune and reputation.

In the next paragraph, he wryly admits to being "a somewhat less than reliable and trustworthy witness" (283). This ghost addresses us as "you, the living" from beyond the grave, although, as Tom Whalen observes, he seems to lack the omniscience customarily assigned to ghosts and spirits; either he cannot "illuminate the novel's central mystery" and tell us how Marlowe was killed, or, for some reason, he prefers not to (Whalen 95). *Entered from the Sun* would have been a very different novel if the narrator's feelings about Marlowe and himself had been a dominant presence; instead, they appear momentarily, as one perspective among many.

Garrett reopens a "closed" event, investing Marlowe's mysterious death (often thought to be related to his activities as a spy on the continent) with an "afterlife," an ongoing intrigue that draws its inspiration from historically documented surveillance activities. In a conspicuous departure from the detective fiction conventions that shape the narrative, he leaves the ending unresolved; the reader never learns who hired Hunnyman and why, nor the "real" identity of the narrator. Indeed, "we know nothing more at the end of the novel concerning its central mystery than we did at the beginning," as Whalen observes, adding that Garrett seems to be implying "that 'history' can teach us nothing"; his two spy-historians, in their efforts to reconstruct the past, "find no answers, only more mystery, deception and death the deeper they descend into the labyrinth" (98). This kind of postmodern fiction, in the words of Frederick M. Holmes,

> suggest[s] not only the vexed character of our knowledge of the past but also our freedom from the apparent constraints of history. If events are not final, if we are not locked into a single irrevocable sequence . . . then history is not the coercive force which it appears to be. (31)

London in the year 1583 provides the setting for *Firedrake's Eye* by Patricia Finney, a very accomplished historical novelist who, astonishingly, began her career at the age of nineteen.[1] To Garrett's preoccupation with surveillance and power politics Finney adds another Foucauldian element, the representation of madness. Rather like the narrator of *Entered from the Sun*, her narrator is at once an omniscient narrative voice and a character with seemingly limited opportunities to know what goes on inside the lives and minds of other characters. But this voice mixes fairly straightforward storytelling techniques with the extraordinarily poetic ravings of a Bedlam beggar. He is Shakespeare's Poor Tom come to life, and, according to the historical note at the end of the novel, is based on a "genuine" ballad called "Tom O'Bedlam's Song," a ballad that might have inspired Edgar's disguise in *King Lear* (Finney, *Firedrake's Eye* 253).

Finney writes for a reader who can read intertextually, recognizing the Shakespearean traces in the former courtier, poet, and law student who has become a schizophrenic, visionary madman haunted by devils and capable of seeing angels. Although he has forgotten his birth name, Tom is entirely conscious of his two selves, the uncontrollable Tom and the lucid "Clever One." This slippage between overlapping identities constitutes a postmodern revision of our conventional notions about fictional "character," but it is also historically grounded in Renaissance theories about possession. Here is Tom on the opening page, introducing his dual identity:

> First must I ask forgiveness, that this has somewhat of madness colouring it. For my poor skullmate Tom was always at my side, and would often elbow past me and the Courtier to bow to the Queen Moon. . . . And yet Poor Tom has his uses, for his angels make him windows in men's heads to see their souls. So I beg you, forgive his yammerings and do not put all of them aside. Perhaps it is only the weight of the infinite that made him rave. So here also is Tom's madness, woven like gold thread into a good cloth of sense. . . . (5)

Finney uses Tom's "madness" (just as Shakespeare uses madness and folly in *King Lear*) to comment on the corruption and shallowness of a world that, in a different kind of historical fiction, might be romanticized and celebrated.

Tom's narrative style gives *Firedrake's Eye* an unbalanced quality, that sense of being poised somewhere between historical realism and fantasy which is characteristic of magic realism. For example, here he is describing himself inside St. Paul's, the heart of Elizabethan London:

> I myself flew through the nave, borne upon angels' arms, speaking to the faces carved upon the roof bosses [while] Tom capered below and got some pennies for amusing of a Queen's favourite with an argument that it was possible to weigh tobacco smoke. (120)

A couple of days later he speaks of losing all memory of an afternoon that "went missing to join the flock of my lost days in the locked belfry of my mind" (123). When he returned to consciousness of his whereabouts, only to be confronted with the spectacle of violence and death and plotting and threats of torture,

> I went out and up and walked about among the stars, leaving my animal part to rave below, while I trod the dark gritty clouds of London, the

star daemon in my soul conversing pleasantly with the Queen Moon and the Seven Governors of the Sky. (126)

The "I" of this passage invites us to participate in a conception of character that deliberately challenges the seemingly realistic characterization employed elsewhere in the novel.

Finney's narrative strategies bring to mind Catherine Belsey's comment in *Critical Practice* on "deconstructing a text." Belsey notes that "the strategies of the classic realist text divert the reader from what is contradictory within it . . . because [it] represent[s] experience in the ways it is conventionally articulated in our society" (128). The object of deconstructing the text, then, is to "locate the point of contradiction within the text, the point at which it transgresses the limits within which it is constructed, breaks free of the constraints imposed by its own realist form" (104). In the parts of the novel where the narrative is filtered through Tom's fractured and unstable voice, Finney could be said to perform just such a deconstruction of a hypothetical "text" about Shakespeare's England familiar to readers conversant with the period. This "text" is based upon the images, assumptions, and historical details Finney encountered during the years of research she alludes to in her author's note, not to mention the tradition of fictional constructions of Elizabethan England since *Kenilworth*. *Firedrake's Eye* looks like a realistic text at times, but its unconventional narration causes it to "break free of the constraints" imposed by its seeming adherence to the rules of classic historical fiction. This becomes especially evident at the end of the novel, when we discover that Tom is narrating these events after his own death—surely a betrayal of the narrative convention whereby the reader assumes that the narrator is left alive to tell the tale.

An Oxford-trained historian, Finney is very scrupulous about providing historical notes, glossaries of unfamiliar words, and character lists distinguishing invented from historical characters. These supplements to the novel itself reinscribe the distinction between truth and fiction, history and story. The novel is set in 1583 because of Sir Francis Throgmorton's intrigue with French and English Catholics to free Mary Queen of Scots and place her on the English throne. Throgmorton was arrested, confessed on the rack, and was executed as a result of counter-espionage activities directed by Elizabeth's Secretary of State, Sir Francis Walsingham. In Finney's version of the events of 1583, the plot to assassinate Elizabeth in the midst of the Accession Day festivities does not end with Throgmorton's arrest (accordingly, the historical note tells the reader that "[T]he central story of this book, an assassination attempt during the 1583 Accession Day Tilts, is entirely invented" [253]).

Using information on the Tilts of 1582, biographies, and historical records, Finney invents a decentered cast with Elizabeth and the court at the periphery and two fictional characters as the protagonists: Simon Ames, a fictional member of the historical Jewish mercantile family headed by Dunstan Ames, and David Becket, a former soldier in the wars in the Netherlands of the 1570s with contacts in the London underworld, who is licensed to teach the use of arms and is the self-proclaimed "best sword-and-buckler man in London" (21). The plot is thwarted, at the very last moment, by the combined efforts of Ames (a skilled cryptographer), Becket, and Poor Tom, who loses his life to save the queen's. (*Firedrake's Eye* will be discussed further in chapter 7.)

In 1998 a sequel to *Firedrake's Eye* appeared, emphasizing women characters, both real and invented, and relegating Becket and Ames to less active roles. *Unicorn's Blood* displays what Elisabeth Wesseling describes as the cross-fertilization between historical fiction, detective fiction, and counterfactual or alternate histories, whereby the lost possible divergent paths history could have taken are recuperated; this kind of "postmodern counterfactual conjecture" speculates about "the malleability of historical reality" (100, 113). The conjecture in *Unicorn's Blood* centers on the possibility that Queen Elizabeth became pregnant at the age of fourteen, a theory that has been in circulation since her own lifetime. Like its precursor, *Unicorn's Blood* is intermittently narrated by the delusional alter-ego of one of the characters, in this case an aged crone named Mary. Mary is a former nun and the mother and grandmother of whores; as the narrator, she assumes the persona of the Virgin Mary and refers to Elizabeth as "my usurper," which, given the Protestant iconography of the age, she was. (*Unicorn's Blood* will be discussed further in chapter 5.)

Mary often disappears as the narrator in *Unicorn's Blood*, rather as the mysterious narrator of *Entered from the Sun* does. In neither case is the author willing to limit the perspective to one character's viewpoint, as realistic novels narrated consistently in the first person do by constructing a narrator who serves as the filter through which incidents must pass. Eva Figes solves the problem of first-person narration in *The Tree of Knowledge* by writing an essentially plotless short novel set entirely in a room where the narrator receives visitors. A feminist critic, scholar, editor, and novelist, Figes uses her narrator's tale to disrupt the way traditionally inscribed British history views one of its icons. Inspired, perhaps, by Robert Graves's *Wife to Mr. Milton*, Figes takes on the Milton establishment in a fragmentary narrative that views Milton and his age from the perspective of his daughter Deborah.

Deborah is not exactly a narrator; she is a speaking voice, the only one in the novel. *The Tree of Knowledge* consists of a series of one-sided conversations, rather like an epistolary novel in which the reader is provided with only one side of the correspondence. Unlike *Wife to Mr. Milton* and other classic historical fictions, *The Tree of Knowledge* makes no obvious effort to help readers establish their bearings: it offers very few names, no dates, no exposition or panoramic descriptions of the world beyond the room that holds the speaking voice. The reader has to read intertextually, bringing knowledge derived from conventional Milton biographies to the experience of *this* reconstruction of the way biographical information is collected.

> Pray be seated, sir, and pardon such humble surroundings. This room must serve both as schoolroom and for living in, and I fear it is but a shabby place to receive visitors. You see how bare it is, and lacking in comfort, but children make rough work of household chattels. . . . (1)

These are the opening sentences of *The Tree of Knowledge*. The "sir" of the first sentence, we gradually infer, is a visitor who has come to hear the aged Deborah's reminiscences about her famous father. "I would not have you think me bitter," she says to the gentleman. "I have long since forgiven him. All I have in my heart now is a kind of love and much sorrow, that there should have been so little of it when he lived. But we cannot undo the past, can we, sir?" (2–3).

Ironically, Figes intends to do just that, to "undo" a version of the past handed down by generations of male biographers and scholars who never thought to look at Milton from the perspective of the daughter he disinherited, allegedly after teaching her to pronounce, but not understand, Latin and Greek so that she could read aloud to him. Speaking of her father's feelings about the restoration of the monarchy in 1660, she describes him as enraged "that we, the few, should now return to slavery, because the many choose not to be free." Then she adds, in a bitter comment on her father's inability to apply his principles to his own family, "Besides, sir, that which I endured, my sisters also, was it not a kind of slavery, and brought about by him that spoke of freedom?" (111). Speaking through Deborah's voice, Figes instigates a subversive re-vision of Milton's writings, the historical "sources" for much of her novel.

Little by little, a multigenerational family portrait comes into focus, as Deborah rambles on about the past. First she talks to the professor, and, after an unspecified period of time, to another visitor who comes to get a box of pamphlets she has managed to save from being used for the fire that is so important in this drafty, uncomfortable room. We know this only because she says, "Your name sir? I have no recollection of it, and the professor has not been here for some time" (55). Between visits, Deborah's one-sided dialogue is directed to her daughter Elizabeth, who is "lately risen from childbed" (16) and mourning the death of her infant when the novel begins, and to Elizabeth's daughter Liza, who dies at the age of eight during the novel's indeterminate timespan. The narrative captures the largely undocumented experience of being born female in the seventeenth century through the kind of family history, laced with moralizing sayings and homilies, that women pass on to the young as they go about their household duties.

The Tree of Knowledge solves the problem of the first-person narrator's access to events beyond her own experience by giving Deborah memories that reach back to before she was born, derived from what she heard from her father, her lawyer uncle, and her much older husband. As Deborah observes, "what we hear in childhood stays with us forever, image and language both" (76). It is through these images and language, preserved from childhood onward, that Figes reconstructs "history" as viewed from the underside and preserved by oral transmission, told from a perspective of partial and fragmentary knowledge—knowledge that comes, as Deborah says at the very end of her long monologue, from eating the fruit of the trees of knowledge and of life, which are "but one and the same" (138).

The fragmentary narrative of still another old woman is one of several voices in Jeanette Winterson's *Sexing the Cherry*, an eclectic, postmodern fiction by a writer whose earlier, critically acclaimed *The Passion* is a magic-realist historical novel set during the Napoleonic wars. In *Sexing the Cherry*, Winterson interweaves the reminiscences of Jordan and his adoptive mother, the Dog Woman, set in the 1640s and 1660s, with a feminist revision of a folktale called *The Twelve Dancing Princesses*. The twelfth dancing princess, Fortunata, is the object of Jordan's quest and desires. The Dog Woman shares some of the magic-realistic characteristics of Finney's narrators: early in the novel, after describing the way she found Jordan "so caked in mud I could have baked him like a hedgehog" in the Thames (in a deliberate allusion to the biblical Moses [3]), she remarks,

> I was invisible then. I, who must turn sideways through any door, can melt into the night as easily as a thin thing that sings in the choir at church. Singing is my pleasure, but not in church, for the parson said the gargoyles must remain on the outside, not seek room in the choir stalls. So I sing inside the mountain of my flesh, and my voice is as slender as a reed and my voice has no lard in it. When I sing the dogs sit quiet and people who pass in the night stop their jabbering and discontent and think of other times, when they were happy. And I sing of other times, when I was happy, though I know that these are figments of my mind. . . . (8)

The Dog Woman takes pride in her grotesqueness: she is heavier than an elephant, so much so that "When I was a child my father swung me up on to his knees to tell me a story and I broke both his legs," but is nevertheless loved by Jordan, who "was proud of me because no other child had a mother who could hold a dozen oranges in her mouth at once" (21). Can such a narrator be reliable in the conventional sense? This is one of many questions Winterson's fiction poses.

More than any of the other novels I have been discussing, *Sexing the Cherry* participates in a number of postmodern conventions: it integrates history and the fantastic, parodies and borrows from other texts, and breaks down and makes fluid the boundaries between genres, mingling stretches of continuous narration with the testimony of the princesses and other labeled fragments (McHale 90; Hutcheon 9). For example, a list of seven "lies" appears out of nowhere, epigrammatic pronouncements that, in a different fictional world, would be truths:

> LIES 1: There is only the present and nothing to remember.
>
>   · · ·
>
> LIES 3: The difference between the past and the future is that one has happened while the other has not.
>
>   · · ·
>
> LIES 6: Reality as something which can be agreed upon. (90)

Later, we come across "PAINTINGS 1"; then "TIME 4," in which Jordan asks, "Did my childhood happen? I must believe it did, but I don't have any proof. My mother says it did, but she is a fantasist, a liar and a murderer. . . ." He concludes that "I will assume that I had a childhood, but I cannot assume to have had the one I remember" (102). A page or so later, Winterson interrupts her narrative with

> MEMORY 1: The scene I have just described to you may lie in the future or the past. Either I have found Fortunata or I will find her. I cannot be sure. Either I am remembering her or am still imagining her. But she is somewhere in the grid of time, a co-ordinate, as I am. (104)

Fragments like this one serve as a skeptical critical commentary on the rest of the narrative, calling into question the nature and knowability of history.

Historiographic metafiction, according to Hutcheon, "problematize[s] both the nature of the referent and its relation to the real, historical world by its paradoxical combination of metafictional self-reflexivity with historical subject matter" (19). Narrative conventions are "installed and subverted"; the narration is disrupted and denied closure, and the speaking subject lacks "confidence in his/her ability to know the past with any certainty" (121–22, 117). All of these characteristics are evident in *Sexing the Cherry*, particularly in the novel's final pages, where Winterson introduces two "new" twentieth-century characters. Nicholas Jordan is pretty clearly an avatar of the seventeenth-century Jordan; more puzzling is a nameless woman, "a chemist with a good degree . . . an attractive woman whom men liked to work with," (142) as she describes herself, whose being seems at times to merge with the enormous, earthy, murderous Dog Woman's. "If I have a spirit, a soul," she says, "it won't be single, it will be multiple. . . . It may inhabit numerous changing decaying bodies in the future and in the past" (146). This is a more radical and surrealistic version of Figes's strategy of layering of one "period" over another. Figes lets Deborah mythologize past and present, contrasting "those distant times [before the Commonwealth when] men thought that great events were brought about by God . . . " with her listener's present, in which "the Bible is now like some ancient tale. . . . " (110). Winterson, more skeptically, has one of her narrators say on the novel's final page that "the future and the present and the past exist only in our minds, and from a distance the borders of each shrink and fade. . . . " (167).

The most common form of first-person narration is the principal character's account of his or her life or a portion thereof. When the narrator is an historical figure and the reader comes to the novel with some knowledge of history, the reading experience entails a suspension of disbelief: the reader sets aside "history" and enters into the narrator's version of events, or else reads ironically with a constant awareness of the narrator's bias. In Robert Nye's *The Voyage of the "Destiny,"* the conventions of retrospective narration shape Sir Walter Raleigh's account of his final months, with backward excursions to earlier events in a patchwork pastiche that presumes upon the reader's knowledge of history.

The fictional Raleigh is writing a mixed text; part letter to his thirteen-year-old son Carew, a child he never knew, and part journal, starting in February 1618 from the ship *Destiny* near the end of his third and last voyage to the New World (which ended disastrously). A letter of "instructions" Raleigh wrote to his son and "to posterity" is embedded within the novel; this mixing of fictional and historical documents is a recurring characteristic of the New Historical Fiction. The letter is reminiscent of Bacon's *Essays,* Machiavelli's *The Prince,* and Polonius's famous leave-taking speech to Laertes in *Hamlet,* and includes advice about friendship and trust, the selection of a wife, the dangers posed by flattery, lying, vanity, excess, and so forth. Its formal and prescriptive style is quite different from the speaking voice Nye creates in other parts of the novel. The weakened narrator, plagued with illness and devastated by the death of his older son Wat during the abortive invasion of a Spanish garrison, writes a text that is "both more than a Journal and less." "What will it be?," Raleigh asks. "I don't know. I am writing it partly to find out. It will have to be something like the truth." He speculates that it will be "some kind of confession. The story of my days past and the story of my days present. What I was and what I am" (5).

The untitled chapters are dated in the manner of journal entries and contain a mixture of accounts of the "present" in 1618 with allusions to the past. Metacommentary suffuses the novel, as Raleigh reflects on the nature of his text. In a nearly page-long parenthetical aside that interrupts an account of a cockfight at James I's court, Raleigh alludes to the limitations of first-person narration as he explains the method and purpose of his text:

> (It occurs to me that my method in this writing is most curious, yet necessarily so. I am recreating past scenes for you, Carew, and to some extent for myself—the better to get to the bottom of them. Yet sometimes they are scenes in which you perceive I play no part, not having been present to witness with my own eyes what things were done nor hear with my own ears what things were said. So do romancers write, who make up fictions for the entertainment of empty minds. My purpose is different. I am trying to get at the truth of certain past events that have bearing on my situation now. Truth needs no audience, but he who would tell it is helped to keep straight by a listener he loves. . . .
>
> I tell you what Winwood told me. Where Winwood told me what *he* thought and *he* felt, I repeat that. For the rest, I report just the outward events and remarks to the best of my memory. There can be no steel glass in these passages.) (Nye 72)

Like many of the other novels I will be discussing, this one "focus[es] attention on history not only by containing episodes set in the historical past but also by featuring characters' attempts to reconstruct the past" (Holmes 53). Holmes observes a similar tendency in hybrid fictions such as A. S. Byatt's *Possession* or Peter Ackroyd's *Chatterton*.

Nearly two hundred pages after the previously quoted passage, Raleigh realizes that his book is "the log of three voyages"; rather like Renaissance allegory, it is at once a day-by-day record of the present, a tale of "my life and fortunes," and finally, a metaphorical voyage through "the fog of memory, the storm brewed where past and present waters meet only to make a whirlpool in the mind," on "an unfathomable ocean [where] there's no crew but myself . . . " (248). As Nye's Raleigh probes further and further into his past, he begins to address others, such as Queen Elizabeth and his wife Bess (221ff; 226–33). The last hundred pages of the novel contain other texts, giving the journal the character of a commonplace book. Nye includes the King's Proclamation giving Raleigh license to undertake the voyage to Guiana (265), the last entry from the ship's log (267), the full text of Raleigh's well-known poem "The Lie" (269–71) and excerpts from other poems, an account of the voyage by the Reverend Mr. Samuel Jones, (chaplain on the *Destiny*) (281–87), the warrant for Raleigh's arrest in July 1618, and letters and documents from the final days before his execution on October 29, 1618. Nye is particularly given to this sort of inclusiveness in his novels; his *Falstaff* and *The Late Mr. Shakespeare*, while quite different in some respects from *The Voyage of the "Destiny,"* are even more inclusive and encyclopedic in character. ✖

Raleigh's bitterness about Queen Elizabeth and King James I contrasts sharply with the tone of another experiment in first-person narration, Rose Tremain's *Restoration*. Tremain's account of the years from 1664 to 1667, as viewed through the consciousness of Robert Merivel, is a seemingly "realistic" narrative that only gradually reveals its strangeness. Some of this strangeness is due to the very historicity of the novel, for Tremain manages to capture an aspect of the past that is utterly foreign to twentieth-century Western readers: the quasi-sexual, lover-like devotion and absolute trust the narrator feels for the king, regardless of his flaws, and the god-like intuitive knowledge that the king—again, despite his flaws—seems to possess.

Merivel's "story" has "a variety of beginnings," numbered one through five, starting at five different points in his earlier life. This strategy draws attention to the constructedness of the narrator's tale, and so calls into question the reliability of autobiographical accounts. In the fifth beginning, the most comically improbable of them all, Merivel abandons his medical studies to become resident physician for the eighteen Royal Dogs, having accidentally saved the life of one of them by falling asleep, thus allowing nature to effect a cure (5–17). This fifth beginning proceeds swiftly in the space of three or four pages to Merivel's marriage, at Charles II's command, to Celia, one of the royal mistresses. Merivel becomes Sir Robert Merivel, and the king's "loyal Fool" (49). His love for the king, and his mistaken belief that the king returns his love, are cruelly shaken in the course of the narration, but the reader is made to feel little or no sympathy for this comically helpless, physically inept, indolent and self-deprecating character who remarks halfway through the novel, "Well, you know me intimately by this time" (174). Knowing him intimately is a curiously uncomfortable, even disorienting, experience, though; for while Tremain *seems* to be writing a fairly conventional, albeit exaggerated, historical fiction, she breaks an unspoken rule of classic realism by giving us no inkling that the person who is recounting this story has changed, grown, become someone to listen to with respect. An abrupt shift occurs when Merivel is cast out of his "Paradise" and forced to resume his medical career. "I shall not say *adieu*," the king says to him, as he dispossesses him of house and title and wife, "for who knows whether, at some time in the future, History may not have another role for you?" (183–84). And History does.

Thus the novel undergoes a radical shift of scene and tone, in an implicit rejection of the premise that an "age" has consistent and defining characteristics, a premise associated with both the "old" historicism and classic historical fiction. Breaking off his narrative to address the reader directly,

Robert tells us he has "passed from one life to another," and admonishes us to let go of the past in the same way he has:

> Under these things you may draw a line: my house at Bidnold, the colours of my park, Celia's face at my table. Neither you nor I will see them again. They have been consumed, not by actual flames . . . but by the fire of the King's displeasure. I must thus imagine them turned to ash, and so must you, for you will not be returned to them. (203)

In his subsequent life among the Quakers at Whittlesea Hospital, he tries hard to believe "in the death of Merivel and his replacement by Robert," although Merivel, his physical, sexual side, cannot be "entirely quiet" (257). The dual identity the narrator experiences is somewhat like Tom's in *Firedrake's Eye* inasmuch as it is historically grounded. Tremain's re-creation of a seventeenth-century conversion experience makes Merivel's improbable transformation fictionally acceptable; in a less extensively researched novel, it might seem unconvincing. Her research also enables her to "translate" medical treatises and other sources of historical information so as to invent a fully realized picture of what it was like to be a physician, to work in a hospital for the insane, and to *think* in the terms and vocabulary that medical science afforded at that time.

In the final chapters, Robert survives the Great Fire of London, and is granted a "restoration" and a reconciliation with his beloved king, in a strange parody of the reunions of lover and beloved at the end of historical romances. As he anticipates the reunion, Robert uses language that evokes the union between man and God:

> And this is what I believed: I believed that if, one day, the King *wanted* to find me, he would find me. I did not know how. I could not even imagine how. I only knew that he would. And that it would not prove to be very difficult for him, for such is his power that surely no corner of his Kingdom is invisible to him and no person within it beyond his reach? (356)

Like most of the writers I've discussed here, Tremain exhibits an ability to reproduce the thought patterns of the past and the language which constitutes our primary means of access to them in her narrator's first-person account of his life. Although we come to know Robert Merivel well by the end of the 370-page novel, he always remains psychologically unlike us. Compared, for example, with the medieval or Renaissance protagonists of more conventional historical novelists, such as Gillian Bradshaw, Rosemary Sutcliff, or Dorothy Dunnett, he does not invite the identification and engagement that occur when a character fulfills a reader's expectations about the way people conduct and reflect upon their lives.

We arrive, by a circuitous route, at the historical subject who occupies this book's shifting center, William Shakespeare. Shakespeare, it need hardly be said, appears in countless historical fictions and fiction-biographies; indeed, his life became the object of imaginative invention and mythologizing not long after his death. Anthony Burgess set the standard for subsequent myth-debunking historical novels about Shakespeare's life and loves in *Nothing Like the Sun*, one of many innovative novels Burgess wrote during his long career (see chapter 3). John Mortimer's *Will Shakespeare: The Untold Story* surpasses *Nothing Like the Sun* as absurdist comedy, although is is ultimately less innovative as historical fiction. Mortimer employs a narrative strategy that Nye and Burgess would subsequently adopt in *The Late Mr. Shakespeare* and *A Dead Man in Deptford*, respectively: he invents a boy actor whose proximity to Shakespeare enables him to narrate his untold story from the remove of many years.

Mortimer's narrator introduces himself as "I John Rice, at one time little Jack Rice, Snotnose, bare arse, runabout Rice, and at one other time, at the best time the Lady Anne, Queen to Crookback Richard, and sweet Viola, fair Rosalind. . . . " He then begins again in the present: "I John Rice, 'Praise the Lord and Let His Enemies be Smitten' Rice, at present sexton, key-holder, grave-tender and singer through the nose on Sundays at the Church of St. Barnaby . . . " (11). Writing clandestinely during the Commonwealth period, "emboldened by Holy Wine," Rice looks back fondly on the flourishing of the theaters from a present in which "a two-hour sermon on the Evils of Fornication is the nearest we come to Comedy" (13). He describes himself as "a playmaker in secret," who composes his account of Shakespeare's life from "my own knowledge," tales he picked up from "Dick Burbage and the other actors and the servants of my lord Southampton," visits to Stratford, and inventions based on "all I knew of Will and his probable manner at the Court and in the Ale House . . . " (13). Like Nye's Raleigh, this first-person narrator makes a point of accounting to the reader for the way he acquired his material.

The ensuing "Comical, Tragical History of William Shakespeare" includes an enormous cast of characters: Shakespeare's neighbor Hamnet Sadler, upon whose testimony Rice relies; Christopher Marlowe, who puts Shakespeare to work writing parts of *Henry VI* in a collaboration that launches Will's career as a playwright; Shakespeare's fellow actors Richard Burbage and Will Kempe; the Earl of Southampton, who goes about in the disguise of "Hal the Horse-Thief" and becomes the subject of Shakespeare's sonnets; and many others. Rice intersperses accounts of his own performances, often beginning his chapters in the present and then leading the reader back through a sequence of reminiscences to the subject of his memoir, as in this opening paragraph of chapter 15, "Of What Was Revealed By The Death Of Tybalt:"

I was giving my Lady Juliet, one of my favourite roles and for which I shall long be remembered. (I saw old Master Pennybroker, our Rector's father, look quaintly at me in Church last Sunday as if trying to recollect something. Did he see me down a misty corridor of memory as a Star Crossed Lover, married at fourteen, hauling her husband up a balcony to spreadeagle her upon an Italian mattress on a hot night in Verona? Did his thought grow so hot in memory that he would have crossed the aisle to pinch my aged buttock? As we passed in the graveyard I thought I heard him whisper, "A rose by any other name would smell as sweet." It was like a password given by allies lost in battle. . . . (103)

The novel's gossipy renditions of hearsay and fragments of recorded history owe something to the style of John Aubrey's *Brief Lives* or Samuel Pepys's *Diary*, both written at about the time during which Rice is telling his tale. Characterizations of historical figures are frequently exaggerated and mocking, such as this description of James I, a marked contrast to Merivel's worshipful descriptions of Charles II in *Restoration*:

The King's head seemed ever too large for his body, his eyes were damp and his tongue lolled. As he spoke he could not control a dribble at the corner of his mouth (which they say was almost the only watering his face received, for he ever denied himself washing as Christians deny themselves meat in Lent). As he walked the room he for ever plunged his hand into his breeches to worry his codpiece (these same breeches being well padded behind so as to protect his rump, it seems, from sudden assault by assassins and their daggers). (227)

In its less frivolous moments *Will Shakespeare: An Untold Story* speculates about how Shakespeare's plays were regarded in their own time; in a chapter on the company's performance of *King Lear*, for instance, Rice remarks of Oswald that "I could see so little good in the man that I thought how far had Will Shakespeare gone in his hatred of time-servers and double-dealers" (243). When the performance is over one of the actors tells Shakespeare that the company was "sore afraid" that "the King and his Courtiers might take some offence at it" (245). The play was a success, however, for as Will wryly observes, "the more we rail the more they smile at us! We show them their Ingratitude, their Hypocrisy, their short, strutting, empty Authority and Insolence in Office! And they smile and put their hands together and say, 'Thank you, actors, there is beef and small beer for you in the Lower Servants' Hall'" (246). Reading this, a reader might return to King Lear with new insights about the way it might have been received by its seventeenth-century audience.

Robert Nye's *The Late Mr. Shakespeare* is much longer and more inclusive than *Will Shakespeare: An Untold Story*. Like Mortimer, Nye has written a playfully postmodern parody of conventional biographies, one that satirically takes on the Shakespeare legends and embellishes them to the point of absurdity. The novel is an eclectic melange of researched and invented mock-history presented as the reminiscences of another fictional sometime boy actor who, much as Mortimer's Rice does, narrates from the novel's present (in this case, the Restoration). The narrative style is similar to that of *The Tree of Knowledge*; the speaker, nicknamed Pickleherring, addresses his rambling account to unnamed listeners called "Sir" and "Madam," whose voices we never hear (although as a result of Pickleherring's remarks, they gradually acquire personalities).

Speaking through Pickleherring, Nye offers historiographic metacommentary on the kind of biography he is composing. In the fifteenth of the novel's one hundred short, numbered chapters, entitled "What This Book Is Doing," Pickleherring draws the reader's attention to the way his inventions "make you remember certain things I tell you. . . . I want you to think for yourself about all of them." (54) Later, he distinguishes between "two ways of seeing" and thus, "two ways of historicizing":

> There is *town* history and there is *country* history.
>
> Town history is cynical and exact. It is written by wits and it orders and limits what it talks about. It relies on facts and figures. It is knowing. . . .
>
> Country history is faithful and open-ended. It is a tale told by various idiots on the village green, all busy contradicting themselves in the name of a common truth. It exaggerates and inflames what it talks about. It delights in lies and gossip. It is unwise. Wild and mystical and passionate, it is ruled by the heart. . . .
>
> Easy to mock, it always strains belief. But sometimes it catches the ghostly coat-tails of what is otherwise ungraspable. It is the only possible way of accounting for Mr Shakespeare. (67–68)

There are no notes or other indications of the sources Nye used, only a postscript that begins: "This book contains quotations from (and variations on) the lives and works of," followed by an alphabeticized list of some seventy-five names, from John Aubrey and W. H. Auden to John Dover Wilson and Ludwig Wittgenstein (400). This strategy of teasing the reader with unmarked quotations and allusions had been used by Peter Ackroyd in the postmodern hybrid *English Music*, inspired by the memoir of the Victorian medium, Daniel Home. *English Music* begins with an acknowledgments that offers this arch remark about what is to follow:

> The scholarly reader will soon realize that I have appropriated passages from Thomas Browne, Thomas Malory, William Hogarth, Thomas Morley, Lewis Carroll, Samuel Johnson, Daniel Defoe and many other

English writers; the alert reader will understand why I have done so. (n.p.)

By the time one reaches the postscript of *The Late Mr. Shakespeare*, the list has become a familiar recurring motif; at one point late in the novel, Pickleherring lists all the things "which it is now too late to work into the fabric of my book," and we are left to wonder what these one hundred and fifty or so alphabeticized words and phrases signify in the life of Shakespeare: familiar ones like "alarums" and "cross-gartering," unfamiliar ones like "fewmets" and "pantofles," ordinary things like "oats" and "onions," and places and names like "Ireland" and "Inigo Jones" (Nye 375–77). Both this list and the postscript act as mocking affronts to the scholarly practices of scrupulous footnoting and quotation, so that the novel becomes, in retrospect, a puzzle that invites solving. The reader wonders who is Warren Hope or the Comtesse de Chambrun? or why are Edgar Allen Poe and Dylan Thomas on this list? The withholding of information both frustrates and challenges; it tests the reader's knowledge not only of Shakespeare and the cumulative Shakespeare "biography," but of subsequent writers who may not have been referring to Shakespeare at all in the unmarked allusions Nye playfully incorporates into his text.

In a self-reflexive moment, Pickleherring observes "that every attempt to find out the truth of another man's life, and to write his Life, throws light on the person who makes the attempt, as much as on the man biographied" (144). Just as *The Tree of Knowledge* is at once Milton's story and the story of his daughter and her daughter and granddaughter, so *The Late Mr. Shakespeare* is also Pickleherring's story. He composes his narrative in a little attic room above a bawdy house during the Plague and periodically reminds the reader that he writes from a Restoration perspective:

> I know the modern taste calls him vulgar and crabbed, an uncouth spirit . . . [but] I predict that one day Mr William Shakespeare and his works will be so popular and so revered that children will be required to study the subject in schools and universities. You find the notion crazy, sir? Preposterous, madam? (117)

As Figes does in her multilayered historical fiction, Nye demonstrates the ways in which the past has been successively reinterpreted and reevaluated. His clairvoyant Pickleherring is ahead of his time because he is a creation of ours.

Nye addresses the issue of the biographer's source material by giving Pickleherring a room filled with boxes of notes and documents. One box, for instance, contains the full text of "Tom O'Bedlam's Song" which Nye, like Finney, associates with *King Lear* ("It is a ballad sung by Edgar in *King Lear*. We used it to cover the noise of scene-shifting between the third and fourth scenes of Act II. For some reason it does not appear in the plays as printed in the Folio" [357]). The randomness of the boxes' contents helps account for the seemingly random organization of the novel. Box number forty-three contains the bard's famous calf-killing speech, copied from a mourner's remarks delivered at Shakespeare's funeral, a bit of pure nonsense embellishing the hearsay collected by Aubrey. Samuel Schoenbaum includes Aubrey and many others in his comprehensive *William Shakespeare: A Documentary Life* and *Shakespeare's Lives*; reading *The Late Mr. Shakespeare* and Schoenbaum's works side-by-side reveals Nye's strategy of appropriating the stories about Shakespeare from the time of Robert Greene's "upstart crow" reference onward. Nye repeats almost verbatim, without attribution, Samuel Johnson's version of a legend that the young Shakespeare held horses for wealthy spectators at the theatre, which explains how the phrase "Shakespeare's boys" became the term for horseholders, a tale Mortimer had also embellished in his account of how Shakespeare got his start as an actor (Nye 22).[2]

Speaking of his method in a chapter entitled "About This Book," Pickleherring asks "Who is Shakespeare? What is he?" (a parody of the song *Who Is Sylvia* from *Two Gentlemen of Verona*). He continues: "that is the question my book is trying to answer. . . . How can we tell the man from the work, and both from the stories about him?" (38). At this moment, he sounds like a serious biographer. He ends the chapter with the Delphic utterance that his story is inspired by "a desire to come at the truth by telling lies" (41). Remarks like this are delivered in a speculative, associative manner reminiscent of Montaigne, particularly when Pickleherring reflects on his own writing process:

> sometimes the mind works strangely, but I count this the best way to remember. The trouble with thinking about something often is that it becomes more and more your memory of the thing rather than the thing itself remembered.
>
> What my mind thinks my pen writes. I respect matter, not words. With Mr Shakespeare it was otherwise. (46)

Montaigne is not listed in the postscript, but John Florio, his Elizabethan translator, is. Another early modern writer to whom Nye is indebted is Robert Burton, whose *Anatomy of Melancholy* has a similar encyclopedic quality, mixing folklore, etymology, early science, and metaphysical speculation. Nye also uses the work of the modern scholar Caroline Spurgeon, as when he traces a word through the plays: for example, his riff on crickets with quotes from a half a dozen plays (101) or the miniature essay on the language of flowers and weeds in Shakespeare as contrasted with Milton (130–31). This excursion occurs in a chapter that speculates about the drowning of Ophelia and her derivation from a Katherine Hamnett or

Hamlet who drowned in the Avon in 1579. According to Schoenbaum, Edgar Fripp, "a distinguished scholar in the great Stratford antiquarian tradition" is the source of this theory (*Shakespeare's Lives* 689). Sure enough, Fripp's name appears in the postscript.

Unlike virtually every biographer of Shakespeare, Pickleherring dwells at length on his subject's imagined childhood, so much so that Shakespeare's marriage to Anne Hathaway doesn't occur until halfway through the four-hundred page novel. This strategy of devoting more than half of his mock-biography to the parts of Shakespeare's life about which we know practically nothing is clearly central to Nye's satiric mythologizing. In a parody of biographers who extrapolate from the works to reconstruct the life, Pickleherring tells us that Bottom in *A Midsummer Night's Dream* was inspired by the amateur actor who played Arion in the revels at Kenilworth in 1575 (141). (According to Schoenbaum, "some biographers have toyed with the pleasing and not implausible notion that Alderman Shakespeare pressed in among the throng with his eleven-year-old son" [*William Shakespeare* 89].)

Pickleherring cheerfully admits that he "infers from the plays and the poems" (96) and at times the inferences are rather astute, as when he speculates that Shakespeare probably knew very little about chess, because "In *The Tempest* he has Miranda say that Ferdinand is cheating—and it isn't easy at all to cheat at chess" (97). It is tempting to take Nye seriously when he theorizes about the circumstances in which the author's works provide clues to the biographer. Pickleherring speaks disdainfully of those whose "trick is to take certain bits and pieces from Mr Shakespeare's plays and to press these passages into service as if they could be made to illustrate Mr Shakespeare's private life." He explains that his "method is to *only use those bits that do not fit*"; (219) an example of this is a line spoken by the Shepherd in *A Winter's Tale*. Referring to his son, the old man says: "I would there were no age between ten and three-and-twenty, or that youth would sleep out the rest; for there is nothing in between but getting wenches with child, wronging the ancientry, stealing, fighting." Pickleherring deduces from this that Shakespeare left Stratford at the age of twenty-three. The line is self-revelatory precisely because it does "not belong where our playwright put [it]" (216).

As Nye proceeds to tackle the most provocative aspect of the Shakespeare biography, the supposed autobiographical allusions in the sonnets, he once again assumes the persona of a bona fide Shakespeare scholar. After taking up and dismissing a number of theories about the identity of the Dark Lady, he asks the reader to "consider for a moment" that there is no Dark Lady, no Friend, "nor indeed a constant and unchanging (but strangely colourless) 'I,'" but instead "patterns" who in the last and most serious analysis . . . have no existence save as the words they are, black marks on a white page." Thus, he argues, using the sonnets as his evidence, the Rival Poet is sometimes Marlowe, sometimes Chapman, and the "I" and others in the sonnets are "in one sense *parts* created by Shakespeare" (287). Here and elsewhere in the novel, one could almost believe that this is a serious fiction-biography that acknowledges the difference between known facts and inventions, unlike some of the other historical fictions discussed in this chapter.

And yet these moments are mingled with the most outrageous bawdiness and broadly comic excursions. Nye is disarming; he can be foolishly self-indulgent and yet can equal in poetic eloquence the most powerful moments in Finney's or Garrett's fictions. "Be sure that fiction is the best biography," Pickleherring proclaims, and then offers up a list of numbered "fictions" in a style reminiscent of *Sexing the Cherry*. Number four reads as follows:

> Mr Shakespeare in his youth heard singing masons building roofs of gold. Mr Shakespeare in his middle years drank a drop of happiness, an old brown drop of golden wine. Mr Shakespeare in his last years looked down a well of eternity—the joyous, awful noontide abyss. (304)

The final chapters of *The Late Mr. Shakespeare* employ an approach similar to that described by Holmes, who notes that "a structural feature prominent in numerous contemporary novels [is] textual fragmentation or deformation." Often, he adds, postmodernist novels "present themselves as unintegrated agglomerations of different kinds of documents." He calls this "textual hybridism" (34–35). The Shakespeare biography, based as it is on so few extant documents, lends itself to a kind of textual hybridism, with much speculative filling in of gaps. Many of the efforts to reconstruct Shakespeare's life have turned on his will, a document Nye reproduces in full as chapter 96. The will, complete with old spelling, is annotated by Pickleherring, whose footnotes serve as a mock-scholarly commentary on the text. Chapter 100 takes up Shakespeare's gravestone inscription and subjects it to metrical analysis and close reading which purport to prove, by comparing phrases with their counterparts in the plays, that the four-line poem was written by Shakespeare. In the final pages of the novel Pickleherring reveals his identity: he is Robert Reynolds, a Papist, and he is quite certain that Shakespeare was a lapsed Catholic who was reconciled to the Church at his death. And then the old man ends his narrative, as the city burns around him in the Great Fire of 1666, the event that played so important a role in Winterson's and Tremain's novels. He has metamorphosed through the many women's parts he played into his final role, the hermaphrodite Ariel: "at the end the late Mr Shakespeare kindly made me Ariel. This is Pickleherring's great secret. I am a spirit. I can fly away." Like Finney's Poor Tom, Pickleherring will "rise above the city where it burns," and with this, he says "Farewell" to the reader, having "concluded what I promised I would do" (398).

Ambiguously magic-realist elements such as this ending often occur in the New Historical Fiction, but more importantly, postmodern historical fiction breaks with tradition by virtue of its very historicity, a historicity that blurs the boundaries between context, or setting, and foreground, or characterization, in ways analogous to the critical practices of the New Historicists. The historicity of the New Historical Fiction is, as I have tried to suggest, as much a matter of the voice and mentality of the narrator as it is a matter of research and descriptive detail. After describing the way he immersed himself in medieval chronicles in *Postscript to The Name of the Rose*, Eco said that he wanted "to acquire their rhythm and their innocence" so that he could "narrate *in* the Middle Ages" (511). Once you "construct a world, the words will practically come on their own." "The first year of work on my novel," he continues,

> was devoted to the construction of the world. Long registers of all the books that could be found in a medieval library. Lists of names and personal data for many characters, a number of whom were then excluded from the story. . . . It was not necessary for the reader to know them, but I had to know them. (513)

Reimagining another age entails a certain loss of autonomy, however, for the "constructed world will then tell us how the story must proceed." At this point, Eco declares, "the narrator is a prisoner of his own premises," for "the characters are obliged to act according to the laws of the world in which they live" (515). I suspect that the fiction writers I have discussed here would take issue with Eco on this last point. Their narrators and other characters are hardly the modern people in fancy dress one often finds in even the best of much popular historical fiction, but neither do they belong entirely to an internally consistent, historically constructed past, for all of these historical novels experiment in one way or another with suspending the laws of their constructed worlds.

Chapter 3

Historical Novelists at Work

George Garrett and Anthony Burgess

*I*n 1953, when graceful, belletristic essay-writing flourished and popular historical fiction and fiction-biographies provided ordinary readers
with a window into the past, a writer for the *Sewanee Review* named Andrew
Nelson Lytle compared the historian and the historical novelist:

> both must do the research necessary to recover manners and customs,
> codes, public and private disciplines, all those habits and rituals which
> make up a pattern of culture. But the novelist must go further than the
> historian. He is not in search of principles and causes but of people. He
> must become the research; like Alice must walk through the looking
> glass of time and be there, where strange manners are no longer strange
> but familiar, at least acceptable. He metamorphoses the pastness of the
> past into the moving present. The reader becomes the witness. He is
> there; he sees; he tastes; he smells—if the author succeeds. This involves
> all the technical knowledge and vision which goes into the making of
> any good novel; but when the fiction assumes the past, it places an extra
> burden upon the artist. And this pressure makes another value which
> raises the sense of contemporaneity to a higher power: you have not only
> the illusion of the present, but the past permeates the immediacy of this
> illusion; the fictive personalities take on a certain clairvoyance; the action
> a double meaning, as if the actors while performing disclose the essential

meaning of their time, even of all time (this is possible). This is literary
irony at a high level, an irony that restores vitality to tradition—the past
is not dead but alive; the contemporary scene then seems merely one
division of an accumulation of the segments of time, wherein live people
act out their private destinies in the context of a common destiny which
is their history. (411-12)

George Garrett, a southern writer who was a graduate student in the 1950s,
may well have read this essay; Anthony Burgess, who was a civil servant
teaching and writing in Malaya at the time, probably did not. Lytle's eloquent injunctions regarding what the historical novelist "must do" seem to
speak directly to and about the work of these two remarkably prolific writers,
whose historical fiction constitutes only a small part of their collected written
works, yet who together have brought the age of Shakespeare and Marlowe
and Raleigh to life as few other novelists can claim to have done.

This pairing is inspired in part by some curious echoes and conver-
gences. George Garrett started writing a biography of Raleigh as his doctoral
dissertation in the early 1950s, but found that so many good biographies of
his subject had appeared in recent years that he turned to fiction instead. He
began writing *Death of the Fox* in 1964, the same year that Anthony Burgess
produced his provocative novel about Shakespeare's early life, *Nothing Like
the Sun*, "composed somewhat hurriedly to celebrate in 1964 the quartercentenary of his birth" (9). Garrett's enormous and encyclopedic Raleigh
novel was finally finished in 1970, the year Burgess published his short biographical study *Shakespeare*. (A comparison of the biography with *Nothing
Like the Sun* reveals the historical fiction writer at work, transmuting fragments of fact into fictional gold). Burgess relates in the author's note to *A
Dead Man in Deptford* that he hadn't initially set out to write about
Shakespeare, however, for *his* university thesis dealt with Christopher
Marlowe. He never finished his thesis, for, as he observed wryly, after quot-
ing Doctor Faustus's line "I'll burn my books. Ah Mephistophilis!", "the
Luftwaffe was to burn my books and even my thesis." Over fifty years later,
at the end of a long career, he finally wrote the Marlowe novel which he had
"determined some day to write during the dark hours of the Battle of
Britain" (271). *A Dead Man in Deptford* appeared in 1993, shortly after
Garrett's Marlowe novel *Entered from the Sun* was published in 1990. These
years saw a flourishing of Marlowe books, including Charles Nicholl's *The
Reckoning: The Murder of Christopher Marlowe* and Judith Cook's *The Slicing
Edge of Death: Who Killed Christopher Marlowe?* Both Burgess and Cook
acknowledge the influence of *The Reckoning*, a fascinating investigation of
the mystery of Marlowe's death that blurs the boundaries between fiction
and nonfiction, particularly in the way evidence is pieced together and pre-

sented to the reader. (Nicholl won the Crime Writer's Gold Dagger Award for nonfiction thriller.)

The writer of historical fiction stands "in a peculiar relation to his reader," observes Mary Lascelles in *The Story-Teller Retrieves the Past*. "By the nature of his undertaking, the story-teller who draws on history impels us to ask what he has been reading in the course of his search for access to the past" (20). Too often, historical fiction writers are frustratingly close-mouthed about what and how they read. Happily, Garrett and Burgess have written essays about the experience of creating their historical fictions, and both provide some information about what they read. This particular assemblage of texts, then—Burgess's *Shakespeare* and *Nothing Like the Sun, The Reckoning*, both writers' Marlowe novels, *The Death of the Fox*, and the Raleigh biographies Garrett was reading in the 1960s—can serve as a laboratory in which to explore the way the storyteller draws upon and then transforms the material provided by the historian, the archivist, and the biographer. The Garrett and Burgess novels, written from 1964 to 1993, also exhibit the innovations in historical fiction writing that a number of novelists were introducing into a genre often thought of as old-fashioned and conventional.

In the foreword of *Shakespeare*, Anthony Burgess engages in the traditional ritual of telling the reader what his book is—and is not. "What I claim here," Burgess asserts boldly, "is the right of every Shakespeare-lover who has ever lived to paint his own portrait of the man." Unlike *Nothing Like the Sun*, in which there is "some invention that has no basis even in probability," *Shakespeare* "contains conjecture duly and timidly signaled by phrases like 'It may well be that . . . ' or 'Conceivably, about this time . . . ' but it eschews invention." Burgess goes on to lament the absence of "laundry lists" and letters and "the minutiae of daily life which build up to a character" (9–10). The absence of those "minutiae" may have hindered Burgess the biographer, but it freed Burgess the novelist to invent a Shakespeare whose "love-life begged to be probed with the novelist's instruments." In his essay "Genesis and Headache," Burgess recounts the daring hypothesis that gave shape to his novel: in an aggressively iconclastic affront to the "quasi-religious attitudes" that informed the quartercentenary celebrations, his sexually adventurous Shakespeare would become afflicted with syphilis (29). Like an archeologist decoding an ancient text, Burgess found his dark lady's name, "Fatimah" "acrostically presented" in a sonnet that speaks of sickness and appetite (Sonnet 147: "My love is as a fever, longing still / For that which longer nurseth the disease, / Feeding on that which doth preserve the ill . . . "). He imagines her to be a prostitute from the East, a brown woman "like one of the Malays or Achinese or Bugis I had been hotly attracted to during my times as a civil servant" (30, 32).

After a false start involving an "insincere sounding" first-person narrator, Burgess settled on a third-person narrator whose approximation of Elizabethan English would be "protected from sneerers and carpers by a sort of built-in irony," for it would be the voice of a character "vaguely playacting because partly drunk" and taking liberties with language in bursts of Joycean inventiveness ("Genesis and Headache" 33). He would refer to Shakespeare by the neutral initials "WS," a name "purged of all the harmonics of greatness in a novel which has no concern with that greatness" (34). And so the novel begins with an inscription that reads in part as follows, printed in a manner that deliberately evokes the much-debated dedication of the sonnets:

MR BURGESS'S
farewell lecture to his
special students [here a long list of names
follows] who complained that Shakespeare had nothing
to give to the east . . .

He then thanks them for three bottles of *samsu*, adding "I will take a swig now. Delicious" (*Nothing* n.p.).

While the sober biographer's voice in *Shakespeare* contrasts markedly with the inebriated lecturer of *Nothing Like the Sun*, it can also serve as a gloss on the novelist's strategies:

For my part, I seize on the song in *Love's Labor's Lost* to visualize the sister Joan as a greasy girl who spends much of her time washing pots and pans in cold water. Gilbert I see as dully pious and possibly epileptic, the source of the falling sickness that comes in both *Julius Caesar* and *Othello*. . . . Richard III and Claudius conjoin in the real brother Richard. He may have been sly and lecherous, and, in Will's absence in London, ready to post to incestuous sheets. He may have limped. On the other hand, he may have been an upright well-made young man who loved his eldest brother and respected his sister-in-law. (*Shakespeare* 25)[1]

This last sentence is a tongue-in-cheek comment on novelistic invention. Burgess defends his license in his essay "Genesis and Headache" as follows:

Needless to say, there is no documentary justification for . . . making young Gilbert Shakespeare epileptic, moronic, and afflicted with religious mania. What I have to do is wait until somebody can prove that he was *not* these things. I will have to wait a long time. (35)

In the opening pages of *Nothing Like the Sun*, WS and his siblings are on a "glove-delivering walk" on "A Good Friday, sure. '77? '78? '79?" (3). Burgess's imagined thirteen- or fifteen-year-old WS resists the "kidskin slavery" of his father's trade, and is all-too-conscious of his mother's Arden heritage (8). Whereas Burgess the biographer cites the 1596 application

Shakespeare made for a coat of arms, with its reference to his mother as "the daughter and heir of Arden, a gentleman of worship" (18), Burgess the novelist conveys this information to the reader in an entirely different way, through the racing thoughts of the resentful WS:

> Oh, the ancient glories of the Ardens, long before the Conqueror came. The Arden lands, the Arden hauteur. The pigeon-house at Wilmcote, with its coocoocooing of more than six hundred pair. ("And and and," cried his mother, all Arden, "they passed through Stratford, mine own cousins, and they would not call, not for a glass of wine, no, nor to give a word of family news. Oh, the shame, the shame. I have married beneath me. I was taken unawares by a rogues's eye. I was ruined.") Tears came to the eyes of WS. It was, he feigned, the spring wind freshening. They had best get home to their dinner, greasy Joan and the great lady their mother and their anxious smiling father. (5–6)

And so, in a few deft strokes WS's parents are depicted: this mix of stream-of-consciousness fragments and associations, transcribed sounds ("coocoo-cooing"), parenthetical interruptions, remembered scraps of dialogue, and two- or three-word characterizations ("anxious smiling father") is typical of Burgess's novelistic style.

A few chapters later, WS takes refuge from his troubles in an alehouse, which comes to life in the descriptions of its inhabitants' appearances, smells, and fragments of speech, as observed from the perspective of the resentful adolescent aspiring poet:

> The alehouse was full tonight, choked with the low and their stink, bad breath, black teeth, foul loud holes of country mouths. He saw, of a sudden, an image of proud high London, red towers over a green river with swans. He pushed himself room on a settle next to an old smocked shepherd who reeked of tar, his nail-ends swart crescents, crying rough speech in this blanketing thick air and noise to one who squinnied, thin, ancient, nodding, chumbling gum and gum (And then what dost think a done? A laid all on board and quotha, "A groat an inch in warranty," quotha, main.') The girl who brought for him had a may-sprig in her bosom, fat, spongy tits thrust high as they were sacks on a man's back; she leered at him with country teeth. (25)

As WS becomes drunker his perceptions become angrier and more colorful, and the language correspondingly vivid and experimental:

> Drink, then. Down it among the titbrained molligolliards of country copulatives, of a beastly sort, all, their browned pickers a-clutch of their spilliwilly potkins, filthy from handling of spade and harrow, cheesy from udder new-milked, slash mouths agape at some merry tale from

that rogue with rat-skins about his middle, coneyskin cap on's sconce.
Robustious rothers in rural rivo rhapsodic. Swill thou then among them,
O London-Will-to-be, gentleman-in-waiting, scrike thine ale's laughter
with Hodge and Tom and Dick and Black Jack the outlander from
Long Compton. (26)

Burgess, like Shakespeare, is a compulsive coiner of words, with an ear for
sounds that makes you want to read a passage like this one aloud.

Mixed in among the neologisms, word pictures, and bizarre sound
effects are unmarked quotations from Shakespeare poems and plays, such as
the phrase "country copulatives" from *As You Like It*. In her discussion of
intertextuality and parody in historiographic metafiction, Linda Hutcheon
notes the recurrence in modern and postmodern texts of ironic allusions and
"recontextualized quotations" (126). Burgess mines the Shakespeare canon
for words and phrases, assuming a reader who will recognize and appreciate
the wittiness with which he recontextualizes them. For example, WS
emerges from the tavern "Mewling and puking" (another *As You Like It* quotation) and some hours later, finds himself in the arms of a woman; this is
how Burgess reinvents the first encounter with Anne Hathaway. WS asks
himself: "In God's name, though, what had he done in that great void of
unmemory? Never never never never never would he come more to that. He
would be a moderate man" (28). This appropriation of one of Shakespeare's
most daring and powerful lines, the five "never"s from Lear's final moments
of tragic anguish, is playfully provocative, to say the least. Yet it also suggests
a decisive, even tragic turning point in WS's life, for he will be forced to
marry the pregnant Anne by her thuggish relatives some months later.

There are actually three distinct kinds of Elizabethan, or pseudo-
Elizabethan, verbal strategies in Burgess's writing. First, the direct quotation,
such as Lear's "Never, never, never, never, never" or "Reply, reply" from the
casket song in *The Merchant of Venice* (33), or, in reference to the hastily
arranged wedding, "so what was to be done was to be done quickly" (36), an
appropriation from Macbeth's famous soliloquy which begins "If it were
done, when 'tis done, then 'twere well / It were done quickly." The reader's
recognition of the quotation evokes a comparison of the murder of Duncan
and the marriage to Anne, another signal that WS is embarked on a deed
with tragic consequences. The second kind of Elizabethan utterance recurs
throughout the novel on nearly every page; in this category are commonplace
words and phrases that appear frequently in the writings of Shakespeare and
his contemporaries. For example, in the second part of *Nothing Like the Sun*,
which deals with the events of 1592 to 1599, the actor Will Kemp, speaking
of a rival acting company, says "They are naught. They are but a sort of lawful
ruffians" (79). After a performance WS is sent for by Robert Devereux and

"Master HW or WH," who says "You are welcome hither" (91) and later, "Well, I am chided . . . let us have this poem, by all means" (94). Such mimicry of early modern English phrasing occurs in many historical novels, but few writers can do it as adeptly and naturally as Burgess does.

The third kind of diction in Burgess's arsenal could be described as "Joycean-Elizabethan"; in these instances, Burgess uses words and phrases that sound like the wilder excesses of the Elizabethans, playfully updated, as in Anne's angry words to WS: "you have time enoow, oh aye, for the miowling of kitticat poetry like a struck fool. . . . " (41). Commenting on early reviews of his novel in "Genesis and Headache," Burgess notes that

> I was accused of inventing words when all I had done was to steal from Elizabethan chapbooks, pamphlets, and Shakespeare's own plays. Where I was most serious I was supposed to be most facetious; where I merely transcribed documentary truth I was said to be wildly and implausibly inventing. (43)

Burgess does confess to a neologism, however. In the novel's second paragraph, the peevish WS is described as kicking "the turves of the Avon's left bank, marking with staring-up spaniel's eye the spurgeoning of the back-eddy under the Clopton Bridge" (3). Burgess calls this "the first of my literary tricks," explaining in "Genesis and Headache" that

> this word *spurgeoning* is . . . derived from the name of Caroline Spurgeon, a modern scholar, who, in her work on Shakespeare's imagery, noted that he introduced the peculiar behaviour of the Avon under that bridge as a simile in "The Rape of Lucrece." (35)

Burgess assumes that at least some of his readers will be sufficiently learned to pick up "tricks" like this one.

Postmodern historical fiction writers take great pleasure in making cryptic intertextual references of various kinds. Explicit, often jesting allusions to other works and Bakhtinian heteroglossia, or the conscious use of different types of speech, both included by Menton among the characteristics of the New Historical Novel, are present throughout Burgess's writing, as they are in Nye's. Although he does not mention *Nothing Like the Sun*, Menton includes a reference to Burgess's *Napoleon Symphony*, which presupposes a knowledge of the Napoleonic period and is based on the *Eroica Symphony* (24-25).

Shakespeare provides more glimpses of the intertextually adept writer at work, with its references to the many other texts of the period Burgess read and absorbed. In his chapter "Poets' War," Burgess lapses into fiction-writer mode, as he imagines Will Kemp's parting thoughts as he leaves the Lord Chamberlain's Men in 1599:

Kemp said, doubtess, that he had been in the profession before most of them were wiped, and as for Shakespaw here, butcher's boy hence Not Without Mustard, had he not taught him all he knew while he was still unhandily botching plays for the Queen's Men? A sort of ingrates, the lot, but Shakebag especially. Well, he would be glad to be out of it, the theatre was not what it had been all words words words now, honorificabillibus, and no wooing of the muse of improvisation. . . . He planned to dance from London to Norwich, with his trill-lillies on his legs, and make himself rich by opening a book (three to one he couldn't do it) and later writing one. (158)

The book, Burgess goes on to explain, was *Kemps Nine Daies Wonder* and he quotes from the part in which he found the word "trill-lillies" and an eccentric spelling of Shakespeare's name: "onely tricker of your Trill-lillies, and best belshangles between Sion and mount Surrey" and "my notable Shakerags" (158). Elsewhere, he refers explicitly to his quest for wonderful-sounding words: in Ben Jonson's *The Poetaster* he found "*spurious, snotteries, turgidous, ventocity*" (164).

Burgess had clearly become enamored of the word "trill-lillies" back in 1964 when he was writing *Nothing Like the Sun*: "Hast not heard of Dick Tarleton? And that with him is Gemp or Camp or Kempe or suchlike, trill-lillies jinging round's calves" (71) (the playful inclusion of variant spellings of names is a Burgess trademark). Tarleton's patter is recreated as follows:

Hark, all, your doubtful worships are royally bidden to a feast of wrong-doing (oh, you will like that well enough for all your long faces) and thereto will be added for good measure a good measure, nay a treasure of good measures, viddy or skiddy lissit a jig, aye, a jig. Here is your only jigmaker. And it will be tomorrow, you whoreson scurvyrumps, you cheesefoots, you heavenhigh stinkards and cackards. (72)

This virtuoso re-creation of Tarleton's voice takes off from the historical traces provided by Elizabethan texts, but reaches new heights of verbal ingenuity, as in the mocking approximation of the Latin term *vide licet*.

Not all of Burgess's experiments with language are comical. *Nothing Like the Sun* contains a powerful description of London during the plague of 1588 that in a single paragraph accomplishes more than whole pages of conventional history writing:

The city baked in its corruption; flies crawled over the sleeping lips of a child; the rats twitched their whiskers at an old dead woman (shrunk to five stone) that lay among lice in a heap of rancid rags; the bells tolled all day for the plague-stricken; cold ale tasted as warm as a posset; the flesher shooed flies off with both hands before chopping his stinking beef; heaps of shit festered and heaved in the heat; tattered villains broke into houses where man, woman, child lay panting and calling feebly for water and, mocking their distress, stole what they had a mind to; the city grew a head, glowing over limbs of towers and houses in the rat-scurrying night, and its face was drawn, its eyes sunken, it vomited foul living matter down to ooze over the cobbles, in its delirium it cried *Jesus Jesus*. (85–86)

This succession of phrases, all linked by semi-colons, has the rhythms of verse, and with its alliterative echoes (heaps . . . heaved . . . heat) and nightmarish images, resembles a prose poem. Indeed, some of Burgess's prose betrays the influence of Anglo-Saxon alliterative verse, like this excerpt from a paragraph in *Shakespeare* that evokes the daily life of Tudor Stratford in a long, encyclopedic series of phrases: " . . . seasonal ceremonies, cows lowing in labor, the felling of bobby-calves, the sticking of swine, flies in summer, frozen pumps in winter . . . ways foul after rainfall. . . " (49).

Historical fiction has traditionally provided descriptions of other times and places that both transport and educate the reader. Another, perhaps more important way in which historical fiction brings the past to life is by offering explanations or speculating about cause and effect. At the end of a chapter in *Shakespeare*, Burgess remarks that "Infuriatingly, whenever Shakespeare does something other than buy a lease or write a play, history shuts her jaws with a snap" (166). Undaunted by the dearth of information, Burgess the novelist constructs more or less plausible accounts of pivotal moments in Shakespeare's early life. For example, he spins a story around the composition of *The Comedy of Errors*, quite possibly Shakespeare's first play—and significantly, the one most closely indebted to its source, Plautus's *Menaechmi*—to account for Shakespeare's arrival in London as an actor-playwright. Perpetuating the novel's theme that all of WS's life choices are made unwittingly, Burgess imagines WS in a moment of drunken abandon signing an indenture to be tutor to the five sons of a Master Quedgeley. When his new employer suggests that the boys translate the *Menaechmi*, WS goes off to Bristol to buy copies of the play, but loses them in a whorehouse where he meets his first dark lady. And so WS reconstructs Plautus's play himself, passing it off as his pupils' translation, which explains the inexpert rhymes and "clumsy lines, each pinned to each by a device out of Seneca, not Plautus" (*Nothing* 63). WS will lose his tutoring job after still another sexual indiscretion, but in 1587, when the Queen's Men come to Stratford, he "takes his few hundred lines of pseudo-Plautus" and joins the acting company (75).

Burgess discusses this incident in his essay "Genesis and Headache," calling it "a device for making him write, against his will, *The Comedy of Errors*" (37–38). His version of the event in *Shakespeare* is similar in its conclusions but differs significantly in presentation. Burgess the biographer adeptly reviews the anecdotal evidence that places Shakespeare as a tutor in

Gloucestershire during the years before he arrived in London, then speculates about a "teaching experiment" that involved "acting a play of Plautus
not in Latin but in English" (grammar school students in Shakespeare's time
frequently studied and performed Plautus's plays). What begins as a translation of the *Menaechmi* becomes an original work. Assuming a relatively
uninformed reader quite different from the reader of *Nothing Like the Sun*,
Burgess goes on to summarize and compare the two plays, finally concluding, a couple of pages later, that *A Comedy of Errors* was "a work that had its
origins less in professional dramaturgy than in amateur pedagogy and that it
was the first work of any length that Shakespeare completed." Reverting to
the "I think"s and "might"s of the cautious biographer, he envisions a
Shakespeare who gave his partial draft to a troupe of actors "as an earnest of
what, given the chance, he could do" (47). This is much the same story
Burgess tells in *Nothing Like the Sun*, but stripped of its more sensational fictional elements—the drinking and whoring and the five boys (including a
pair of identical twins, one of whom joins WS in his bed, with predictable
results).

There are other references to the plays in *Nothing Like the Sun*, but no
attempt at the inclusiveness Burgess provides in *Shakespeare*. We hear a fragment of conversation between WS and Burbage, for instance, about the
theory of the humours as a method of characterization. WS sees all too
clearly the method's limitations:

> " . . . But that is just singing one air over and over and then turning to
> another. But a human soul is not just one repeated air, it is many. Now
> even Shylock has many sides—sometimes to be pitied, sometimes
> laughed at, hated at other times—"
>
> "Shylock is a dirty Jew."
>
> WS sighed very deeply. "That is what the people wish to believe,
> they wish him to be a kind of Lopez. That is the way of satire, setting
> up a dirty Jew or an old cuckold or a young lecher or a fantasticated gal-
> lant. But satire is a very small part of poesy." (184)

This is historical fiction of a conventionally instructive kind, with a little lecture in the form of a dialogue on Shakespeare's complex characterization and
departure from his predecessors. A wise and authoritative WS concludes the
discussion with the pronouncement that "a play should be bigger than the
times" (185).

These familiar historical fiction strategies are juxtaposed with characteristically postmodern ones such as the mix of narrative styles and voices,
including a sequence (144–59) in which the text becomes WS's diary entries
from an unidentified year (with plenty of clues for the educated reader). In
the next chapter the now-quite-drunken Burgess lecturer returns, in the role
of a preacher inveighing against "lust and filthy fornication and sodomy and

buggery" in a splendid parody of the sermons and tracts of the times (160). The novel concludes with an epilogue narrated in the first person by a WS dying of syphilis, which becomes an explicit metaphor for the injustices and corruption dramatized in the tragedies and *Troilus and Cressida*: "My disease was a modern disease; it was the same disease as that which cracked order in State and Church and the institutions of both. We have had the best of our time" (230). Like Othello falling into his epileptic trance, the speaker's language reveals the breakdown of reason; he ends with a phantasmagoric stream-of-consciousness muttering, a seemingly random collection of the wonderful-sounding words Burgess loves so much.

In her discussion of "fiction histories," Naomi Jacobs speaks of the fiction historian's awareness that "'all the facts' can never be known . . . [for the] most scrutinized life will include only a small part of 'what really happened.'" Such a writer, she continues, employs

> the free imagination to describe possible thoughts, meetings, and actions for which no evidence could ever exist . . . [and] creates an openly unverifiable, blatantly implausible and even indefensible version of what might be called an epoch's internal experience. (72)

Nothing Like the Sun fits Jacobs's definition of fiction history through its emphasis on sexual escapades for which there is no documentary evidence. When the historical novelist has a much more extensive historical record from which to work, as George Garrett did with the life and dramatically enacted death of Sir Walter Raleigh, there might seem to be fewer temptations to invent fiction history of the kind Jacobs describes.

Like Burgess, Garrett wrote about the experience of inventing a new form of historical fiction; his essay, "Dreaming with Adam: Notes on Imaginary History," was published in 1970, shortly before *Death of the Fox* appeared. He explains that the boom in studies of the Renaissance, which included a number of Raleigh biographies, had rendered his "scarcely begun" biography "out of the question, unnecessary," but the project, "constantly changing shape and form," was never abandoned. A phrase in Agnes M. C. Latham's edition of Raleigh's poems pointed him in the direction he was to take: Raleigh "might have walked out of an Elizabethan play, a figment of the renaissance-imagination" (25). There were very few serious historical novels to serve as models for the fiction Garrett said would have to "be different from any I had known and enjoyed." He does mention *Nothing Like the Sun*, "a brilliant and virtuoso piece," but one that "violates most of the premises" from which he planned to proceed, the most fundamental of these being "to keep to the decorum of fact except in very rare cases where it seemed to me that the evidence was sufficient to be more definite than speculative" (26). To probe the mysteries of the Renaissance imagination and construct a version of the age that went beyond familiar generalizations and conventional images, Garrett immersed himself in the textuality of history, reading and rereading Elizabethan and Jacobean writers so as to become "physically in *touch* with the language, rhythms, the styles of the times." He read randomly rather than systematically, for the latter approach, he felt, though "easier and more efficient . . . would have arbitrarily inhibited the playful process of assimilation" (29).

"Dreaming with Adam" is especially interesting for its account of the way Garrett analyzed and dealt with the issue of style. He aspired to "the creation of a 'new' style, by definition personal," which would "permit the reader to participate" as he conjured up "ghosts and ruins" (28). After reading extensively, he set aside his notes and wrote, using "what remained in consciousness." He then excised "most of the eccentricities" in later drafts, recreating in readable prose "the surfaces of a world and a time" that was "so alien . . . so removed" from his own (29). The result is a style quite different from Burgess's, with an even more conspicuous narrative voice that intermittently addresses the reader directly and employs the present tense to create a sense of immediacy throughout the leisurely and rambling narrative. Approximations of Elizabethan diction mix easily with a more timeless, neutral English in the dialogue, as in this excerpt from a conversation between Raleigh and his friend Thomas Hariot:

> "Are you afraid?"
> "God's name, Thomas, I have been with fear like a whore all day long. My bones feel it. They want to jangle like the keys of a virginal. And all of my hairs would like to stand up at once like the bristles of a boar. My blood is quicksilver and my bowels are a pack of beagles. Can't you tell?"
> "I could not have guessed it."
> "Good," he says. "It belongs to me, then. Will you have a last glass of wine?" (605)

Notice the series of analogies, the first three turning on the word "like," a deliberate echoing of the conceits of the Elizabethan poets, juxtaposed with more modern-sounding phrases like "Can't you tell?" As Monroe Spears remarks in his essay "George Garrett and the Historical Novel,"

> the real challenge is to write like Ralegh or Bacon or Queen Elizabeth so that the reader is not shocked by the transition from their own prose to yours, and Garrett manages this with great success. It works partly because they were such good writers, and when pruned of minor surface anachronisms do not seem at all dated or antiquated. . . . The style then,

is not based on pastiche or fake antiquarianism, but on the solid middle ground of English. (65)

Traces of reading and assimilation are sometimes explicit: for example, Garrett makes a point of acknowledging the textuality of history by invoking a document that countless historical fiction writers have had recourse to (but without remarking on the fact), John Stowe's *A Survey of London* (1598). The old, imprisoned Raleigh of 1618 meditates on the past, his voice set off from the narrator's by italics (Garrett's method for mixing a character's inner thoughts with a third-person narration that adopts various invented characters' points of view). As he recalls his arrival in London as a boy from Devon and his wanderings throughout the city, he regrets "*the loss of a London I never truly possessed.*" He thinks of Stowe, "*this man who has made London forever new by charting it old*" and muses:

> *Yet, thanks be to God and to John Stow, his* Survey of London *restored the freedom of the city to me even as I was penned in the Tower. Thanks to his pen, I could walk those streets again.*
>
> *I could wish you were with me, old man of Three-Needle Street, my companion here and now. To brighten a brief moment with the long-burning light of the past . . . John Stow, I am no prophet, no prognosticator. But I will tell you this. The King is a scholar and he writes books, a rare thing for any king. Still, reason tells me your words will live when his, and mine too, no doubt, are feeding the insatiable worms that love most those books least read.* (193)

As this example suggests, Garrett's research enables him to produce a "voice" that draws the reader into the constructed past; through its locutions and alliterative cadences it reinvents the mentality of the period so convincingly that we experience the *illusion* of reading phrases composed in 1618. This effect is heightened by the novel's intertextuality; as Irving Malin observes in an essay entitled "Hermetic Fox-Hunting," "the entire text is filled with texts—proverbs, riddles, biblical quotations, legal definitions," not to mention all of the excerpts from Raleigh's own writings that serve as epigraphs for the sections of the novel (12).

Death of the Fox deliberately eschews the usual structure of biography by starting at the end of the story, the twenty-four hours leading up to Raleigh's execution on October 29, 1618 (I use this spelling; Garrett uses "Ralegh"). There are several major characters who experience repeated flashbacks, so that the narration is constantly shifting backward and forward in time, always returning eventually to the room in the Tower where Raleigh awaits his death. The effect is sometimes disorienting, for unlike conventional historical novelists, Garrett provides very minimal identifications of historical figures. Details—and there are thousands of them in this dense, 739-page

novel—emerge organically from the characters' recollections, accumulating
through digressions, anecdotes, and lengthy descriptions, a process of world-
building that draws the reader more and more fully into the past. In addition
to Raleigh, characters such as King James and Attorney General Henry
Yelverton take center stage periodically and reflect on their own past lives,
predecessors, and contemporaries, so that through them the reader meets
Robert Cecil, Sir Edward Coke, Queen Elizabeth, the Spanish ambassador
Gondomar, Francis Bacon, and countless others.

The novel's encyclopedic breadth is largely due to Garrett's invention
of an original storytelling strategy. After about 250 pages, the narrator
begins to speak of ghosts and Elizabethan and Jacobean ghost lore.
Although "Walter Ralegh has not much interest in ghosts" (here he quotes
from Raleigh's *History of the World*), the narrator nevertheless announces
that there is "Time, while the old man dozes, to summon up ghosts, imagined and imaginary. . . . Perhaps he will not be offended if they are to be
considered *characters* in the fashion of the types of Englishmen drawn by Sir
Thomas Overbury" (254). Drawing on a distinctive seventeenth-century
genre, the "character," or portrait of a type, Garrett proceeds to invent three
"ghosts" who represent facets of Raleigh's life: the soldier, the courtier, and
the sailor. Each speaks at length in a distinctive idiom, addressing the
reader as "you," as if in conversation;

> you want to know some things about being a soldier. Well, you have
> come to a man who can tell you. There are many around and about—I
> will mention no names—who would tell you a Jordan pot full of lies.
> (261)

The "you" of the soldier's monologue, often addressed as "sir," takes on a
character as well: "There's many a man who needs schooling. I count you
among them. So head up, eyes front, pay attention and listen well" (261).
The ghosts, conceived as garulous storytellers, are rather pleased to be sum-
moned to testify and inform, and they digress freely as the spirit moves them.
Here and elsewhere, Garrett employs witty metafictional strategies, drawing
attention to his novel's design; for instance, his soldier-ghost, after about
twenty pages of Elizabethan military history, interrupts himself with:

> But I see you are impatient. You did not imagine me out of the darkness
> to hear the chronicle of my life or my privy opinions.
>   It is Walter Ralegh you are seeking. (283)

Garrett creates an even more layered narrative strategy with the
courtier-ghost's tale. The outer-frame narrator introduces the courtier by
calling into question the reliability of his narrative, remarking drily that he is
not likely to offer "anything more than the worldly wisdom of a wounded
pride and thwarted ambition" (299). After several pages in which the courtier

and his world are evoked through such devices as paragraphs listing court sounds, odors, and foods, the narrator decides to send his aging, disappointed courtier back to his home in the country and replace him with a younger courtier, "young and unlined," the "child of change" (308). There is a brief exchange between the old and young courtiers, after which the young one embarks on a narrative distinguished visually from the rest of the novel by the dashes with which each paragraph begins (similarly, the sailor's paragraphs are set off by ellipses).

Garrett uses these ghost-narratives to paint an enormous canvas from which Raleigh's life story emerges. In a long sequence about styles of clothing and sumptuary laws, for example, he casually includes—and seems to question the authenticity of—the best-known myth about his subject, while at the same time educating us about the cost of articles of clothing in Elizabethan London:

> —If Walter Ralegh indeed spread a cloak for the Queen at a splashy place, the Queen then walked across a good year's living for an ordinary gentleman.
> —In the reign of the Queen a pair of silk stockings cost more than an entire costume of her grandfather's time. (321)

Each ghost's contribution serves as a partial biography; taken together, they demonstrate the biases, omissions, and shaky hypotheses inherent in the writing of history. At one point, the courtier disputes the soldier's account of Raleigh: "He was not as the braggart captain would have him. Nor as he seems now—an old man, sick and tired . . . " (336). Later, the sailor, whose role it is to tell of Raleigh's voyages to the New World, speaks scornfully of the courtier as "that idle fellow" with "[a]ll his dainty colors and delicate stuffs!" (375). Toward the end of the sailor's tale, in a typically elliptical account of Raleigh's final voyage (the subject of Nye's *The Voyage of the "Destiny"*), Garrett repeats the phrase "some say" as a device for representing the rumors and hearsay and gossip surrounding his subject (317–18). No amount of historical reconstruction can make sense of the mysteries of human behavior, says Garrett through his crusty and skeptical old sailor: "The route and dates of his voyage are record. But who shall know, now or in time to come, the reasons?" (423).

In his prescient essay on the kinds of historical fiction, written just before innovative and unconventional historical fictions began to appear with increasing frequency, Joseph Turner used *Death of the Fox* to illustrate what he called the Philosophical Mode of historical fiction writing, "where the primary concern becomes how, or if, history itself is possible—history *in and for* but primarily *about itself*." In contrast to the Original Mode of historical fiction, in which the principal concern is to create a picture of the past, and the Reflective Mode, in which "the chasm between past and present is recognized only to be bridged," the Philosophical Mode is "the best historical fiction," the kind that is "about man's fate to live in history and his attempt to live in awareness of it" (Turner 353–54). Garrett's ghosts, with their imagined retrospective insight into the past, serve as mouthpieces for philosophical observations the author might hesitate to utter directly, for fear of sounding pompous and didactic. As the courtier says toward the end of his long monologue, "with the changing of the present, the past has changed as well. There have been discoveries of hidden truths which alter the appearance of the past" (367). What better description of historical scholarship and interpretation?

Garrett recommends several biographies in the introductory note to *Death of the Fox*. From them, we can learn something about the way he transformed the historical record into fiction, expanding upon what was already an inherently dramatic story. For purposes of comparison, I looked at the way four biographers and Garrett each treated a relatively minor character, Robert Tounson, the Dean of Westminster, who was the last person to speak with Raleigh before the public execution, and who recorded his experience about ten days later in a letter to Sir John Isham. This letter was available to the biographers, and presumably to Garrett, in E. Edwards's two-volume *The Life of Sir Walter Ralegh, Together with His Letters*, published in 1868. Garrett presents the conversation between Raleigh and Tounson in the form of a ten-page dramatic dialogue, as if it were an excerpt from a play, interrupted by narrative commentary about the two men stressing the psychological and political complexities of the situation and casting doubts on the reliability of the documentary evidence:

> Ralegh may be playing a stage part so that the Dean will report him to have died a good Christian. . . . But [the Dean] does not know, cannot conceive what is true or false in the man. And cannot conceive whether true or false report is expected of him. (709)

Garrett ends the chapter with an ironic commentary, set off in italics to signal a more detached narrative voice:

> *When he has taken the communion Ralegh will rise, seeming more blithe than before. He will eat like a farmer with a long morning's labor ahead, or a man at an inn facing a journey on the open road. And as the day's sunlight begins to stream through the windows and the servants snuff out the candles, he will call for a pipe and smoke it.*
>
> *Leaving the Dean of Westminster to wonder how he shall retell this last gesture.*
>
> *All the world knows how much the King hates the habit of tobacco.*
> *(714)*

The distinctive verb tenses ("will rise," "will call," etc.) and the descriptions of the scene make these sentences sound like stage directions.

Tounson's letter had included the reference to the last pipe of tobacco; the excerpts quoted in Norman Lloyd Williams's 1962 biography indicate that he stressed how "cheerful and merry" Raleigh was and that he "took tobacco, and made no more of his death than if he had been to take a journey" (256). Taking his cue from these words, perhaps, Garrett spins out a long philosophical discussion of death, fear, and religious faith, cast in a debate-like give-and-take between two shrewd rhetoricians. Another biographer, Willard M. Wallace, paraphrases the conversation thus:

> Raleigh baffled Tounson by being so untroubled. In fact, he made so light of death that Tounson reproached him for it. Raleigh replied that he did not fear death, and greatly preferred to die by the ax than by a wasting fever.

Wallace quotes the phrase "cheerful and merry" as well as Tounson's reference to "this extraordinary boldness" of Raleigh's, and goes on to paraphrase other parts of the conversation, including Raleigh's insistence on his innocence. Wallace characterizes Tounson as "a brisk, businesslike cleric, an ambitious man not above being presumptuous" (311). Garrett, by contrast, evokes a much more lifelike, uncomfortable Tounson, acutely aware of the significance of the moment and conscious that "he must trust himself that much, be faithful to his version of this world even if he doubts it" (*Death of the Fox* 710).

Garrett's complex and curiously sympathetic portrait of Tounson is even more striking when compared with still another biographer's account. Margaret Irwin, herself a historical novelist whose work includes three novels about the young Queen Elizabeth, creates a rather different Tounson. Her "brisk, rising young cleric" bustles in during "a busy week with me" (this last phrase is from the letter, though not identified as such, and is quoted out of context[2]), "full of self-confidence, on his official mission of religious admonition and comfort . . . just the sort of whipper-snapper busybody that Ralegh and his arrogantly intellectual friends used to mock at" (303–04). Her version of the final pipe of tobacco is very close to Garrett's, and may have inspired the "punchline" effect of his final sentences:

> Not only did the pipe rather shock the Dean in itself, but so did the thought of how his tobacco-loathing King would be sure to take this for a last carelessly defiant gesture. (306)

Irwin's novelist's instincts lead her to construct an unsympathetic Tounson who is "officious to the end" as he accompanies Raleigh to the scaffold and asks him "if he would not lie facing east for our Lord's rising" (312), a suggestion Garrett assigns to the headsman, Gregory Brandon, in his dramatic rendering of Raleigh's final moments. Raleigh responds, "So long as the heart is right, it is no matter which way the head lies" (*Death of the Fox* 738). All the biographies contain this memorable valedictory, with minor differences of wording, and all have Raleigh say to the headsman a variant of Garrett's "What doest thou fear? Strike, man, strike!" (739). Clearly, the historical record gave novelists and biographers alike some wonderfully dramatic material with which to work.

With the exception of A. L. Rowse's 1962 biography, *Sir Walter Ralegh: His Family and Private Life*, the four biographies I looked at end climactically with the execution scene, rather like the final frames of a film. The severed head is put in a red leather bag to be conveyed to Raleigh's widow, the screen goes dark, and the credits roll. Garrett ends his novel similarly, but the final page of his treatment of the scene takes the reader, for the last time, inside Raleigh's consciousness, as italicized excerpts from the Lord's Prayer alternate with his sensory experience of the seconds before the ax falls (738–39). Altogether, Garrett's rendition of the execution scene is much longer and more vivid than the biographers' accounts, with more characters (the sheriff, Brandon's son Richard, to whom Raleigh gives a ring) and more dialogue, although Garrett skips over some of the details the biographers include. Apparently Raleigh made a long final address, a retrospective of the events that brought him to the scaffold. Garrett chooses not to linger over the address, which Williams had reconstructed in his biography, collated from several contemporary accounts (257–63 and notes, 276); rather, mimicking a reporter on the scene, he passes over parts of the speech in a series of summarizing phrases, such as:

> And now, in the form of a story, his version of what took place. Much the opposite of all report. How he was kept close prisoner in his cabin by mutineers. How they had forced him to take an oath, or be cast into the sea, that he would never bring them home to England. (730)

The theatrical character of the event is made explicit: "like the chorus in an English play [Raleigh] has painted scene after scene more palpable than anything they see" (732). The scaffold is his "stage," where "in one step [he] dismisses trivial present time, like a magician with a wand of words" (731).

Garrett, too, is a magician with a wand of words, a conjurer who brings his subject to life more vividly than the biographers, for all their considerable narrative and synthesizing skills. He calls his three Elizabethan novels the "imaginary past," and as Spears remarks,

> there is no way of automatically reconstructing it (or them, for the past is not one but many, of course) from facts—but it is solidly based on a thorough knowledge of what historical facts and documents are available

. . . this kind of historical novel is a kind of communal product, in a sense, not based on the limited scope of one man's imagination, but on the productions, fiction and real, of many people's minds—a kind of collective reality created by all of them together. (69)

Garrett continued his fictional explorations of early modern England with *The Succession: A Novel of Elizabeth and James*, published in 1983. This is in some ways a more unconventional novel than *Death of the Fox*, for it ranges backward and forward in time in disconnected and seemingly randomly organized chapters. The chapters are presented from the points of view of frequently unnamed characters at different times, and always circle back to 1603, when James VI of Scotland became King of England upon the death of his cousin Elizabeth. Garrett draws attention to chronology (marking each chapter by year) only to disrupt it. John Banville uses a variation on this strategy in *Kepler*, the middle third of which is an unannotated sequence of letters from the sixteenth- and seventeenth-century astronomer Johannes Kepler to various friends and colleagues; the letters are organized from Ash Wednesday 1605 to April 1612 and then, disconcertingly, from December 1611 backwards to Easter 1605 (Banville's narrative organization is based on Kepler's theories about time). Garrett goes even further in fracturing and deconstructing historical sequence through sixteen chapters, varying from five to over one hundred pages long, that leap from 1566 to 1603 to 1626 and back again, in a mix of narrative styles, all the while constructing a world through description whose density far exceeds even the most detailed of historical fictions. James and Elizabeth are nearly always just offstage, the objects of speculation, the catalysts of events, but not the subjects of fiction-biography in the conventional sense. Their chapters ("Queen: March 1603," "King: March 1602–1603," and "Christmastide: 1602–1603") are quite short in comparison to the fifty-five page "Reivers: 1602" or the eighty-page "Priest: 1587." History, this narrative strategy suggests, is not continuous, or seamless, but an amalgam, a collage of fragments, each with its own point of view. Hutcheon could have been referring to this novel when she describes narrative conventions in historiographic metafiction as problematizing the notion of subjectivity through multiple points of view (121–22).

Garrett explains in a prefatory note that he began with "the letters—first with the actual letters of Queen Elizabeth (weighty in syntax, knotty in thought, generally obscure in their gnarled tangle of motives)" and that his novel was originally meant to be a narrative account of the exchange of letters between James and Elizabeth over the years, "each seeking to come to know and understand the other with a kind of urgent and thorough intimacy that even lovers seldom achieve" (vii). But just as he found himself summoning up the ghosts in *Death of the Fox*, Garrett relates that "I was forced to summon up many others to help me" (vii)—these include both "real" personages like

Robert Cecil or the queen's cousin Sir Robert Carey, and imaginary ones, such as a messenger who carries letters and messages back and forth between Scotland and London in the year James was born and a Catholic priest in 1587 who reacts with shock and sorrow to the execution of Mary Queen of Scots. As Monika Fludernik observes in her essay "History and Metafiction," "there is no real unitary plot to this novel, it is a fragmented collection of vignettes which are linked by the reader's knowledge of historical events." She continues: "Instead of a retelling, an ordering of historical events, one gets a series of personal experiences which allow an insight into the Elizabethan *mentalité*," yielding a "multi-perspectivism" that is metafictional inasmuch as it "reflect[s] the absence of unitary meaning" (98–99). *The Succession*, she concludes, belongs to a "new paradigm or genre" that could be described as the "new non-fabulist historical novel." Since historical novels "imitate the ways of *writing* history . . . it should therefore come as no surprise that postmodernist attempts at the historical novel imitate both fictional innovations and historiographic developments" (101).

In many ways *The Succession* is a novel about what constitutes history: history as gossip and hearsay, history as letters; history as the opinions of interested parties like Robert Cecil, who stakes his future on James's succession, history filtered through the lens of ideology, as in the priest's narrative; history from the perspective of the nameless reivers on the Scottish border who sit around the fire telling stories. No two stories will ever be the same, for "the English have their [tales] and tell [them] their own way. And the Scotsmen have as many versions . . . as there are tellers." Each story "keeps changing with the passing of time" (237).

Garrett expects the active participation of his readers, who must piece together the fragments of information and provide the missing links. In effect, the readers contribute to the process of constructing a world, bringing to the experience not only their knowledge of the period but also their ability to make sense of seemingly unrelated fragments of text. For example, nowhere in the first "Messenger 1566" section (there are five of them, scattered throughout the novel) is the reader told what the messenger's message is; only gradually do we infer that he is bringing news of James's birth to William Cecil. As R .H. W. Dillard observes, the reader is "required by the text to become a spy . . . reading over shoulders, listening in on private thoughts, assembling the data, adding them up for private reasons" in an involvement far "beyond that of a detached, even if excited reader" (115).

The two Cecils are the link between Elizabeth's and James's reigns. Robert Cecil, the frail, lame son who succeeded his father as the queen's secretary and chief adviser late in her reign, spends a long night in 1603 rereading letters in the chapter most closely derived from Garrett's original plan. As he orchestrates the succession, Cecil "can understand the contradictions of the King," for whom he "has a deep sympathy . . . albeit a sympathy gently but firmly modified by the necessary sense of his own superior abilities" (*Succession* 302–03), abilities honed during his years of service to Elizabeth. The five chapters that bring the messenger closer and closer to delivering his message obliquely emphasize the importance of the role Robert Cecil inherited from his father. In the last of these chapters, when the messenger finally arrives in London, he reflects on the machinations of court that play so large a role in the novels about Shakespeare's England:

> And then he thinks he would, if he could, prefer to change his situation. Change the nature of his services to his master. He, like Cecil's other spies and secret agents, is generously rewarded. No one pays more for information and service. No complaint there. He can be sure he will receive a sum of money amounting to more by far than the yearly income of several of Cecil's most senior servants. . . . (487)

Then the narrative perspective shifts to William Cecil, who speculates about how the queen will receive the news, and what it means for the "question of the Succession, which is pressing and serious," since "She has not only avoided making any clarification of the complex matter of the rights of a possible Successor, but has also refused to allow it to be discussed" (488).

When this fifth "Messenger: 1566" chapter ends, the reader is abruptly transported to "Christmastide: 1602–03," the novel's final chapter. Among the others she recalls as she presides over the feasting, Queen Elizabeth remembers William Cecil, a man "In so many ways closer and nearer (and dearer) to her than any favorite or even lover could ever be" (527). Characteristically, Garrett addresses his final paragraphs to an unspecified "you" (whom the reader finally realizes is a happily drunken plowman) who is "full of food and drink and gratitude" from the Christmas feast, wishing the world "nothing but well. Nothing but good fortune" (538). The birth of the infant James, which the five messenger chapters subtly construct as a analogy to the birth of Jesus, is celebrated, in the novel's skewed chronology, by the Christmas festivities of 1602–03. Three months later, James VI of Scotland will be reborn as King James I of England.

Experimental as *The Succession* is, it has more in common with *Death of the Fox* than either novel has with the third work in Garrett's triptych, *Entered from the Sun*, a metafiction that enacts the process by which historical research and the reconstruction of events and motives attempt to make sense of the past and sometimes fail to do so. Marlowe's death in a Deptford tavern on May 30, 1593, was and continues to be one of the most intriguing mysteries in the literary history of Shakespeare's England. Although scholars have probed the Marlowe biography, the extant documentary evidence consists mainly of court records; there is nothing like the wealth of information available about Raleigh, Elizabeth, and James—except, of course, Marlowe's plays and poems, which have been inspiring biographical inferences ever since his contemporaries began likening him to the atheist Tamburlaine, the Machiavel Barabas, and the homosexual Edward II.

Marlowe is not a character in *Entered from the Sun* in the way that Raleigh, Elizabeth, James, and the others are characters in the two earlier novels. Rather, he has been dead for some four years, long enough for the event to have become shrouded in mystery, but recent enough so that witnesses and evidence are still accessible. Garrett's two amateur detectives, Joseph Hunnyman and Captain William Barfoot, accept their assignments unwillingly, fearing that they are being set up and that the Marlowe investigation may be only a pretext for something more sinister and threatening. Like the ghosts of *Death of the Fox* and the invented characters of *The Succession*, Barfoot and Hunnyman begin as character types, but become more three-dimensional as the novel proceeds.

Entered from the Sun playfully adapts espionage and detective fiction conventions, mixing them with conventions borrowed from other forms; for instance, Garrett includes ghost and dream lore reminiscent of magic realism. Brian McHale's definition of "the postmodern revisionist historical novel" sounds very much like Garrett's method: "First, it revises the *content* of the historical record, reinterpreting the historical record, often demystifying or debunking the orthodox version of the past. Secondly, it revises, indeed transforms, the conventions and norms of historical fiction itself." To do so, the writer operates in the "dark areas" of history, and "supplements the historical record, claiming to restore what has been lost or suppressed" (90). But *Entered from the Sun* is even more complicated than McHale's definition would suggest, for Garrett is using historiographic as well as fictional resources to "demystify or debunk" the several "orthodox" accounts of Marlowe's death. Moreover, the reconstruction of the murder is only ostensibly the "subject" of the novel, and hardly enters the narrative until more than half-way through its 350 pages. Just as *Death of the Fox* and *The Succession* jump back and forth between shifting pasts and presents, much of *Entered from the Sun* consists of retrospective accounts of the earlier lives of Hunnyman, Barfoot, and Hunnyman's lover Alysoun.

Alysoun is a curious mix of the Elizabethan and the modern: a beautiful and independent young widow who presides over her deceased husband's print shop, she revises conventional depictions of gender inequality in the past by being far wiser, shrewder, and more successful than the hapless Hunnyman, and looks forward to some of the women to be discussed in chapter 5. In a richly ironic chapter that presumes the reader's knowledge of literary history, Hunnyman refuses her offer to set him up with his own acting company, since he predicts that plays and players have had their day, and that Shakespeare has "shot his bolt" and will soon retire to Stratford (*Entered* 254). Alyson's sexual independence provides an opportunity for scenes that help "sell" historical fiction, but they also help link the characters' discrete stories, which unfold discontinuously through a variety of digression-laced strategies.

As the novel draws to an end, the "mystery" of Marlowe's death remains unsolved, although Garrett does offer an inconclusive resolution of the mysteries surrounding Barfoot and Hunnyman's shadowy employers, who turn out to be Raleigh and his enemies, the Cecil and Essex factions. This strategy of interweaving historical characters with entirely fictional ones in a plot that has no basis in history was a new departure for Garrett, and it sets *Entered from the Sun* apart from the other Marlowe books of the early 1990s as well.

It would be interesting to know whether Charles Nicholl read *Entered from the Sun*, for his book could be viewed as an extended gloss on Captain Barfoot's assessment of "this our age of spies," an age in which "we can never know where their loyalty or allegiance may lie," and in which "even the best among them must be assumed to have played on both sides of everything" (*Entered* 275). Nicholl's biography indicates that he read extensively in the primary documents and secondary scholarship, but *The Reckoning* often reads like a novel and is documented without footnotes (phrases in bold and page numbers identify endnotes) so that the scholar's methods remain unobtrusive. Nicholl had written a study of Elizabethan alchemy and a biography of Thomas Nashe before tackling Marlowe, and so, like Burgess and Garrett, he was already steeped in the rhetoric and culture of the age when he began his research. He was attracted to the Marlowe story because, as he says in his introduction, "an unsolved murder does not really age. It continues to require our attention, our questions, our unease. We may never find the truth, but we can dig away some of the lies" (3). He was also drawn by the puzzle-like quality of the evidence, and describes his book as "an attempt to fill in the spaces: with new facts, with new ways of seeing old facts, with probabilities and speculations and sometimes with guesswork" (3). Burgess and Garrett could have described their historical fictions in much the same way.

The "we" of Nicholl's introduction remains a strong presence throughout *The Reckoning*, and it has the effect of drawing the reader into the process of investigation and reconstruction, much as Garrett's use of the word "you" does. A distinctive narrative persona emerges, that of the investigative reporter–detective who challenges the literary-historical establishment and embarks on a journey of discovery that begins with a portrait, rather like Josephine Tey's well-known detective fiction about Richard III, *The Daughter of Time*. Nicholl takes us with him to the dining room of Corpus Christi College, Cambridge, to view what is now widely accepted as a portrait of Marlowe, painted in 1585, when he was twenty-one years old. He relates his conversation with the head porter, who delivers the received opinion of Marlowe, "He died in a drunken brawl!" (7), just as the nurse in *The Daughter of Time* tells the bedridden detective Grant that Richard was a "murdering brute" who "did away with his two little nephews" (39). Nicholl frequently resorts to questions, and here, too, the effect is to draw the reader into the story: "What really happened? Who was responsible? And—looking at this handsome aspiring young man in velvet and gold—what went wrong? These are the questions we owe the dead man" (9).

Another characteristic feature of Nicholl's narrative style is his way of calling attention to what he is doing and how his book differs from other accounts of Marlowe's murder. He does so with the novelist's flair for pictorial detail, as in this artful paragraph that brings the first chapter, titled "Deptford 1593," to a close:

> This is a story of the underside of Elizabethan politics, not the glittering propagandist surface. It is part of the unauthorised version. It has the feel of history in the raw, history as it suddenly happens. A man is walking in a garden in Deptford on a summer afternoon. The smell of the garden is sweet, but a breath of river-breeze takes the sweetness away, and there is the familiar stink: fish, pitch and sewage, the dung-boats and the dog-kennels, the slaughter-yards busy for some stately banquet, the blood running down Bow Ditch and into the river. (16)

Writers of Cold War thrillers and recent historical novelists attracted to Shakespeare's England have this in common: they are fascinated by what Nicholl calls "the secret world" of espionage and counter-espionage, assassination plots, surveillance, entrapment, and interrogations. For example, numerous historical novels have been written about sixteenth-century conspiracies to assassinate Queen Elizabeth and place Mary Queen of Scots on the throne. Nicholl goes to great lengths to reconstruct the secret world presided over by Sir Francis Walsingham, Elizabeth's "spymaster." He proceeds from the premise that the border between the criminal world and the secret world is a shifting one, as he depicts the shady characters who moved back and forth between England and the continent, passing information to their employers, making their fortunes, and betraying one another as the occasion required. He likens the secret world to the most illusory and unsettling kind of theater, warning the reader that

> there are no clear answers, only a juggling of different questions, an assortment of different masks. You have to take it as a kind of theatre, a political house of games in which everything is potentially different, potentially reversible. (114)

In thirty-five short titled chapters, most of them organized around a participant in the extended drama of Marlowe's activities in Walsingham's service, Nicholl builds his case as a lawyer would, sifting and interpreting the available evidence, sometimes comparing his work with that of his predecessors. For example, in a chapter on William Vaughan, author of *The Golden*

Grove (1600), which contains an account of the stabbing of Marlowe at Deptford, Nicholl comments that "none of Marlowe's biographers has investigated Vaughan, or asked how he might have acquired this information" (78). On one level, *The Reckoning* is a study of historiography and a critique of the way conventional literary biographies have treated Marlowe's death as "a separate and rather puzzling side-issue" (265). On another, it is a contribution to revisionist history writing that insists on a clear-eyed, unromanticized reconstruction of the age of Shakespeare. As Nicholl sums up his account on the first page of the book's sixth and final section, titled "The Frame,"

> it is not a pretty view of the Golden Age of Elizabeth, and it is not a pretty view of Christopher Marlowe either. In these fragments which record his involvement in the secret world—the Privy Council certificate, the Sidney letter from Flushing, the Kyd deposition—there is a common thread of falsehood. They record his pretences, his masks. He is a militant Catholic "determined to go to Rheims", he is a seditious coiner with "intent to go to the enemy", he is a propagandist stirrer going "unto the K of Scots", and yet we find he is really none of these things, that these appearances of commitment are only to cover—or as they said it, to "colour"—his role as a spy, a deceiver, a politic meddler. . . . It is a world of gestures, of alterable meanings: the "secret theatre." (265)

These words could almost have been spoken by one of George Garrett's ghosts or by Captain Barfoot or indeed, by the ghost-narrator of *Entered from the Sun*, who toward the end of the novel chides us, the twentieth-century readers, for the "brutal and boundless pride" with which we pass judgment on his characters. He then asks pardon for his "untoward interruption" in which, "chorus-like," he came "on this stage" sounding like a preacher (328).

Anthony Burgess acknowledges having read *The Reckoning*, along with other biographies of Marlowe, in the author's note at the end of *A Dead Man in Deptford*. Like Nicholl, he sets out to show how Marlowe's activities and relationships led to his death at Deptford, and like Nicholl he emphasizes Marlowe's role in Walsingham's spy network. However, Burgess's novelist's instincts caused him to extrapolate and invent, for, as he says in the author's note, "the virtue of a historical novel is its vice—the flatfooted affirmation of possibility as fact" (271–72). He seizes on a possibility Nicholl had rejected: that Marlowe was involved in a homosexual affair with Sir Francis Walsingham's young cousin, Thomas Walsingham. Thomas was associated in various ways with the three men (Nicholas Skeres, Ingram Frizer, and Robert Poley) who were present in the room in Eleanor Bull's house at

Deptford where a quarrel over paying the bill, or reckoning, allegedly led to the scuffle in which Marlowe was fatally stabbed by Frizer, as described in the deposition at the coroner's inquest (Nicholl 17–18). In his chapter on Walsingham, Nicholl dismisses "certain fanciful versions of Marlowe's death" in which Walsingham "has some sinister, puppet-master connection with the killing," and goes on to say, rather sarcastically, that "[i]t is too vague and easy to put him up as the schemer behind the scenes. It is possible, but there is not real evidence for it. The same goes for that other pleasant pipe-dream, which makes him Marlowe's lover." It is more likely, albeit "more prosaic," Nicholl adds, that Thomas Walsingham was Marlowe's friend and protector, and that he had been one of Marlowe's contacts in the intelligence service (118).[3]

Burgess, with his penchant for vividly described sex scenes and the torments of unfulfilled love or lust still evident thirty years after the composition of *Nothing Like the Sun*, makes the Marlowe-Walsingham relationship the shaping event in the short life of his fictional Marlowe. He suggests early on that Frizer, Tom's bodyguard and companion, developed a jealous homophobic hostility toward Marlowe, and so casts him as the "villain" of the novel. Burgess's Marlowe is a sympathetic character, though he is also a self-destructive one—arrogant like Tamburlaine, skeptical like Faustus, and recklessly given over to forbidden love like Edward II. His death is a deliberate execution, prompted by his unwillingness to continue in the service; like a defector in a modern spy novel, he is eliminated because he knows too much. *A Dead Man in Deptford* is thus a more conventional fiction than *Entered from the Sun*, inasmuch as it fills in a number of gaps and orders the fragments of information to make sense of Marlowe's life and death according to recognizable fictional plot elements.

Although he had rejected first-person narration in 1964, Burgess evidently felt differently in 1993, and here he may have been influenced and encouraged by the successful use of first-person narration in the New Historical Fiction written during the intervening decades. His nameless narrator is a boy actor when he first encounters "Kit," as he calls Marlowe, and he soon becomes Kit's bedmate, which accounts for his intimate knowledge of Marlowe's life (a narrative device Nye subsequently uses with Pickleherring in *The Late Mr. Shakespeare*). Burgess begins his novel by having his narrator address the reader much as Garrett's various narrators do: "You must and will suppose (fair or foul reader, but where's the difference?) that I suppose a heap of happenings that I had no eye to eye knowledge of or concerning" (*A Dead Man in Deptford* 3). He repeats the word "suppose" insistently several more times on this first page and throughout the novel up to the very end, where he concludes, "So I suppose it happened, but I suppose only" (267).

The narrator's metafictional comments on his own discourse and on "the impossibility of ascertaining the true nature of history" are, as Menton points out, a characteristic of postmodern historical fiction (25).[4] The boy actor acknowledges his playful rhetoric: "I see . . . that I am in danger of falling into the dangerous orbit of the playman Jack Marston and being betrayed into use of the most reprehensible inkhornisms" (3). A couple of pages later, he pauses before launching into his tale by asking "how will you have your dialogues, reader? I will follow the foreign fashion and indent and lineate" (5). Burgess persists in calling attention to the textuality of his novel and the unreliability of early modern written records by including variant spellings of Marlowe's name, just as he had done with Shakespeare in *Nothing Like the Sun*. For instance, when Kit introduces himself to Thomas Watson, he calls himself "Christopher. The other name is unsure. Marlin, Merlin, Marley, Morley. Marlowe will do" (9).[5]

Burgess uses his actor-narrator as a vehicle for providing glimpses of the world of Elizabethan theater. Like so many New Historical Fictions, this is a novel for readers familiar with the period, one that playfully nudges the knowing reader with passages such as this, in which the narrator casually remarks that

> I had abandoned the Lord Admiral's Men through dislike of Alleyn's imperiousness and had discovered the talent of song with Lord Strange's Men. . . . And I was lodged now with the new player and playmaker (botcher, collaborator) from Warwickshire, a mild man but ambitious, who sucked me dry, but ever with a mild smile, of all I knew of the craft. He moaned this Christmas, indeed wept, because he was absent from his three children that had ever loved the games of the season and the gifts. He moaned less that he was absent from his wife. (194-95)

Just as we are expected to recognize this mocking portrait of Shakespeare, we are expected to recognize phrases from Marlowe's plays, as in this description of the audience, viewed through the eyes of the arrogant and contemptuous Kit:

> Were they then to be taught naught but gross comic murder, language mere noise (but was it more in the endless Sunday sermons they were whipped to attending?), history a gallimaufrey of rivalry and blood? They wished diversion, no more. Diversion filled no empty heads, save with ride in triumph through Persepolis and avaunt avoid Mephistophilis and (so it would be now) master I'll worship thy nose for this. (196)

In describing historiographic metafiction, Linda Hutcheon speaks of the way documentary sources, "the traces of the past," are intertextually incorporated into text (121–22). Garrett does this in an unusual way in *Entered from the Sun*. The novel contains four short sections that appear unexpectedly in the text entitled "Present Difficulties of This Time" and, near the end of the novel, a fifth called "Words of Christopher Marlowe and Others." These sections are reminiscent of Elizabethan commonplace books; each consists of excerpts from documents in different typefaces printed in double columns like a newspaper. The first "Present Difficulties" collection is devoted to "Apparel," the second to "Plays, Players, and Playhouses," the third to "Matters of Religion," and the fourth to "The Court," and they are interspersed among the other chapters with no explanation. Together, they set forth the issues and controversies of "this time," while illustrating the rhetoric and idioms and syntax that Garrett so skillfully adapts. Included among the fragments of text are snippets of famous poems like Raleigh's "The Lie" ("Say to the Court it glows / And shines like rotten wood"), Royal Proclamations, Elizabethan sermons, the Book of Common Prayer, pamphlets by Dekker, Nashe, Stubbes, and Gosson, John Manningham's *Diary*—all familiar to scholars and testimonials to the extensive research that Garrett undertook during his thirty-year immersion in the sixteenth and seventeenth centuries.

Interestingly, postmodern theories are seen to have Elizabethan counterparts—in one of the "Present Difficulties" sections, Garrett quotes Sir Thomas Overbury on "The Character of an Actor": "All men have been of his occupation; and indeed, what he doth feignedly that do others essentially. This day one plays a monarch, the next a private person. Here one acts a tyrant, on the morrow an exile" (*Entered* 100). Anticipating the Overbury passage in an earlier chapter, Garrett uses the metaphor of the actor as the basis for Hunnyman's character. In a self-justifying dialogue with himself, Hunnyman remarks that "here [in London] all men are players of one kind or another. . . . In such a world how can anyone tell and separate the truth from the false?" (73). This sounds very like the shifting and multiple subjectivities both Nicholl and Burgess ascribe to Marlowe. Nicholl's Marlowe may not have realized this about himself, but Burgess's Kit does: "Listen to me, Kit said, and he knew, saying it, that the me to which he referred was one of a parcel of many within, and he felt a manner of despair or at least desperateness in not knowing well which was to speak" (161). The reader unfamiliar with Overbury (or Montaigne, or other writers of the period) might be tempted to dismiss this introspective moment as the kind of psychological anachronism novelists can produce when, as Elisabeth Wesseling observes, they "attempt to detail the workings of the minds of characters from previous epochs." She cites an oft-quoted letter from Henry James to Sarah Orne Jewett written in 1901, in which he condemns the historical novel because of its inability to represent the "old CONSCIOUSNESS, the soul, the sense, the horizon, the vision of individual in whose minds half the things that make ours, that make the modern world, were non-existent" (58).[6] If this moment in *A Dead Man in Deptford* is convincing, I would suggest, it is largely due to the way Burgess uses diction to approximate the Elizabethan consciousness.

Burgess's and Garrett's innovations and attention to diction and style are thrown into sharp relief when one compares their novels with Judith Cook's *The Slicing Edge of Death: Who Killed Christopher Marlowe?* and Stephanie Cowell's *The Players* (a fiction-biography that uses Shakespeare's sonnets as the basis for reconstructing his love life). Like *A Dead Man in Deptford*, Cook's novel was published in 1993, the four-hundredth anniversary of Marlowe's death. Cook is much more direct and unambiguous in representing the characters' motives: the "thesis" of her novel is that Robert Cecil ordered Poley to orchestrate Marlowe's death at Deptford because Marlowe knew dangerous information about Cecil's relative Anthony Bacon. Cecil manipulates Thomas Walsingham into persuading Marlowe to go to Deptford on the fateful day; afterwards, he justifies the murder as a form of social control:

> Most of those who go to the playhouses, Thomas, are ignorant and unlettered. Suddenly, they are exposed to new ideas, ideas of a blasphemous, immoral, even of a treasonable nature, ideas they would never have dreamed of had they not been presented with them in so immediate and vivid a way. What might Marlowe have gone on to write? (224)

Cook thus ascribes to Cecil the attitudes toward theaters and players set forth by moralists of the day (good examples can be found in the documents in *Entered from the Sun*) and implies that Marlowe was killed partly to prevent him from writing more plays. This is an improbable theory, to say the least, particularly to anyone who has read *The Reckoning*. It is also a suspiciously neat way to account for Marlowe's death, by selecting Cecil from among the available cast of historical characters and transforming him into the conventional scheming villain.

Just as jarring to readers of Garrett and Burgess is Cook's use of contemporary diction, particularly in her dialogue, which is indistinguishable from the language of fiction set in the present. Here is Marlowe in conversation with Thomas Walsingham:

> "You know you can come to me for anything you need."
> "I don't want to be always your debtor, Thomas."
> "I'd infinitely prefer that to your involving yourself with such as Cecil and Poley. Robert Cecil is no Francis Walsingham, nor do I have any such influence over him as I had over my uncle. Poley is . . . well, Poley. I don't have to tell you what kind of a man he is. Surely now with your success in the playhouses, my patronage and the place you've made

for yourself in society, there's no need for you to grub around in that dirty world?"

Marlowe tries to reassure Walsingham, saying

> "I think you worry over nothing."
> "I hope so."
> "You sound doubtful."
> Walsingham sighed then came and put his arm round his friend. "I have a gut feeling—it's no more than that Kit—call it if you will a feeling of unease, of something not being quite right."

To which Marlowe replies "God's wounds, Tom . . . what are you suggesting?" (132). The phrases "God's wounds" comes across as an effort to impose an Elizabethan veneer on an otherwise utterly un-Elizabethan sounding passage. It is a phrase Garrett and Burgess never use; it sounds too stagey, too clearly an Elizabethan cliché. Period dialogue is difficult, to be sure, and it is only fair to say that the novel is more convincing in stretches of third-person narration presented from the point of view of Richard, still another invented actor who serves as observer and chronicler of events.

Stephanie Cowell, author of two earlier historical novels set in Shakespeare's England, follows much the same trajectory as *Nothing Like the Sun* in *The Players: A Novel of the Young Shakespeare*. Her young William is forced to marry the pregnant Anne in the second chapter of the novel; by the beginning of the third, he has run off to London to live with his friend, the printer Dick Field, and join the actors he had met in Stratford. Cowell's dialogue relies on words like "art," "doth," "hast," "thee," and "wouldst" for its Elizabethan sound, but they are used inconsistently and the effect is somewhat contrived in comparison to Garrett's and Burgess's. Here, for instance, is her Marlowe in a confiding mode:

> Christopher leaned back and narrowing his eyes said, "Art witty enough, could write thyself! You could do many things, William, and yet you stand apart observing it all. . . ."
>
> "Christ's love, the bricklayer's son hath driven all sleep from me! Sometimes I am awake until dawn and never think to sleep for two nights more. Life rushes by so quickly, and one is struck down and all is over. . . ."
>
> "I am not a man like thee, Will. I fancy boys—I want them until I am sick with wanting, and then having had them, I am sick with that too and go into my mind. If only we could love without knowing the other's name, without having to look into the eyes. . . . (68–69)

Following A. L. Rowse, to whom the novel is dedicated, Cowell constructs a love triangle among Shakespeare, Henry Wriothesley, and the Italian musician Emilia Bassano, assuming the autobiographical authority of the sonnets, several of which are reproduced in full in the historical notes. *The Players* is a sexy, steamy treatment of her characters' tangled relationships, with very brief references to the early plays. After a final encounter in which Shakespeare give Wriothesley the packet of sonnets, Cowell leaves us with the saddened playwright who "wanted more than anything to write again" sitting down to work on *King John*, "this story of the dissatisfied king who could not love" (236–37). Like *The Slicing Edge of Death, The Players* is a little too plot-driven in the way it imposes a narrative on the gaps in the historical record, and in comparison with Burgess's and Garrett's novels, a little too predictable in its use of the strategies of popular historical romance. Together, these novels illustrate the difference between reasonably well-written conventional historical fiction and the innovative and experimental New Historical Fiction.

Cook's and Cowell's attempts to approximate the diction and tone of Shakespeare's England serve as a reminder that it takes a great deal of reading, and an ability to reproduce the structures of early modern English, to write a sentence like Garrett's "In your case, better be sure your journey is not taken stark naked at a cart's arse or upside down on a hurdle, dragged to some hanging place" (*Entered* 261). This sentence unobtrusively communicates information about the cruel theatricality attendant on executions (also described at length in *A Dead Man in Deptford*). The crude phrase "at a cart's arse," or behind a cart, wittily reinforces the shocking image of nakedness, while the expression "stark naked" is a good example of a memorable Elizabethan phrase still in common use (Shakespeare used it in *Twelfth Night* and *Antony and Cleopatra*). Burgess and Garrett were each blessed with a remarkable ear for the sounds of the past, and the distinctive idioms they created use sonorous words and phrases, syntax, and, most importantly, the mentality of an earlier time to create the illusion of realness that is one of the most endearing qualities of good historical fiction.

The historical novelist's imaginative reconstruction of the mentality of the past can assume an irony directed to the modern reader, as, for instance, in Burgess's depiction of Marlowe's introduction to tobacco. Burgess's Raleigh of 1587 offers us still another side of the complex figure Garrett recreates in *Death of the Fox*. He introduces Kit to "the nymph tobacco" in an extended conceit that evokes both the exotic novelty of tobacco and the associations with sexuality which still cling to tobacco consumption:

The aroma sidled towards Kit; Kit coughed gently. Aye, you will cough more when you kiss her. But the cough will be in the manner of a cleansing, a disgorgement of the grosser humours, you may even vomit them up. There is a bowl beneath that table. And then no more coughing, only the bliss of inhalation. (127)

Despite his body's initial revulsion, Kit becomes enthralled by the hunger for the nymph, or as his thinks of it, the "buggery of the lungs" (132). Prophetically, he senses that "the drawing in of this divine smoke was an ecstasy and men would in time perceive it as a great benison to the world." But "the daily ravishing of the nymph" is also a need no "trugging house . . . no baker or vintner could satisfy." Marlowe realizes that he has become dependent on Raleigh, "the keeper of many keys" (133). A scene like this one accomplishes one of the many goals of historical fiction, namely, to link present conditions with their origins in the past. If there is an element of what Brian McHale calls "creative anachronism" (90) in Kit's awareness that he has become addicted (though he does not use that modern term), it only serves to intensify the scene's pungent irony.

In 1970, Garrett observed in "Dreaming with Adam" that the historical novel had declined in prestige and popularity since midcentury in America, and that this was a "national singularity" that went "against the grain of much highly regarded foreign writing" (22–23). By the mid-1990s, this was no longer the case; complex historical fictions by known and unknown writers had appeared on the bestseller lists (e.g., Toni Morrison's *Beloved* and Charles Frazier's *Cold Mountain*) and novelists not known for writing historical fiction (like Jane Smiley, Kathryn Harrison, and Rose Tremain) were producing extensively researched historical novels. Both Burgess's and Garrett's later novels were refined and shaped by the influence of nearly three decades of experimentation in serious historical fiction. Whereas the "character" of Burgess's WS was largely constructed around imaginative inferences drawn from the sonnets, his Kit explicitly repudiates the biographical fallacy and denies that his creations are projections of himself:

> —I must create men and women and eke create voices for them, but they are not my voices.
> —If you create them they must of necessity be yours.
> —No, Sir Walter. There may be a directive will, Plato's charioteer, but there are many horses and they pull diverse ways. I may dream atheism and solidify that dream in *personae* that stalk the stage, but it follows not that I proclaim a damnable *non credo*. (137)

Speaking through Kit, Burgess thus participates in an ongoing dialogue about how historians and biographers use the evidence available to them in order to reconstruct the past.

As Turner observes, historical novels "are frequently structured to highlight the problems of historical interpretation" (340). When Garrett takes the form of the historical novel in a different direction in *Entered from the Sun* he does just that; his novel is in a very real way an exploration of the way amateur detectives, like historians and novelists, locate, piece together, interpret, and embellish the historical evidence. Indeed, *Entered from the Sun* serves as Garrett's own metafictional demonstration of the research he himself undertook when writing *Death of the Fox* and *The Succession*, complete with the "primary" texts in the "Present Difficulties" sections and the excerpts from Marlowe's plays and poems and the documents pertaining to his death, which Garrett provocatively withholds until after most of the speculation has taken place. What Turner says of Faulkner's *Absolom, Absolom* anticipates Garrett's strategy in *Entered from the Sun*:

> the meaning of history and possiblility of recovering it become the primary concerns in Faulkner's novel. Determinations of fact, assessment of documents and oral reports, interpretations of motive—these are all methodological issues for the historian, as they are for Quentin. Thus by predicating a gap between the narrator and his story, Faulkner raises the issue of how it is to be closed. Herein lies the difference between many invented historical novels and other fiction: in realistic novels, though the narrator may pose as a historian, attention is usually diverted from the problem of how the narrator can know his story; in invented historical novels, by contrast, that very possibility is often brought into question, turning the novel into a reflection on the way we know history. (340)

Turner's distinction between "realistic novels" and "invented historical novels" speaks to some of the differences between conventional novels and the New Historical Fiction. Garrett and Burgess comment on the historical method at unexpected moments in their novels, often by casting their characters in the historians' roles. Thus, for example, as they attempt to reconstruct Marlowe's mysterious death, Barfoot and Hunnyman exemplify two contrasting ways of gathering information:

> Barfoot by papers and the words of shepherding clerks; Hunnyman by talking and listening to other players as if he were cast in a minor part, a role designed mostly to cue and to prod others into recollection, all part of a strange play that will end, bloody and mysterious, with the death of its hero—both of them able, by inclination and experience, to read through the text, the outward sense of what they are learning, to the kernel of meaning. . . . (*Entered* 215)

Garrett's metaphor of the past as a playtext is a richly ambiguous one, for it places the invented characters at once in the roles of playwrights, actors, and audience.

   The alternative scenarios Barfoot and Hunnyman produce in the chapters that lay out their hypotheses at once illustrate the unknowability of the past and the subjective bias each historian/detective brings to his reconstruction of

it. Barfoot's "texts" (his letters to his brother, one of many narrative strategies
in this mixed media novel) view Marlowe's death through the lens of his own
role as agent and spy in what he calls "the sin-ridden, vice-haunted, cynical
world" (274). He speculates that Marlowe was either planning to flee to
Scotland or, alternatively, was refusing to do so, and was killed because he
would not follow orders. Raleigh, Barfoot's mysterious employer, offers a third
interpretation, "that Walsingham, true to the ways and means of his blood kin,
planned on the precaution of stopping Marlowe's mouth before he ever had
the chance or the temptation to utter anything against his patron" (321).

This is still a different Raleigh from the Raleigh of *A Dead Man in
Deptford* or the Raleigh of *Death of the Fox.* One of the pleasures of reading
historical fiction, here as elsewhere, is that of seeing the same historical figures come to life in various ways. These texts have given us several
Marlowes, several Raleighs, several Shakespeares, not to mention lesser
characters like Robert Greene, Ingram Frizer, and of course, Queen
Elizabeth herself, who makes at least a cameo appearance in every novel set
in the age that bears her name.

Chapter 4

Barry Unsworth's *Morality Play* and the Origins of English Secular Drama

Among the narratives about Shakespeare there is one that goes something like this: when Shakespeare was born in 1564 secular drama barely existed in England; then, in the 1580s and '90s, with the help of a few contemporaries like Marlowe, Kyd, and Greene, Shakespeare virtually invented the forms that would dominate the English literary landscape until the closing of the theaters in the mid-seventeenth century. Apart from a few private entertainments like Sackville and Norton's *Gorboduc* (1562) or Udall's *Gammer Gurton's Needle* (1553), the only identifiable precursors of the plays of Shakespeare and his fellow playwrights were the mostly anonymous morality plays and biblical cycle dramas, the St. George mummers plays, and holiday festivities that were performed through the cities and towns of medieval and early modern England. Where we might expect a gradual accretion of forms and conventions, as for example, in the case of the sonnet or the novel, we find instead a stunning breakthrough which, in a decade or so, produced some of the most brilliant and complex dramas known to Western culture. Narratives such as this one are necessarily constructed from the existing evidence, evidence that is fragmentary and incomplete and subject to the vagaries of recordkeeping. For every fourteenth- or fifteenth- or early sixteenth-century playscript that has survived, there must be countless that did not.

Historical fiction writers are attracted to gaps in our knowledge of the past; indeed, the filling in of gaps is among the principal self-ordained functions of serious historical fiction. What a historical novel "does is to extrapolate from the historical knowledge of the actual world by 'filling in' the interstices in that knowledge with imagined states of affairs which *could well have been* actual of that world at that time," Doreen Maitre observes in *Literature and Possible Worlds*. The reconstructed history the novelist devises "may have no historical authentication, but at the same time it is *compatible with* such historical facts as are known" (88). Some writers of the New Historical Fiction would disagree with Maitre; as we have seen, their fictions take considerable liberties with "historical facts" and even call into question the assumption that such facts are irrefutably "true." Many contemporary historical novels not only address the gaps in our knowledge of history, but go further to question the very assumptions upon which historical and anthropological reconstructions of the past proceed. "The redefinition of the historical novel as a means for inquiring into the epistemological problems of historiography" (in Elisabeth Wesseling's words), "has proved to be modernism's most enduring legacy to succeeding writers of historical fiction" (88).

Wesseling and Maitre would both agree that historical fiction can contribute to ongoing revisions and adjustments in our understanding of the "actual world" through positing "possible non-actual worlds" (Maitre 118). The cross-fertilization between historical fiction and detective fiction, the latter "the epistemological genre *par excellence*" (Wesseling 89), produces a conflated form Wesseling calls "self-reflexive historical fiction," in which the supposedly direct relationship between *res gesta* or actual deeds, and *historia rerum gestarum*, or narratives about these deeds, is disrupted (vii). The inaccessibility of the past is in a very real sense the starting point of such fictions, or "alternative versions of history" (82). The fiction writer is thus "inspired by the notion that any given historical situation implies a plethora of divergent possibilities that far exceed the possibilities that happen to have been realized" (100).

The imagining of divergent possibilities characterizes two astonishing and very different historical novels by Barry Unsworth. Unsworth's Booker Prize-winning novel *Sacred Hunger* imagined an eighteenth-century slave ship revolt that led to a utopian mixed-race settlement in Florida. His subsequent novel, *Morality Play*, reached further into the past: in it, a fourteenth-century troupe of traveling actors stumbles upon a murder and in the process of investigating it they invent a new kind of drama. *Morality Play* contains no afterword or historical note detailing the author's research, and unlike Garrett, Burgess, Renault, Yourcenar or Eco, Unsworth has not, to my knowledge, written about his experiences and methods as a historical novelist (although he did answer some of my questions in e-mail correspondence). Reading *Morality Play* against the extant scholarship on morality plays and other early English drama thus becomes in itself a process of probing unanswered questions and filling in gaps.

In order to reinvent the moment of transition from didactic, allegorical drama to secular, topical drama, Unsworth casts his players as amateur detectives who, in keeping with murder mystery conventions, come to the defense of the unjustly accused suspect and identify the murderer. Their play, which undergoes revision as new pieces of evidence emerge, is a hypothetical reenactment of the crime that also becomes a vehicle for eliciting information from the spectators, rather like Hamlet's "Mousetrap." Like "The Mousetrap," too, it is an adaptation of an old play to fit the circumstances at hand. The play also serves as a metacommentary on the role of the drama in the world of the novel, much as Shakespeare's plays-within-plays do. The leader of the troupe, Martin, is the primary agent of change. At one point, Unsworth endows Martin with the ability to speak from the vantage point of the future: "It has been in my mind for years now that we can make plays from stories that happen in our lives. I believe this is the way that plays will be made in the times to come" (79). The other characters are fearful and resistant; from their perspective, Martin's "pride of mind" leads him to "usurp the bodies of living people," for it is a "damnable proceeding" to "make a play of a true thing" (76, 123).

Unsworth's narrator, a renegade cleric named Nicholas Barber, joins the acting company at the beginning of the novel, and his initiation into the art of playing becomes the reader's initiation as well. George Garrett calls him "an ideal narrator, being educated and intelligent, empathetic and understanding, yet he is an innocent in the world who needs to learn much that others simply take for granted" ("The Historical Novel Today" 460). In contrast to the other players, he is an outsider who asks questions, receives instructions, and recounts his experiences; moreover, he is a fascinated but reluctant participant who embodies the resistance to innovation that invariably accompanies change. These, as Richard Humphrey observes, are familiar traits of historical fiction: the traveler or "go-between," analogous to a detective, who has a foot in two places or cultures, and the report or memoir inscribed by an amateur historian have characterized the historical novel since the nineteenth century (22–30). In escaping from his dull and solitary life as private secretary in a nobleman's household, Nicholas experiences the shift from a medieval, Church-dominated society to a world poised on the brink of the Reformation and the social and cultural changes that accompanied it. As his life changes, so does the play.

The earliest known morality play, *The Pride of Life*, is variously dated at 1350 (Happé 10), the late fourteenth century (Harbage and Schoenbaum 8), and 1400 to 1425 (Houle 121). Only a fragment survives, but since the prologue summarizes the play, we know that the plot deals with the approach of death, a recurrent subject of morality plays. Proud and boastful, the King of Life dismisses the warnings of his queen and bishop, relying instead on his knights, Strength and Health, and his messenger, Mirth. He eventually meets Death in combat and is conquered by him, but at the request of the Virgin he is granted salvation in heaven (Houle 121–22). Unsworth would have found a reference to this play in one of the books he consulted, Glynne Wickham's *The Medieval Theatre*, in the chapter "Drama of Moral Instruction" (118). His background reading in Wickham's book and elsewhere would also have familiarized him with the plague-ridden fourteenth-century's preoccupation with death as a harvester leading souls to their graves in the Dance of Death (111). Nicholas speaks of death as an allegorical figure as he watches the players huddled around their dying fellow-actor Brendan in the opening pages of the novel:

> Then the sound ceased and I saw them shift back to make space for Death, a thing very wise to do, Death being less provoked when at large than when confined. It was like that scene in the Morality Play when the besieged soul flies free at last. It was then I saw that one of the men had a badge of livery, the emblem of a patron sewn to his cap. (9)

Impulsively, Nicholas takes the dead man's place in the troupe, though, as he says,

> I had no thought in the beginning of taking part in their plays, of practicing their shameful trade, *artem illam ignominiosam*, forbidden to us by Holy Church. My only thought was to travel with them and this because of the badges the leader wore, which meant that the company belonged to a lord and had the lord's letter of license and would not be set in the stocks or whipped for vagabonds as happens to those accounted fugitives or masterless men and this has also befallen men in Holy Orders who have no warrant from their bishop. (13–14)

These two passages illustrate Unsworth's approximation of the medieval mentality and diction in his narration: the word-ordering of the phrase "a thing very wise to do," the scrap of Latin, the series of "and"s and expressions like "whipped for vagabonds" and "masterless men" evoke the sounds of the past without seeming contrived.

The speaking voice of a first-person narration is better suited to the reconstruction of the mentality of the past than an omniscient narrator's voice, which frequently will lapse into the diction of the present, describing people and events with the psychological insights of a later age. As Hella

Haasse, author of the splendid historical novels *In a Dark Wood Wandering* and *The Scarlet City* notes, the "certainty" an omniscient narrator offered seemed "utterly antiquated" during the early modernist period, and so historical fiction writing, which was more dependent upon the omniscient narrator than any other text type, was largely abandoned (quoted and translated from the Dutch by Wesseling, 69). Unsworth, whose novels are set in a variety of times and places, exhibits the serious historical novelist's willingness to immerse himself in period texts in order to in recreate the sounds of the past.

In the passages just quoted Unsworth introduces the term "morality play" and provides the reader with information about the patronage and protection which actors continued to rely upon in Shakespeare's time. The first historical records of the acting profession date from the early fifteenth century, when "Interluders" appeared before King Henry VI in 1427. These troupes were known either by the name of their leading actor or by that of the nobleman whose endorsement protected them as they traveled. The early acting troupes competed with traveling minstrel bands whose repertory included tumbling, sleight of hand, conjuring, music, and possibly, says David Bevington, dramatic farce (11). Unsworth alludes to these performers when his actors arrive in the town and hire a barn adjoining the innyard where they plan to perform, only to find that a band of jongleurs, complete with a fire-swallower and a family of tumblers, had arrived earlier and laid claim to the best performance space. Nicholas, whose training as a scholar inclines him to the kinds of explanations historical fiction is known for, observes that

> Jongleurs travel in groups and entertain people wherever they can, in great halls, at tournaments and archery contests, at fairs and marketplaces. In this they resemble players, but unlike us they have no leader and there is no general meaning in what they do, they can combine together or break away. (45–46)

Notice that he does not use words like plot or characterization, but rather, distinguishes the players from the jongleurs with the vague word "meaning," to signify the structure and purpose of the moralities and miracle plays.

Although Unsworth titles his book *Morality Play*, the plays in his actors' repertoire seem closer to what Bevington calls "Biblical redaction containing elements of moral allegory" (13). One of the earliest historians of medieval drama, Thomas Warton, describes a process of evolution whereby "the Miracle-Plays, or Mysteries [which] . . . tamely represented stories according to the letter of scripture" began to require "the introduction of allegorical characters, such as Charity, Sin, Death, Hope, Faith [and] at length plays were formed entirely consisting of such personifications." These plays, the Moralities, "indicate the dawnings of dramatic art." For Warton, "the gradual transition to real historical personages was natural and obvious" (quoted in Happé, 12). Unsworth takes issue with the evolutionary theory of cultural change and reimagines it as abrupt and dangerous, motivated by a mixture of pride, love, inquisitiveness, moral outrage, and sheer accident.

In addition to Nicholas, the players are Martin, Springer, Tobias, Straw, and Stephen, each of whom has particular talents and can play multiple roles. They are accompanied by Margaret, a sometime whore attached to Stephen, who washes, mends, and cooks but also, interestingly, bargains with the innkeeper for their performance space, collects and manages the money, and contributes to the players' information-gathering. When the players first arrive at the unnamed town where they plan to bury Brendan, they perform *The Play of Adam*, a hybrid that contains a Devil and Devil's Fool (Nicholas's part), as well as God, the Serpent, and Adam and Eve. Unsworth's fascinating account of the performance, as Nicholas experiences it, includes details of staging and costuming and snatches of speeches:

> Now it was time for Stephen to appear as God the Father and make his slow majestic way through the people. In order to increase the impact of his presence he walked on six-inch stilts, tied to his legs below the robe. The gait of a stilt-walker has a sway of majesty about it, something stiff and slightly hindered, as God might move among men, and quarrelsome Stephen looked truly like the King of Heaven with his gilded mask and triple crown, as he paced from light to dark and back again, delivering his monologue.
>
> > "I, God, great in majesty
> > In whom no first or last can be
> > But ever was and aye shall be
> > Heaven and earth is made through me
> > At my bidding now be light. . . ." (49)

Like many of the extant morality plays, *The Play of Adam* is a temptation story, with a yellow-wigged Eve who is played with comic lewdness by the boy actor, Springer. Nicholas describes the masks, the doubling of parts and rapid costume changes in the barn, the songs and the audience's reactions. But most important, he recounts his own rapid metamorphosis, from a broadly comic creature who "hissed and jabbed and made sorties among the people and flipped up my spiked tail behind" to a daring improviser who changes the play so that "[i]t was the Fool tempting the Devil with the World, a reversal of roles. Something new" (51).

With this phrase "something new" Unsworth introduces his theory of the transformation medieval drama underwent in order to withstand the competition of the jongleurs and the guild cycles. How, the visionary Martin asks, can the "poor players who travel with the Mysteries" match the guilds in Wakefield and York, with all their wealth and resources (61)? Their problem, he realizes in a flash of inspiration, is that "the story of the Fall is an old one, the people know how it ends. But supposing the story were new?" (61). The other players vehemently resist innovation. "Play the murder?" Tobias asks. "Who plays things that are done in the world?" "It is madness," Straw exclaims. "How can men play a thing that is only done once? Where are the words for it?" "There is no authority for it," insists Tobias. "It is not written anywhere." But Martin is determined and "[i]n the end," Nicholas relates, "it was our destitution that won the day for him" (73–74). As in other aspects of life, a species must adapt in order to survive, and so the players reluctantly embrace change, although they justify their decision in characteristically fourteenth-century terms: "God cannot wish us to starve while we wait for him to give us the meaning," says Springer (75). The play about the murder of Thomas Wells breaks with the past by degrees, adhering to religious structures first and then becoming increasingly secular. "It can be made a type for all," Martin explains. The familiar plot structure of the *psychomachia*, in which Virtues and Vices battle for the soul of an Everyman or Mankind, is "the same battle in each separate soul, in ours and in that of the woman who robbed Thomas Wells and killed him." The learned Nicholas then explains to the reader that the *Psychomachia* of Prudentius, with its battle over the soul, had been giving form to stories for a thousand years (75).

Were Unsworth writing a scholarly study rather than a novel, he might acknowledge that by the early fourteenth century the vernacular sermon had come to include one or more *exempla* employing entertaining storytelling techniques and drawing on secular events. As Wickham observes in *Early English Stages*, "the *exemplum* often eclipsed in length the whole of the rest of the sermon . . . and frequently became very fanciful, dramatic, or both"; "The Tale of the Tempted Monk" and "The Tale of the Bloody Child," both referred to by Robert Mannyng of Brunne in his 1303 manual of sermons (*Early English Stages*, 129), could well have served as inspiration for Unsworth's players.[1] By making his narrator a cleric turned player, Unsworth draws attention to the uneasy kinship between preaching and playing. Just as the well-known morality play *Mankind* begins as a sermon preached by Mercy as prologue and "the play that then unfolds is, in effect, the *exemplum* attaching to Mercy's sermon" (*Early English Stages* 133), so the pieced-together narrative of the murder serves as an *exemplum* as well, though the moral principle it illustrates is not as clearly delineated.

The secular mimes and minstrels were also contributing to the emergence of topical drama, as were the university students, who began composing witty satirical dramatic texts in the thirteenth century. By the close of the fourteenth century, says Wickham, a growing middle class had begun to patronize and even devise "secularly oriented comic drama," so much so that the Bishop of Exeter "felt worried enough to address a mandate to the

Archdeacon forbidding a proposed performance of a play satirizing the exorbitant profits being made by the leatherworkers in the city under pain of excommunication (*Early English Stages* 191)." Adapting the preacher's satirical rhetoric, early playwrights transformed biblical characters such as Caiaphas or Pilate or the Pharisees into bishops or magistrates or lawyers, and so invested the English cycles, moralities, and saint plays of the fourteenth and fifteenth centuries "with a realism that is at times grimly ironic and at others farcically comic" (Wickham, *Early English Stages* 192). There is a strong thread of social protest in these comedies, as there is in the *Play of Thomas Wells*. Unsworth's players, the Wyclifite Weaver who fuels their indignation, and the townspeople who contribute important pieces of information to the play's evolution represent the various participants in the development of secular drama.

By having Martin refer to morality plays centering on characters named Everyman or Mankind, Unsworth is taking some liberties with literary history, for there is no textual evidence of a fourteenth-century play with a character named Everyman, and the sole Mankind in a fourteenth-century text is the protagonist of *The Castle of Perseverance*, one of the three Macro Moralities that constitute the only extant examples of pre-1475 morality plays. *Mankind* is generally dated at 1461–85 and *Everyman*, the best-known English morality play, at 1480–1500. Not every reader of *Morality Play* would know this; as Umberto Eco observes, each "text presupposes a reader's Encyclopedia" or fund of knowledge that the model reader brings to the reading experience. In Eco's way of thinking, "one of the basic agreements of every historical novel is that however many imaginary characters are introduced into the story, everything else has to more or less correspond to what happened in that era in the real world" (Eco, *Six Walks* 107–08). The operative phrase here is "more or less"; Unsworth, I expect, was presupposing a reader knowledgeable enough to recognize some references to medieval and early modern acting conventions, including, for instance, a passing reference to the early Italian improvisational comedy (*Morality Play* 93), but not so steeped in literary history as to distinguish narrowly among late fourteenth-, fifteenth-, and early sixteenth-century texts. And if a reader does, say, recognize the paraphrase of the messenger's opening speech in *Everyman* in Mercy's prologue to *The Play of Thomas Wells* (100, 104), that reader might be sufficiently "sophisticated," to use Eco's term, to accept the liberties the novelist takes with chronology in the service of a good story. Indeed, an even more "sophisticated" reader would realize that *Mankind* and *Everyman* may have had predecessors for which no textual evidence survives, for as the editors of a useful edition of English moralities observe,

> we do not know what percentage of the actual corpus of plays is represented by the surviving texts . . . [nor] what relationship the appearance

of a printed text in a given year has to either the time of the writing of the play or to its performance. (Schell xv)

Unsworth invents an interlude called "Way of Life" as the players' sourcetext, drawing upon details from *Mankind* and other early interludes and moralities. *Mankind*, says Richard Southern, is the earliest surviving play that could have been performed by professional players, and it is "secularized about as far as a morality could be" (21–22). Despite the warnings of Mercy, Mankind falls prey to the temptations of Mischief the Vice and Titivillus (i.e., Totus Villus) the Devil. The other three characters in this seven-character play are Nought, New-Guise, and Nowadays, who engage in singing and revelry early in the play; later, they lead Mankind into a state of sin by tempting him to take part in wenching, stealing, and killing. Mankind is eventually saved and the play ends with a speech by Mercy to the audience exhorting them to examine their own behavior. Temptation plays of this type include either a literal sexual seduction scene or an implied one, with the wenches and brothels offstage (Potter 39, 48). The temptation plot is the morality play's most important legacy; as Edmund Creeth argues, it may have had a greater influence on Shakespeare's tragedies of temptation, *Othello* and *Macbeth*, than is commonly recognized.[2]

Unsworth's players embark on their hybridization by adhering to the conventional early morality-play formula. Because a young woman has been accused of murdering the boy Thomas Wells, the players begin by representing her as a temptress, performed by Shaw, the most gifted of the players. Unsworth describes the miming that accompanies the text in detail that far surpasses anything literary history has to offer:

> For the part of the temptress he had devised a strange and frightening way of bending the body stiffly sideways with the head held for a moment in inquiry and hands just above the waist, palms outward and fingers stiffly splayed in a gesture of his own invention. So for a moment, while he made the pause to see the effects of his tempting, he was frozen in wicked inquiry. Then he broke again into sinuous motion, gesturing the delights that awaited Thomas Wells if he would but follow: cakes and pies and sweet drinks and the warmth of the fireside and something more—there was some writhing suggestion of lewdness in it also. (103)

Nicholas, meanwhile, plays Good Counsel, as in the mid-sixteenth-century temptation plays *Lusty Juventus* and *Satire of the Three Estates;* his role is to advise Thomas to resist temptation. The players also incorporate *psychomachia* conventions, with Avaritia and Pieta struggling for the woman's soul, thus transforming her into a mankind figure as well.

After the first performance of the play (which brings in much more money than *The Play of Adam*), the actors resume their amateur sleuthing, for, as Martin declares, "the play we gave was the false play of Thomas Wells. Tonight we will give the true one." Nicholas comments to the reader,

> He wanted a play with strong scenes, one that would disturb the people and send them away changed. Is that a true play? And he wanted money. He won us over, but to win us over was his role. He was prompted in the lines that he spoke, as were we all. Some fascination of power led us to imprison ourselves in this Play of Thomas Wells. (116)

The age-old conceit of the characters as actors whose roles take over their lives so that they "become" their characters runs through *Morality Play*. Onstage role-playing leads to offstage impersonation as Nicholas assumes the guise of the clerk of the King's Justice, an official whose arrival in the town coincides with the players.' Wearing the black cloak used the previous night for Avaritia, he goes to the home of the Weaver, father of the accused woman, and begins to uncover evidence that will lead to the next revision of the play. In this chapter the reader learns about popular Wyclifite revolts against the excesses of the Church. The Weaver denounces the Monk, accuser of the woman and confessor to the Lord of the village:

> "They have wanted to take me for years past because I speak against the monks and friars and especially against the Benedictines, most slothful and debauched of all. This Simon Damian is a minister of Hell, he serves the Lord and helps him to live delicately on our labors and goods. We starve while they feast, we groan while they dance. But they will groan in their turn when the day—" (124)

Martin, meanwhile, goes to the Lord de Guise's dungeon to interview the Weaver's daughter, only to find that she is deaf and dumb—unable, as her father had told Nicholas, to bear witness.

It is at this point that the most fascinating element in Unsworth's re-imagining of medieval drama converges with the solving of the mystery. Early in the novel, Nicholas was initiated into the sign language employed by the players, thirty hand movements that the players use as signals when they improvise parts of the play. For example, Nicholas made the "three-fingered sign to Tobias to show I would speak my own words" when he decided to add "something new" to his role as the Devil's Fool (52). But there is also a vocabulary of mime-like gestures used for comic effect, like the "two-handed gesture of copulation" or the "rapid tongue movements of lechery," as well as conventional postures used to denote character: "And he compressed his lips and made a gesture of the right hand against his cheek to sign blushes, then with both hands the motion of drawing close a shawl, like Chastity in the Morality Play" (52, 63).

Still other gestures resemble the language of the deaf, as when Martin made "the snake-sign of tonsure and belly for the monk; then the swift chopping motion of roof and walls" (63). Martin uses this kind of signing to communicate with the deaf woman, in a scene that is one of the most powerful in the novel. Nicholas watches as Martin questions her about the crime in rapid sign language and she answers him, although they are not always familiar with one another's signs:

> I saw her shake her head and make the sign of the circle, not that slow one that indicates eternity, but hasty and repeated and made with both hands meeting and parting above and below. I did not know this sign, and perhaps it is not one that belongs to players. . . .
>   . . . Martin made the sign of carnal relation, not that brisk one of copulation but the one that also suggests affectionate feeling, fingers interlaced and held straight. Again I think this is a sign only players use, for she did not know it and signified so by frowning and beckoning. He made the sign again, this time also setting his mouth in the shape of kissing. She made a violent gesture of denial, like a sideways blow with the flat of the hand. . . .

Nicholas likens this dialogue to a dance: "The two of them were moving together now, not drawing nearer but stepping and turning in a kind of accord, like a dance, mocked by their own shadows. . . (131–32).

This scene occurs about midway through the novel, by which point the reader is accustomed to the players' use of signs and mime. Some of the movements are little more than familiar gestures still in use, such as "the shrug of sorrowful resignation, with arms half-raised" (105). The really interesting ones, however, are those that suggest a private language for communication among the players, not meant to be seen by the audience. These hand movements, as one of my students pointed out, are more analogous to the private signals used by baseball players and their coaches to communicate game strategies than they are to the gestures that add emotional emphasis for the audience's benefit.[3] The most important signal is the sign of changing discourse, a twisting of the hand that signifies a player's decision to take the story in a different direction. This device allows the players to improvise, which in turn enables what began as formulaic drama to grow and adapt. When the play comes dangerously close to the truth Martin "signed to Tobias to continue and make speed," and then a little later, "under cover of his body, he made to us the sign of supplication," a signal to the other players to fall back, since the "great rule of players [is] that he who is speaking must not be obscured" (176–77).

In the course of a discussion about the genesis of the novel, I asked Barry Unsworth about the origin of the hand signals. He replied:

several years ago, in casual conversation, I was told [by an Italian actor; Unsworth lives in Italy] that traveling players here in Italy, in the nineteenth century, used to try to find out some event of importance in the town where they happened to be and improvise a curtain-raiser to attract custom. I made a note of this at the time and then forgot it for quite a long time. But from the beginning it was the dramatic nature of the narrative that attracted me—the stumbling on a dangerous truth. The thematic elements came later, in the process of writing. And the details of secular drama etc. later still. The hand signals struck me as inherently probable and I might well have used them without any research material to back me up. Above all they were *necessary*—the process of discovery happened mainly on stage and there had to be the drama of the unexpected in the course of the performance. (letter to author, 3 Oct. 1999)

Earlier, Unsworth had told me that he had seen some illustrated hand gestures

going back, I think, to pre-Roman times. These were intended to emphasize the points that the speaker was making or to accentuate emotions he desired to arouse in the audience. I adapted these for my own purposes, without any authority except my own sense of inherent probability. (letter to author, 11 Sept. 1999)

I had found illustrations of the gestures he was referring to in B. L. Joseph's *Elizabethan Acting*; they first appeared in John Bulwer's *Chironomia* and *Chirologia* (1644), on pages divided into twenty-four checkerboard squares, each containing a line drawing labeled *A* to *Z* (*J* and *U* are omitted) and a Latin phrase identifying the gesture. Five of these pages are reproduced by Joseph, who discusses them at length. Many are quite familiar and still used in our time, such as the handshake for *reconcileo*, the hand grasping another's wrist for *impedio*, the hand covering the eyes for *pudet* ("he is ashamed"), the hands coming together in prayer or for applause, or the counting off on the fingers (48, 50), (which Unsworth uses in *Morality Play* when he has Straw raise his right hand "in the sign of counting, thumb tapping at the finger ends" [156]). Others are more complex, involving manipulation of the fingers as in the sign language used by the deaf. The majority of the examples reproduced in *Elizabethan Acting* are rhetorical in nature, designed to express exhortation, approval, indignation, amplification, negation, contempt, and so forth. Stephen uses a sign of this sort in *Morality Play* when he utters his lines "with extraordinary force and conviction," accompanying the words with "the sign of insistence, hand held out with fingers loosely curled, thumb and first finger touching, little finger extended" (174).

Joseph believes that Bulwer's compilations resulted not only from his reading and knowledge of oratorical conventions, but also describe "what he saw done around him by ordinary men and women of all ranks and callings and by actors on the stage" (14). Bulwer supplemented his account of what was done in his own day with "a history of each gesture with quotations relating to it from the Bible and secular writings of the past," including Shakespeare (57).[4] Nothing in Joseph's study suggests that the signs were used for covert, or secret, communication, however. Rather, when employed by actors the signs enhanced verbal effects or facilitated dumbshows.

Our exchange about the hand signals led to larger issues concerning the writing of historical fiction. Unsworth observed that

> it is not primarily the period that is important, or even the reconstruction of manners or styles of thought. It is the shape of the story that comes first. In the case of *Morality Play* the driving force in the narrative was the process by which the players stumbled through, by trial and error, to a sort of truth. This seemed to me to represent the process of art, or the process of creative imagination, to reach truths not accessible to the unaided reason. This being so, it was absolutely essential for me to make the theatrical business as believable as possible because it is through this that the process of discovery is realized. All the invented or intuitive interactions among the players are designed to serve this central purpose. (letter to author, 19 Sept. 1999)

With gentle irony, he remarked that "[n]ovelists, unlike academics, are generally content with an appearance of truth and once that is achieved they tend to look around for something else for the imagination to seize upon." (letter to author, 11 Sept. 1999).

Ever the academic, I tracked down the book in which Unsworth had found the illustrations of the hand gestures, *Entertainment and Ritual 600–1600* by Peter A. Bucknell. This unusual text ranges widely from Western to Eastern drama, and is extensively illustrated by the author, whose drawings, as described in the acknowledgments, are based upon material in museums and institutes and are sometimes an imaginative composite of multiple sources. *Entertainment and Ritual* is unusual inasmuch as it is at once scholarly and what the book trade might call "for general readers"; it contains a very sketchy index and no notes or bibliographical references. Bucknell was evidently a well-known figure in mid-twentieth-century England: his lectures on "The History of World Drama," presented from the viewpoint of a director who was also a theater designer and teacher of design, "have been renowned for the past thirty years," according to the 1979 jacket copy. Clearly, Bucknell's book helped Unsworth immerse himself in the origins of English drama in a highly imaginative and visual way. From the first page, Bucknell writes very much in the spirit of innovative historical fiction: the preface begins:

Any history, and in particular that of the performing arts, can at its best be only partially true. If an attempt be made to seek for a pattern of development there are so many gaps in extant material available (and much of this can be quite unreliable), imagination and conjecture must be exercised. (9)

Bucknell's illustrations are marvellously detailed monotones, mostly in the style of early woodcuts, and include a wide range of images: achitectural drawings and floorplans, maps, catalogues of emblems, musical instruments, symbols and signs, coats of arms, imaginative reconstructions of medieval staging (labeled "conjectural"), and adaptations of paintings, manuscript drawings, stone carvings, and other objects from churches and museum collections. Among the illustrations is one that adapts some of Bulwer's illustrations, without acknowledgment, on a page containing twenty gestures, as in Bulwer's texts, with the drawings labeled in English rather than Latin (with one exception, *supplico,* copied from gesture "*A*" in figure 2 in *Elizabethan Acting* [Joseph 48]. It is very likely that Bucknell used Joseph as his source, since the gestures he includes appear among the ones Joseph reproduced.

With the license of the fiction writer, Unsworth had appropriated the Italian actor's account of the "systems of signs and signals [that] were developed among actors to indicate changes of intention" (letter to author, 11 Sept. 1999). This system undoubtedly originated in the commedia dell'arte. The commedia, with its masks and stock characters and comic business improvised from "scenarios" inherited from the Roman Atellane had survived the vogue of mystery and miracle plays in France and Italy during the thirteenth and fourteenth centuries and, unlike the English moralities, persisted well into the eighteenth century. Detailed eyewitness accounts, illustrations, scenarios, cast lists, and other documents provide a vivid picture of the drama, much of it captured in Pierre Louis Duchartre's landmark study *The Italian Comedy* (although Duchartre makes no mention of hand signals).

The novelist Ken Greenhall used Duchartre for an episode in *Lenoir,* a historical fiction inspired by a comment about the subject of Ruben's painting *Four Heads of a Negro* which Greenhall found in Julius S. Held's *Rubens and His Circle.* Greenhall invents a freed African slave who poses for both Rembrandt and Rubens, among other adventures that include employment with a traveling commedia troupe. The actors cast Lenoir as a Zanni, and teach him how to pretend to catch a fly and eat it, a bit of comic business suggested by a phrase in Duchartre (Greenhall 146).[5] Like Nicholas in *Morality Play,* Lenoir is an outsider narrator who describes the actors, each called by his or her commedia name; he observes their behavior from a stranger's remove, although his accounts are much less detailed and learned than Nicholas's, in keeping with his character. Greenhall invents a cross-cultural adjustment in the commedia's stage business prompted by Lenoir, who suggests that the *salame* he is required to wear should be a big snake instead, because "A male organ is often called a snake in my homeland. There are many quite funny jokes about it." Pantalone responds; "Yes, I can see that there is more character, more dignity in a snake than in a mere sausage," and Columbine agrees to change the costume (144). As in *Morality Play*, the actors are receptive to outside influences and the drama evolves accordingly.

In the *Postscript to The Name of the Rose* Umberto Eco remarks that the made-up events and characters in historical fiction tell us things "that history books have never told us so clearly." He goes on to say that a historical novel should "not only identify in the past the causes of what came later, but also trace the process through which those causes began slowly to produce their effects" (534). Unsworth recognizes the cause-and-effect relationship between the performance conditions acting companies devised for themselves and the structure and dramatic effects of their plays. Many books have been written about Elizabethan performance spaces, using the traces of information that have survived the accidents of time, such as the famous de Witt sketch of the Swan Theatre that is reproduced in every student edition of Shakespeare's plays. Similar efforts to reconstruct the Elizabethan theater's predecessors—the pageant wagons, innyards, great halls, and so forth—have preoccupied scholars like Richard Southern, who devotes twenty-five pages in *The Staging of Plays before Shakespeare* to scrutinizing *Mankind* for clues to its performance conditions. Some of the details in *Morality Play* seem indebted to *Mankind*, such as the way the actors change costumes quickly in a concealed space, "push through the people ('Make room sirs!')" and collect money from the audience, as indicated in the line, "We intende to gather mony yf yt plesse yowur neclygence" (Southern 29).

Unsworth's reimagining of the emergence of secular drama is deftly interwoven with a reconstruction of the way the acting space evolved. When Nicholas and his fellow actors perform their *Play of Adam* on their first day in the town, they "pass through the people" from the barn, their changing room, to the corner of the innyard where they have set their scene, indicated by a "Fatal Tree [set] against the wall, with a paper apple stuck on a twig" (48). Although most accounts of outdoor drama up to and including Shakespeare's time indicate daytime performances, this one occurs at night. Martin, ever the innovator, has torches set "against the wall so that the people would see us edged by light, beings of flame" (48). The use of torch-light also enables Adam to seem to disappear under his dark cloak after delivering his prologue, and then appear suddenly when Tobias,

> in his first role of an attendant angel, in wig and half mask and wings briefly borrowed from the Serpent, came through the people with a

flame and lit all the brands along the wall and so made a flood of light over everything. (49–50)

When they perform the first version of the *Play of Thomas Wells*, however, Springer, the boy actor, is fearful of passing among the people. The players solve the problem by placing a curtain against the wall of the innyard to serve as a barrier between the actors and audience, who respond viscerally and noisily to the players' accusations (110). It also allows the offstage actors to whisper among themselves as they improvise their script. There was some precedent for this in the curtained scaffolds behind which players retired when "offstage" in the Coventry, or N-Town Plays (Craik 7). The acting space evolves further in the second performance, now called *The True Play of Thomas Wells*; this time the curtain posts are set farther apart and the playing space is marked with pegs and a rope. All this, Nicholas adds, was Martin's invention.

Even more radical, however, is Martin's impromptu decision to cast off his mask and cloak, "showing himself as a plain man," no longer the allegorical figure of Avaritia. The actors are taken completely by surprise, recalls Nicholas: "It is my belief that he intended to shock us, along with the people, and take the guard from our tongues" (148). The others remove their masks and lapse into prose intermingled with remembered lines from interludes as they improvise frantically. Says Nicholas, "We were all without masks now—our sense of the roles we played was shifting, changing" (149). Their metamorphosis into more realistic characters, no longer stereotypes in fixed masks, accompanies the shape-changing the play undergoes, from allegorical *psychomachia* to a sordid tragedy involving a murdered child, a corrupt monk, planted evidence, false accusations, and behind it all, the looming presence of the deadly plague. In its final form, the play looks ahead to domestic tragedies involving murder like *Arden of Feversham* (1592) and *A Yorkshire Tragedy* (1608).

Until now I have said very little about the audience, the townspeople who have lost not one but five young boys to mysterious death in recent months. From everything we know about the audiences of Shakespeare and his contemporaries, they were active, often vocal participants in the drama. The moralities and interludes, because of their didactic intent, engage with the audience more directly than secular drama does, in what Bevington calls "a close and vigorous contact between player and spectator"; he quotes several direct comments to the "good Christian audience" in *Lusty Juventus* (1547– 1553) by way of illustration (18, 21). Robert Potter argues that morality plays are "communal works of art" (33) that invite the audiences' participation: "the plays are the acting out of a complex psychological experiment aimed at catching the conscience of the audience and evoking the repentance they advocate" (36). Southern, in his reconstruction of a fif-

teenth-century performance of *Mankind*, draws attention to the frequency
of direct address to the audience, as when Myscheff turns to them to boast
of how well he has "brought Mankynde to myscheff & to schame" (37). In
his account of Henry Medwall's interlude *Nature* (c. 1495), Southern cites
the moment when Pride singles out a member of the audience and asks him,
"'I pray tell me whych way shall I hold?'—and then, making capital of the
poor fellow's discomfiture, he turns aside . . . in pretended disgust" (89).
Moments later, another character, Worldly Affeccyon, snaps, "Get me a
stole [stool]" to a bystander (90).

Taking his cue from what he learned about the extant morality plays
and interludes, Unsworth imagines a truly interactive drama in which the
audience participates in the solving of the mystery. When Straw, as the las-
civious woman, seduces Thomas Wells in the first performance of the play, a
woman's voice cries out: "'It was not thus,' she shouted, 'My boy did not go
with her'. . . 'My Thomas was a good boy.'" Her voice is joined by other
shouts from among the people, and there is "a rustle of violence" that fright-
ens the players. Martin quickly put on the hood of Mankind and "faced the
people, turning his wrist as he did so in the sign of changing discourse.
'Good people, why did he go with her?' he shouted" (105). The actors continue to pose questions to the audience in the second performance, as they
come closer and closer to reconstructing the crime, until, finally, the play is
interrupted by external events. Nicholas quickly resumes the role of Good
Counsel and preaches a moral in order to calm the shouting crowd. The performance reaches a pitch of emotion and becomes more and more of a dialogue among the actors and the audience, until, at the climactic moment, the
play is halted and the players are forcibly taken to the castle to present their
play for the third and last time as a private performance for the Lord de
Guise.

In his discussion of the Tudor interludes Potter notes the "the dramatic
methods which had originated in a religious context were gradually detached
from that context and adapted to new purposes" (58). In John Skelton's
Magnificence (1515), for example, the Mankind figure is replaced by a noble
prince surrounded by dissembling intriguers. In *The Cradle of Security*, a lost
morality vividly described in a seventeenth-century account (one of the very
few surviving eyewitness accounts of a morality play in performance), the
Prince "did personate in the morall, the wicked of this world" (quoted in
Potter, 68). Unsworth takes liberties with the historical record, fragmentary
as it is, when he locates this transition much earlier. Courting danger,
Martin changes the *Play of Thomas Wells* in the final command performance;
as Superbia, or Pride, he says,

> "I am called by many names . . . As Pride and Arrogancy, Lordship and
> Sway. But what care I for names so I keep my dominion?"

He was using a voice not his own. It came through the cruel and bitter mouth of the mask, slow, deliberate, with a sound of metal in it: it was the voice of the Lord. (178)

Once again, we are reminded of Hamlet's "Mousetrap." The play is interrupted by the entrance of the Lord's daughter and the Lord looks coldly at the players and says, "Perhaps I have seen enough" (181).

I will not spoil the pleasure of reading the novel for those readers unfamiliar with it, except to say that, as in a morality play, Justice, "who sets all things right in the end" restores order and doles out rewards and punishment (191). But when Nicholas turns to the Justice in the final moments of the novel and says, "This is an example of the King's justice. . . . What of God's?" we are reminded that life is not as simple and easily ordered as a play. "That is more difficult to understand," replies the Justice (205).

There is a distinctive subgenre of contemporary fiction that purports to discover previously unknown texts, and another that builds on fragmentary texts or other forms of archival evidence. Some of these fictions are hybrids, juxtaposing past and present, such as A. S. Byatt's *Possession*, in which two modern scholars uncover the letters of a pair of nineteenth-century poets, or Wilton Barnhardt's *Gospel*, which posits a fifth gospel that becomes the object of an adventurous worldwide quest, or *The Name of the Rose*, with its huge library containing an invented text by Aristotle. In each case imaginary documents are modeled upon what we know of the genre from surviving texts, as in Unsworth's novel. Two earlier, more conventionally constructed historical novels based on actual textual fragments are more similar to *Morality Play* in respect to their sources, however. The classicist and sometime literary journalist Peter Green undertook his only venture into the realm of fiction with *The Laughter of Aphrodite*, a novel about the poet Sappho of Lesbos, whose character has been mythologized in ways analogous to Shakespeare's or Marlowe's. In a postscript, Green speaks of his project:

> Since *The Laughter of Aphrodite*, though a novel, attempts to recreate a famous historical character as faithfully as the evidence at our disposal will allow; and since the evidence is so mutilated and fragmentary that much invention has been necessary, while hardly one statement fails to involve historical detective-work; and since, lastly, the figure of Sappho is one round which curious myth and violent moral prejudice have clung since at least as early as the second half of the fifth century B.C.—for all these reasons it may be desirable to give the reader some idea of how much fact and how much fiction my novel contains.

Green goes on to discuss his sources, and to liken his task to "that of an archaeologist reassembling some amphora from hundreds of sherds—of which more than half are missing" (267). *The Laughter of Aphrodite* also contains fragments of text, incorporated into Sappho's first-person narrative, as one discovers when reading the novel alongside the poetry.

Another historical novel constructed from ancient and fragmentary evidence is Rosemary Sutcliff's *The Shining Company*. The novel was inspired by *The Gododdin*, the earliest surviving North British poem, an epic describing the raid by Mynyddog, King of the Gododdin and his three hundred warriors against the Saxons in 600 A.D. As Sutcliff explains in her author's note,

> one of the few survivors was the poet Aneirin, who rode with them and recorded the whole epic tragedy . . . but since Aneirin was really more interested in producing a string of elegies for young men killed in battle than in telling us what actually happened, I have had to invent a good deal of the story line for myself. (295)

At the very end of the novel Sutcliff provides excerpts from the epic, which stand out sharply from the modern diction of the young first-person narrator, Prosper, the only invented character in the novel.

Although Green and Sutcliff are using emerging literary forms—the lyric poem and epic—as source material, neither is interested in the form itself in the way that Unsworth is. This is one difference between the old historical fiction and the new. The real protagonist of *Morality Play*, clearly, is the play, and the murder mystery elements in the novel are ultimately in service to the more interesting project of reconstructing the origins of secular drama from the point of view of the participants. While Nicholas's narrative voice does reveal some traces of modernity, he is more convincingly a creature of the fourteenth century than Sutcliff's Prosper or Green's Sappho are of their respective eras. Yet even as he goes to great lengths to capture the sounds and mentality of medieval England, Unsworth has also written a novel about contemporary moral issues. Philosophers of history from Nietzsche to Hayden White have argued that historians are primarily interested in the past inasmuch as it bears some relation to the concerns and values of their own age. Thus they suppress, highlight, and employ characters, motifs, point of view, and descriptive strategies much as the novelist does in order to create a story that, in Bernd Engler's words, "reflects the very questions the present asks of the past" (21).

Morality Play is akin to this kind of history-making, but it is also a story of origins, modeled on the myths and tales by which cultures recount the origins of practices, places, dynasties, or traditions. The multiple revisions of the *Play of Thomas Wells* participate in the process of making sense of the past that has been part of the literary enterprise since ancient times.

Unsworth's narrative doesn't set out to displace an existing story of origins, but rather to invent a hitherto unwritten, imaginary supplement to the historical record. In contrast to other historical novels discussed in this book, *Morality Play* contains no "real" or documented historical people or places or events, but the types—the players, the Lord, the Monk, the Weaver, the Knight, the Justice, the innkeeper, the beggar and others who people the novel—are modeled on their nameless precursors, defined by class or occupation and seldom singled out for individual treatment by historians. Unsworth brings them to life with a vividness and illusion of realness few historians could match.

Chapter 5

Fictional Queen Elizabeths and Women-Centered Historical Fiction

*E*lizabeth I may well be the most written about monarch in Western culture. In an unlikely instance of the cross-fertilization among popular genres, her life has even served as a model in the advice book genre. The jacket blurb of Alan Axelrod's *Elizabeth I CEO: Strategic Lessons from the Leader Who Built an Empire* emphatically proclaims the queen to have been "the CEO who managed history's greatest 'corporate turnaround.'" The book consists of thirty-eight short sections with punchy titles, purporting to illustrate advice such as "Strength Always Communicates," "Speak Fluent Body Language," and "Get in the Trenches." Historical details and short quotations from primary sources alternate with the bulleted talking points characteristics of the "how to" treatise. *Elizabeth I CEO* employs a strategy writers of the old historical fiction have understood all along, that of appropriating popular genres of the day as vehicles for reconstructing the past. The unwritten rules of the advice book genre assume that calculation, strategic choices, and the deliberate implementation of a master plan are the shaping forces behind a successful life. Axelrod's Elizabeth is a leader whose "preference was always for the practical answer and the direct approach" (219), and "who instinctively shunned quick fixes" (192). By contrast, the historian Christopher Haigh sums up his appraisal of the queen with the conclusion that "we know roughly what Elizabeth did, but she has not told us why she did it" (170). Using the same documents available to writers of nonfiction, historical novelists engage in imaginative speculation about why their subjects "did it" and what they might have been doing during the gaps between recorded events. Queen Elizabeth's life, as we shall see, has proven irresistible to novelists from Sir Walter Scott onward.

Scott is generally regarded as the father of the historical novel; his *Waverley*, begun in 1805 and published in 1814, is the work "without which we might perhaps never have known the historical novel," says Mary Lascelles (37). Scott's *Kenilworth* (1821) investigates an intriguing secondary narrative in Queen Elizabeth's biography, the mysterious death of Amy Robsart, first wife of Robert Dudley, the Earl of Leicester. This incident fascinates fiction-biographers because of its place in the larger narrative of Elizabeth's ambiguous relationship with Leicester, which began, according to some accounts, when the two were about eight years old and continued to his death in 1588. Scott has been criticized for his research, which was attacked by antiquarians in his own time, and for his "strong opinions" which "coloured his treatment of Queen Elizabeth in *Kenilworth*." (Orel 8, 10). Moreover, he plays fast and loose with chronology in the novel, rearranging events so that Amy's death in 1560 coincides with the spectacular entertainment at Kenilworth in 1575.

Scott cannot resist including Shakespeare in *Kenilworth*. Anachronistically, he transports the plays, still fifteen years in the future, to the 1570s and endows the queen with a notable prescience regarding literary history: "And touching this Shakespeare, we think there is that in his plays that is worthy twenty Bear-gardens; and that this new undertaking of his Chronicles, as he calls them, may entertain, with honest mirth, mingled with useful instruction, not only our subjects, but even the generation which may succeed us." As the conversation continues, Sir Walter Raleigh ingratiates himself with Elizabeth by quoting Oberon's speech from *A Midsummer Night's Dream* (frequently regarded as a veiled reference to the Virgin Queen) in which Cupid aims his love shaft "At a fair vestal throned by the west" (205).

Scott's Shakespeare is described as "a halting fellow"; this, notes Samuel Schoenbaum,

> revives the tradition of the poet's lameness initiated in 1779 by Capell's literal reading of Sonnet 89. Scott himself suffered from incurable lameness, the growth of his right leg having been arrested in infancy. Once again we find ourselves in the presence of that alchemical mirror in which the creator, whether novelist or biographer, sees his own reflection assume the lineaments of his subject. (*Shakespeare's Lives* 369)

Schoenbaum's "alchemical mirror" contributes to the portrayal of Elizabeth and other women in Shakespeare's England as well, reflecting not just the authors' own "lineaments" but the attitudes and anxieties of their times.

In his introduction to *Kenilworth*, Scott sets the standard for much subsequent historical fiction with Elizabeth as its subject:

> I have endeavored to describe her as at once a high-minded sovereign and a female of passionate feelings, hesitating betwixt the sense of her rank and the duty she owed her subjects on the one hand, and on the other her attachment to a nobleman who, in external qualifications at least, amply merited her favour. (9)

The introduction also discusses sources and reproduces in full the "Ballad of Cumnor Hall," which evokes the pathos of Amy's final days, replete with several stanzas of dialogue in which she reproaches Leicester for marrying and then neglecting her. The most interesting documents Scott consulted are the detailed accounts of the Kenilworth revels by Robert Laneham and George Gascoigne, both duly acknowledged in a footnote in chapter 30 (328). Scott also provides longer notes at the end of his novel, in which he quotes from these and other sources.

Despite this seemingly scrupulous attention to archival material, Scott freely revises history to suit his plot. He makes Leicester's marriage to Amy a clandestine one, a necessary element in the suspenseful buildup to the climactic scene in the midst of the Kenilworth revels when the disguised Amy appears and reveals herself to the queen. Amy is assisted by the novel's principal invented character, a young man named Tressilian, who in typical romance fashion suffers from unrequited love and is determined to rescue Amy from Leicester's villainous subordinate Varney. Leicester's courtship of Elizabeth, which occurs while Varney is plotting Amy's death, is very nearly successful. When the truth of his marriage is finally revealed, Elizabeth turns on Leicester and accuses him of "a villainy [that] hath made me ridiculous to my subjects and odious to myself" (419). When Leicester tries to excuse himself by claiming that her beauty seduced his frail heart, she responds with brutal sarcasm: "What, ho! my lords, come all and hear the news—My Lord of Leicester's stolen marriage has cost me a husband, and England a King. His lordship is patriarchal in his tastes—one wife at a time was insufficient, and he designed us the honour of his left hand" (421).

Scott's portrayal of Elizabeth promotes the myth of the Virgin Queen who was resolved to "forsake all social or domestic ties, and dedicate herself exclusively to the care of her people" (390). Her trusted adviser Lord Burghley alludes to the myth when he reminds her "that you are a Queen—Queen of England—mother of your people" and exhorts her to "soar far above a weakness which no Englishman will ever believe his Elizabeth could have entertained. . ." (419). Elizabeth's own speeches and letters promoted this image, and it is this image, more than anything else, which has engaged fiction writers drawn to the challenge of recreating the woman behind the myth. The queen's ambivalent relationship with Leicester, her refusal to marry, and her famously changeable temperament, in contrast to the steadiness of Burghley, provide the essential outlines for a large body of twentieth-century historical fiction.

Scott ended *Kenilworth* with the banished Leicester at length recalled to court. Evidently he assumed a reader who was familiar with the period, a reader who, as Umberto Eco remarks, was "supposed both to *pretend to believe* that the fictional information was true and to accept the additional information provided by the author as being true in the real world" (*Six Walks* 94–95) as long as the "real world" status quo resumes at the end of the novel. Lascelles's distinction between fictitious history and historical fiction is useful here; in historical fiction additional characters are invented and "history" as we know it impinges on them, though the novelist had "better not claim that those encounters were in any way responsible for what is known to have happened" (112). Since no one knows for certain how Amy Robsart died of a broken neck at the bottom of a flight of stairs (theories range from suicide to a fall made fatal by bones brittle from the effect of advanced breast cancer), Scott is free to invent his villains' ingenious trapdoor (see Scott 436–37). In fictitious history, Lascelles continues, the author

> offer[s] tales about those historical figures which may be supposed to have escaped the historian's notice—provided these do not run counter to what he has to tell us. But there is now a frontier to be crossed: we are to entertain conjectures of events which could not possibly have befallen the historical characters to whom they are attributed.

She draws examples of this kind of license from Shakespeare: the appearance of Margaret of Anjou at the English court in *Richard III* and the grown-up Queen Isabella (who was in fact a child) in *Richard II* (112–13). Scott, she notes, combines historical fiction and fictitious history in an elaborately interwoven tapestry composed of "embroidery on a given fabric" and a new fabric spun and woven "in defiance of the know facts" (128–29).

A further distinction can be made between historical fiction and fiction-biography, which follows the trajectory of the subject's life without adding new characters or plots. Invented incidents supplement known events and dialogue ranges from paraphrased letters or other documents to modern colloquial conversation. A number of the novels I will be discussing are fiction-biographies, ranging from conventionally narrated old historical fictions to reinterpretations of the historical record that display many characteristics of the New Historical Fiction. These include Margaret Irwin's trilogy about the young Elizabeth, Susan Kay's panoramic novel *Legacy*, and Rosalind Miles's *I, Elizabeth*, narrated by a fictional Elizabeth dictating her memoirs in 1601. In Robin Maxwell's The *Secret Diary of Anne Boleyn*, the newly crowned Elizabeth reads her mother's secret diary as she deliberates her own sexual choices. Although Maxwell invents the device of the secret diary, she does not add major events to Anne's and Elizabeth's lives. By contrast, Finney's invented plot to blackmail Elizabeth in *Unicorn's Blood* interweaves imaginary events with actual ones. In still another hybrid of historical fiction and detective fiction conventions, Karen Harper casts Elizabeth as the amateur detective in *The Poyson Garden* and its sequels, *The Tidal Poole* and *The Twylight Tower*.

These novels were all written by women; taken together, they form a corpus of women-centered historical fiction that, while it frequently focuses on Elizabeth's childhood traumas, romantic and sexual escapades, emotional crises, and relationships with family members and close confidants, also positions her as a self-assertive, politically astute woman in a grand narrative that seldom represents women as leaders. Although male readers can certainly enjoy this kind of fiction, I would argue that the novels speak directly to the female experience, much as many nonhistorical novels circulating in libraries, bookstores, and reading groups do. Elizabeth's story can be written in so many different ways—as colorful costume drama, as dysfunctional family romance, as a long and never-resolved series of ambiguous, manipulative liaisons, as an affirmation of the extraordinary intellectual and political abilities of a powerful monarch, and as the compelling tale of a woman growing old in a role that both elevates and imprisons her. For the writer of historical novels, Elizabeth Tudor's life provides several promising elements: a damsel in distress scarred by the loss of her mother and threatened by political plots and imprisonment in her early years; a flirtatious woman whose sexual activities with her many colorful suitors are clouded in mystery; a young queen asserting her authority over a country beset by political and religious upheaval as she develops a distinctly feminine style of diplomacy; a strong-willed monarch unwilling to name her successor. The years leading to her coronation, in particular, suggest the recurring motifs of woman-centered historical fiction. The Elizabeth of the 1550s overcomes or outwits the obstacles to her succession, endures trials and temptations, learns from experience and advisers, acquires faithful friends and comes to distrust false ones, and finally arrives at the traditional comic conclusion, her "betrothal" to the people of England, who have been the true, nonsexual beloved all along.

Lytton Strachey's *Elizabeth and Essex* is a brilliant early example of the psychologically probing biography that blurs the boundaries between narrative history and fiction. Classified as history in the library catalogue, *Elizabeth and Essex: A Tragical History* nevertheless employs fictional strategies, as its subtitle

suggests. Essex is introduced as a tragic figure in a metaphor that sets the tone
for Strachey's extravagant prose:

> Yet the spirit of the ancient feudalism was not quite exhausted. Once
> more, before the reign was over, it flamed up, embodied in a single indi-
> vidual—Robert Devereux, Earl of Essex. The flame was glorious—radi-
> ant with the colours of antique knighthood and the flashing gallantries
> of the past; but no substance fed it; flaring wildly, it tossed to and fro in
> the wind; it was suddenly put out. In the history of Essex . . . the spec-
> tral agony of an abolished world is discernible through the tragic linea-
> ments of a personal disaster. (2)

Queen Elizabeth is brought to life through vivid descriptive phrases in a portrait that lays the groundwork for the drama to come:

> She swore; she spat; she struck with her fist when she was angry; she
> roared with laughter when she was amused. And she was often amused.
> A radiant atmosphere of humour coloured and softened the harsh lines
> of her destiny, and buoyed her up along the zigzags of her dreadful path.
> Her response to every stimulus was immmediate and rich: to the folly of
> the moment, to the clash and horror of great events, her soul leapt out
> with a vivacity, an abandonment, a complete awareness of the situation,
> which made her, which makes her still, a fascinating spectacle. She could
> play with life as with an equal, wrestling with it, making fun of it,
> admiring it, watching its drama. (17)

Early on, Strachey comments on the "splendid sentences" of Elizabeth's
letters which "proclaimed the curious working of her intellect with
enthralling force" (18). Letters are a principal source of information and
character traits for Strachey, as they are for subsequent biographers and fiction writers who have worked with the enormous archive of records relating
to Elizabeth's reign. Strachey relies on Essex's letters to construct a portrait
of Elizabeth's last favorite, who succeeded his stepfather Leicester as Master
of the Horse. Unlike most fiction writers and many biographers, Strachey
pays homage to his sources:

> That convenient monosyllable [love], so intense and so ambiguous, was
> for ever on his lips and found its way into every letter—those elegant,
> impassioned, noble letters, which still exist, with their stiff, quick char-
> acters and those silken ties that were once loosened by the long fingers
> of Elizabeth. (37-38)

Other letters figure into the story as well, for this curiously novelistic history
is as much a portrait of Francis Bacon and Robert Cecil as it is of Elizabeth
and Essex.

Among Strachey's fictional strategies is his construction of characters around a single defining trait. Bacon possesses

> the detachment of speculation, the intensity of personal pride, the uneasiness of nervous sensibility, the urgency of ambition, the opulence of superb taste—these qualities, lending, twisting, flashing together, gave to his secret spirit the subtle and glittering superficies of a serpent. A serpent, indeed, might well have been his chosen emblem—the wise, sinuous, dangerous creature, offspring of mystery and the beautiful earth. (44)

His eventual disgrace, although it occurs after the text's chronological end-point, is frequently anticipated in speculative moments that reiterate the serpent conceit. This device produces some rather florid prose at times, as when Bacon is described thus: "Inspired with the ingenious grandeur of the serpent, he must deploy to the full the long luxury of his coils" (250). Strachey's last words about Bacon, fifteen pages from the book's end, are "The serpent glides off with his secret" (272).

Robert Cecil, Elizabeth's secretary and closest adviser, is Essex's opposite and enemy; he is the "born administrator," resigned and patient, who is distinguished by his ability to "watch and wait." Cecil, says Strachey, is an "enigma"; in a meditative aside on the gaps in history, he observes

> We can only see what we are shown with such urbane lucidity—the devoted career of public service. . . . So much is plain; but we are shown no more—no man ever was. The quiet minimum of action which led to such vast consequences is withdrawn from us. We can, with luck, catch a few glimpses now and then; but, in the main, we can only obscurely conjecture at what happened under the table. (110–11)

One of the moments shaped by Cecil's instinct to watch and wait occurs when Essex returns from his Irish expedition in 1599, having, as Strachey says, "played all his cards now—played them as badly as possible" (214). He rushes to the queen before news of his humiliating truce with the Irish leader Tyrone reaches her. In Strachey's version of the incident, Cecil could have stopped him, but shrewdly did not. Essex

> was muddy and disordered from his long journey, in rough clothes and riding boots; but he was utterly unaware of any of that, as he burst open the door in front of him. And there, quite close to him, was Elizabeth among her ladies, in a dressing-gown, unpainted, without her wig, her grey hair hanging in wisps about her face, and her eyes starting from her head. (216)

This famous scene is wonderfully captured on film by Glenda Jackson in *Elizabeth Regina* and is based on an eyewitness account. According to the courtier Rowland Whyte, the queen was "newly up, the heare about her face; [Essex] kneeled unto her, kissed her handes, and her faire neck, and had some privat speach with her" (106).[1] Strachey invents the queen's response at the beginning of the next chapter:

> She was surprised, she was delighted—those were her immediate reactions; but then, swiftly, a third feeling came upon her—she was afraid. What was the meaning of this unannounced, this forbidden return, and this extraordinary irruption? What kind of following had the man brought from Ireland? . . .
>   Completely in the dark, she at once sought refuge in the dissimulation which was her second nature. (217)

This passage is a good example of Strachey's most characteristic fictional strategy: the narrated third-person interior monologue, unidentified as such but recognizable from the shift in diction.

A similar shift to the interior monologue occurs when the narrator describes the aging King Philip of Spain, "the weaving spider of the Escorial" (16), watching the chapel priests through an inner window in his oratory especially constructed for this purpose:

> . . . there, operatic too in their vestments and their movements and their strange singings, the priests performed at the altar close below him, intent upon their holy work. Holy! But his work too was that; he too was labouring for the glory of God. Was he not God's chosen instrument? His father, Charles the Fifth, had been welcomed into Heaven, when he died, by the Trinity; there could be no mistake about it; Titian had painted the scene. He also would be received in a similar glorious fashion; but not just yet. He must finish his earthly duties first. (139)

Strachey refers in passing to a nontextual source, Titian's painting, as Philip might view it.

The most extraordinary interior monologue in *Elizabeth and Essex* occurs at the book's climactic moment, when Elizabeth finally, after many delays, orders Essex's execution:

> He had betrayed her in every possible way—mentally, emotionally, materially—as a Queen and as a woman—before the world and in the sweetest privacies of the heart. And he had actually imagined that he could elude that doom that waited on such iniquity—had dreamed of standing up against her—had mistaken the hesitation of her strength for the weaknesses of a subservient character. He would have a sad awakening! He would find that she was indeed the daughter of a father who had known how to rule a kingdom and how to punish the perfidy of those he had loved the most. . . .

. . . her father's destiny, by some intimate dispensation, was repeated in hers; it was supremely fitting that Robert Devereux should follow Anne Boleyn to the block. Her father! . . . but in a still remoter depth there were still stranger stirrings. There was a difference as well as a likeness; after all, she was no man, but a woman; and was this, perhaps, not a repetition but a revenge? After all the long years of her lifetime, and in this appalling consummation, was it her murdered mother who had finally emerged? The wheel had come full circle. (262–63)

With this line from *King Lear* (Edmund's dying recognition that "The wheel is come full circle, I am here" [5.3.175]), Strachey arrives at the diagnosis that subsequent psycho-biographers and fiction writers would invoke as an explanation for Elizabeth's hesitation to execute both Mary Queen of Scots and the Earl of Essex. This is an Elizabeth who has "overthrown [manhood] at last" (263), a woman, who, Strachey notes earlier, suffered from "ailments" of "a hysterical origin" due to the fact that "her sexual organization was seriously warped" (20).[2] In another interior monologue Elizabeth muses that

She was a woman—ah, yes! a fascinating woman!—but then, was she not also a virgin, and old? But immediately another flood of feeling swept upwards and engulfed her; she towered; she was something more—she knew it; what was it? Was she a man? (28–29)

This passage is suggestive of another book published in 1928, Virginia Woolf's *Orlando: A Biography. Orlando* was an early precursor of the New Historical Fiction in its daring and satirical gender-bending and time-traveling disruptions of narrative conventions, and its metacommentary on the historian's role and mocking accoutrements of biography, such as the index and photographs of "Orlando." Early in the novel the seventeen-year-old Orlando offers a bowl of rose-water to "the great Queen herself." This moment, with its close-up focus on the aging queen's hand, is no doubt influenced by the many references to Elizabeth's hands in contemporary accounts.

Such was his shyness that he saw no more of her than her ringed hand in water: but it was enough. It was a memorable hand; a thin hand with long fingers always curling as if round orb or sceptre; a nervous, crabbed, sickly hand; a commanding hand; a hand that had only to raise itself for a head to fall; a hand, he guessed, attached to an old body that smelt like a cupboard in which furs are kept in camphor; which body was yet caparisoned in all sorts of brocades and gems; and held itself very upright though perhaps in pain from sciatica; and never flinched though strung together by a thousand fears; and the Queen's eyes were light yellow. All this he felt as the great rings flashed in the water and then

something pressed his hair—which, perhaps, accounts for his seeing
nothing more likely to be of use to a historian. (22)

In the next paragraph, the narrative perspective shifts to Elizabeth herself, as
Woolf briefly imagines how the historical Elizabeth might have felt during
the political instability of the 1590s.

> For she was growing old and worn and bent before her time. The sound
> of cannon was always in her ears. She saw always the glistening poison
> drop and the long stiletto. As she sat at table she listened; she heard the
> guns in the Channel; she dreaded—was that a curse, was that a whisper?
> (23)

Near the end of the novel, Orlando, now a woman, meditates on the
many selves "of which we are built up, one on top of another, as plates are
piled on a waiter's hand. . . ." The narrator observes that "she had a great
variety of selves to call upon, far more than we have been able to find room
for, since a biography is considered complete if it merely accounts for six or
seven selves, whereas a person may well have as many thousand" (308–09).
The disquisition on selves continues, with a catalogue of all Orlando's incar-
nations through the centuries and an annotated monologue in which the
narrator marks in parenthesis each time "a new self came in" (310). Woolf
takes the notion of the multifaceted self to its farthest extremes in *Orlando*,
and so unmasks the illusion that biography can construct a stable, internally
coherent representation of its subject.

Both *Orlando* and *Elizabeth and Essex* remain in print and are widely
read, unlike the many long-forgotten twentieth-century novels about the
women of Shakespeare's England.[3] Many of these novels revisit the past
from the perspective of women whom conventional historians have largely
ignored. Anya Seton's *Katherine* is a classic in this genre. Seton's author's
note, which describes her research, observes that little was known of
Katherine Swynford, mistress and later wife of John of Gaunt, "except then
her life touched the Duke's and there are few details of that." Seton uses the
word "psychological" to describe her sympathetic treatment of John of
Gaunt, who, she says, has been much "vilified by historians who have too
slavishly followed hostile chroniclers" (ix–xi) (interestingly, Shakespeare had
also parted company with the chroniclers in his portrayal of Gaunt as
Richard II's wise and prophetic uncle).

Another novel that rewrites English history from a woman's perspective
is *The Summer Queen* by the historical fiction writer Alice Walworth
Graham. Graham tells the story of Edward IV's wife Elizabeth Woodville as
narrated by Cicely Bonville, wife of Elizabeth's son by a previous marriage.

The novel ends with Edward's death, from which followed the most vehemently debated ascent to the throne in English history, known to most readers through Shakespeare's *Richard III*. Graham revises the Tudor historians' account by depicting Shakespeare's Machiavellian villain as an understated, neutral character, in contrast to his brother, George, Duke of Clarence, an ambitious and untrustworthy enemy to the Woodvilles. The book contains an editor's note, referring to a journal on which the novel was based, although there is no indication that such a journal actually existed; this, evidently, is another historical fiction predicated on the imagined existence of a hitherto unknown document that contests or adds to the historical record.

The Richard III story receives an aggressively revisionist spin in still another women-centered historical novel, Sharon Kay Penman's nine-hundred-page *The Sunne in Splendour*. The novel covers the grand sweep of Richard's life, from September 1459, when he was seven years old, to December 1485, on the eve of Henry Tudor's coronation as Henry VII. Penman makes a point of inventing personalities and life stories for every possible woman figure in the historical record, with emphasis on their childhoods and relationships with siblings and mothers. Penman's Richard, in a deliberate challenge to Shakespeare's portrayal, is a devoted husband to Anne Neville, and a handsome and heroic leader whose legendary physical deformity is nothing more than the effect of a shoulder broken in "a fall at the quintain" improperly set (480). Like many other traditional historical fictions, this one gives its characters modern sentiments articulated in contemporary diction. For example, Edward IV's daughter, called Bess, who is destined to become Henry VII's queen, comes across as an assertive adolescent, as in this exchange with her mother when they receive news that the two little princes are dead in the Tower at their Uncle's Richard's (i.e., Dickon's) orders:

> "Mama, you cannot believe such a lie! Dickon would never harm Edward or Dickon. They're his brother's children, Mama. Dickon's his namesake, the same age as his own little boy. You mustn't believe their lies, Mama. You mustn't!"
>
> "I don't."
>
> "Please Mama, listen to. . . . What? What did you say?"
>
> "I said I agreed with you," Elizabeth said calmly. She opened the door suddenly, reassured herself that no one was eavesdropping without. "I'm sorry you had to hear that fool Lewis blurt it out like that, but you needn't try to convince me that it's a clumsy lie. I know it is." She laughed, shook her head. "But how very like you, Bess, that whenever you happen to be in the right, you're right for all the wrong reasons!"

As the conversation continues, Elizabeth Woodville astutely sees through what historians call the "Tudor Myth."

"Whatever else the man is, he's no fool. Now if we were dealing with that lunatic George of Clarence . . . but Richard, no. He's shrewd enough to anticipate the reaction of the people to the murder of two innocent boys, to realize it would brand him as Herod. And the crown is already his; why jeopardize it all by spilling the blood of his brother's children?" (774)

The Sunne in Splendour ends with an explicit metahistorical reference to the distortions of history as Grace, one of Bess's sisters, says of Henry Tudor:

. . . your husband has been doing all he can to discredit Dickon's memory, and if lies be repeated often enough, people become accustomed to hearing them, even begin to believe them to be true. I think the day might come, Bess, when all men will know of Dickon is what they were told by Tudor historians like Rous." (926–27)

Penman's challenge to received history follows in the footsteps of Josephine Tey's celebrated mystery, *Daughter of Time*, and other novels that have reopened the case against Richard III, but it also fleshes out the undocumented lives of the grandmother and great-grandmother who attempted to resist the masculine political culture their namesake challenged and transformed during her forty-five-year reign.

In her author's note Penman defends her choices when confronted by conflicting—and biased—accounts: "those chroniclers writing in the early years of Henry Tudor's reign must have known when they crossed over into the realm of creative fiction" (933). The author's note displays the rationalizing and self-justifying traits that frequently appear in this genre; like some of the notes and afterwords I have quoted elsewhere, Penman's offers a revealing glimpse of the author's image of herself and her relationship to traditional history and biography. Penman quotes an unattributed definition of history as "the process by which complex truths are transformed into simplified falsehoods" and adds that this is "particularly true in the case of Richard III, where the normal medieval proclivity for moralizing and partisanship was further complicated by deliberate distortion to serve Tudor political needs." She admits to straying from the facts, but "not knowingly tamper[ing] with basic truths"; instead, she fills in gaps by "com[ing] up with the answers" the medieval historians "neglected to provide." Among the women and children characters she created were the women who bore Richard's two illegitimate children: "I had to fill in virtually all the blanks; nothing whatsoever is known of these women, not even their names" (434–35).

Margaret Irwin's trilogy about the young Elizabeth Tudor has fewer gaps to fill than Penman's or Graham's or Seton's, but the author nevertheless fleshes out the roles of several historical women. Originally published between 1945 and 1953 and reissued in paperback by the United Kingdom publishers Allison and Busby, Ltd. in 1999, *Young Bess, Elizabeth, Captive Princess*, and *Elizabeth and the Prince of Spain* are good examples of the old historical fiction's tendency to teach history by incorporating large blocks of information into the narrative through dialogue or characters' thoughts.[4] Each novel focuses on a relatively brief period in Elizabeth's early life. *Elizabeth, Captive Princess*, for example, begins as Elizabeth's brother King Edward VI is dying in 1553 and ends with her release from the Tower in 1554 during the first year of Mary's reign. Although Irwin is not explicit about this, she is actually telling the contrasting stories of two young women caught in the grip of sixteenth-century power politics, the nineteen-year-old Elizabeth and her seventeen-year-old cousin Jane Grey. Elizabeth is strategically ill and offstage during Jane's doomed nine days as queen, at the end of which the Catholic Mary succeeds her half-brother.

Irwin employs some of the conventions and language of young adult historical fiction in portraying her young characters. Modern-sounding speech patterns that convey attitudes young readers would recognize undermine the novels' period flavor, as when Elizabeth's closest confidante Kat Ashley refers to Lady Jane Grey as "that undersized brat with the freckled nose" in *Elizabeth, Captive Princess* (17). Jane Grey's imprisonment is depicted from a child's perspective, with the focus on unwanted items of clothing:

> Time took twice as long in the Tower as elsewhere, Jane found. She had more than enough means to tell it by. For she had sent for her personal belongings to make her feel more at home, especially her books, and the stupid servants had brought few books, but a mass of things she did not want; among them, mufflers of purple velvet and sable (in this heat!), black velvet hats. . . .

Irwin also employs mid-twentieth-century terms to evoke emotions her young readers would understand, as in this passage:

> Elizabeth knew she would have to choose and comb her words as though to her grandmother; Mary felt how hard and baffling were these young women of the modern generation, so terrifyingly self-assured.

Looking at her sister enviously, Mary reflects "'She thinks me a muddle-headed old maid' . . . and it was no consolation that she thought Elizabeth a brazen young adventuress" (127).

Irwin is capable of transcending the conventions of young adult fiction, however. In *Elizabeth and the Prince of Spain*, a fifteen-page section sandwiched between the two major parts of the novel provides an astute portrait of Queen Mary's Archbishop of Canterbury Reginald Pole. This interlude offers a perspective on the historical events from the point of view of a lesser-known player in the tense events leading up to Elizabeth's accession. Elizabeth's imprisonment in the Tower after the abortive Wyatt rebellion occupies the last seventy pages of *Elizabeth, Captive Princess*. This episode in Elizabeth's youth was transformed into a tale of Protestant martyrdom during her own lifetime by John Foxe, who incorporated a detailed account into the 1563 edition of *Actes and Monuments*, the best-selling work of Protestant propaganda of the sixteenth century. The story was subsequently included in Holinshed's *Chronicles* in 1587. Susan Frye notes that Foxe's representation of Elizabeth as a religious martyr "provides quotations . . . and a wealth of details that only Elizabeth herself could have known"; hence Elizabeth was complicit in constructing herself as a character in a narrative during the early years of her reign. With a compression of events that looks ahead to fiction-biography, "the final two years between Elizabeth's release and Mary's death simply disappear because they interrupt the flow of divine intervention" in Foxe's narrative, as embellished in later editions of *Actes and Monuments* and other accounts of Elizabeth's life from the 1570s onward (Frye 76–77).

The Tower episode lends itself to romantic fictional treatment as well as religious propaganda. According to a contemporary source, the children of the keeper of the Tower brought the princess bouquets of flowers in which were hidden a key so that she could walk abroad (Plowden 170–71). Irwin embellishes the scene by having the children serve as go-betweens, carrying messages from the imprisoned Robert Dudley as well. She adds a passionate love scene which ends abruptly as Elizabeth recalls Thomas Seymour, and exclaims to Dudley:

> "No, no, love brings terror, agony, endless suspicion—not a soul one can trust,—all spies, a thousand listening, whispering spies opening a thousand little secret spy-holes to peer into one's very soul and whisper about it and mutter all together and then shout foul charges, proclaim them through the land and howl, howl for blood." (210)

The Seymour affair included all of the ingredients of lurid romantic historical fiction: a fourteen-year-old princess living in the home of her father's widow, Katherine Parr, her childhood colored by the deaths and divorces which befell Henry's previous wives; a handsome young admiral, Thomas Seymour, recently married to Katherine, who flirts dangerously with Elizabeth, entering her bedchamber and engaging in physical play that has sexual overtones; and finally, Seymour's trial and execution for treason. Both historians and fiction writers dwell on the Seymour affair as a defining event in Elizabeth's life. The historian Alison Plowden sums up the incident in language that sounds very much like a fiction-biographer's:

Elizabeth knew now, at the deepest level of consciousness, that sexual fulfilment was forbidden to her. She could play with physical desire, circle round it, approach it as close as she dared with a sort of delicious defiance but there was a point beyond which she might never, could never go. It was always to be the same type of man who roused this desire—handsome, showy, athletic. (119)

Unlike more recent novelists, Irwin never confronts the great unanswered question; Was Queen Elizabeth a virgin? Susan Kay's *Legacy*, a 560-page novel that covers Elizabeth's life from birth to death, exemplifies the late twentieth-century psycho-biographer's approach, pioneered by Strachey a half-century earlier. Kay represents the Seymour affair and its aftermath as a psycho-sexual trauma that shaped Elizabeth's subsequent relationships with men. *Legacy* won the Georgette Heyer Historical Fiction Prize and the Betty Trask Prize. These awards, along with the author's dedication to her supportive and encouraging husband, place it in the tradition of historical fiction by and for women. So does the blurb on the jacket cover, which describes *Legacy* as a novel "by a young woman who can bring all the intensity, fire, passion and yearning of the young . . . backed by fifteen years of obsessive research" to the story of Queen Elizabeth.

Fire and passion are very much in evidence as Kay describes the climactic sex scene between Seymour and Elizabeth, interrupted by the pregnant Katherine "just in time to stop that moment of wild surrender." Seymour springs to his feet and follows his wife from the room, leaving Elizabeth "alone on the floor, burying her face in the dirty rushes, hiding from a shame that was too great to be borne" (70). Later in the chapter an angry Seymour calls Elizabeth a "taunting jade" and a "bitch" and "slaps her smartly across the mouth" when she sarcastically responds to his declaration of love. "Her taunt was like a burn on his manhood," Kay intones; then she ends the chapter with a prophetic glance forward:

> This morning a woman had sprung to life in his arms, but now that woman had gone, perhaps for ever. It was a child who ran away from him down the narrow gallery of Chelsea Palace; and as he stood and watched that reckless headlong flight he had the morbid fancy that she would go on running for the rest of her life. (72–73)

This episode, Kay implies, contributes to the "childhood legacy" of nightmares and migraines that, Kat Ashley observes inwardly, "could reduce [Elizabeth] to suffocating panic" (131). But the legacy is also Elizabeth's inheritance from her doomed mother. Embellishing a documented incident from Kat Ashley's testimony at Seymour's trial, Kay includes a melodramatic scene in which Seymour slashes Elizabeth's skirts to ribbons. In an invocation of the formula romances known as "bodice rippers," Kay continues: "Finally he took hold of the bodice and ripped it down the front," enraged by the fact that "she was wearing a black dress which reminded him unpleasantly of her mother" (66–67).[5]

Legacy is a more subtle and well-crafted novel than the foregoing quotations might suggest. Despite these and other romance novel clichés, Kay's Elizabeth is a realistically drawn protagonist compared with the Elizabeths of many other historical fictions, and while her romantic entanglements play a prominent role in the novel, she is also depicted as the charismatic queen whose astute self-fashioning enables her to manage the shifting political currents of sixteenth-century Europe. Kay writes in the tradition of extensively researched women-centered historical fiction that rewrites familiar or political history from the perspective of the women characters. Like Katherine or The Sunne in Splendour, Legacy is a hybrid, combining serious historical inference with romance-novel conventions and an attention to women's "issues."

Unlike Katherine Swynford, Elizabeth Woodville, or Anne Neville, who are known primarily as the wives of monarchs, Queen Elizabeth is the subject of some eighty biographies published since 1890, as Christopher Haigh noted in 1988 (175). Susan Kay's bibliography indicates that she consulted two popular narrative biographies by women, Katherine Anthony's Queen Elizabeth and Elizabeth Jenkins's Elizabeth the Great. These biographers, in turn, consulted, among other sources, two earlier efforts to assess the effects of Elizabeth's childhood and medical and sexual history on her character. A "Narrative in Contemporary Letters" entitled The Girlhood of Queen Elizabeth by Frank A. Mumby tells the story of Elizabeth's early life through narrative links and hundreds of letters, beginning with one by Anne Boleyn in anticipation of the "bringing forth of a Princeso," to letters written by agents of King Philip some six months after the queen's accession. Elizabeth's own letters share the narrative with the many dispatches written by Spanish and French ambassadors, as well as personal and official letters written to Elizabeth, Mary, and many others. The introduction announces that

> The conditions of Mary's miserable girlhood, of Elizabeth's unloved childhood, are set forth as they really were. . . . We can judge of the moral dangers which Elizabeth faced with more or less courage and success, at an age when the girls of to-day scarcely know that evil exists, and we can estimate the effect of the physical suffering and the mental torture which hardened the heart of Mary's prisoner in the Tower or at Woodstock. The editor has made no effort to apportion blame or praise; that task is reserved for the reader. (xix–xx)

Another curious early-twentieth-century study, The Private Character of Queen Elizabeth by Frederick Chamberlin, contains chapters titled "Health

for Ever Wrecked by Seymour Affair" and "Medical Record of Elizabeth."
These bring together excerpts from letters and other contemporary documents that refer to Elizabeth's ill health, which Chamberlin then submitted
with a set of ten questions to five medical experts for their opinions. In a
later chapter, Chamberlin compiles documents relating to Elizabeth's alleged
sexual activities under the heading of "The Direct Charges Against
Elizabeth," charges which are then "Cross-Examined" and refuted.

The line of descent from Mumby and Chamberlin through Anthony
and Jenkins to Kay and beyond marks the development of increasingly
embellished psychological portraits of Elizabeth. Kay's title and organizing
theory of Elizabeth's legacy from her parents appears as early as Anthony's
biography, which constructs Elizabeth's inner life much as a novel might.

> Her throne, her extensive wardrobe, her playing on the virginals, her
> dancing, were all sops to her vanity, and the outward measure of an
> abysmal dissatisfaction with herself. She piled her tiara higher, added
> another inch to her ruff, reaped more triumphs in diplomacy, to satisfy
> her pride. But she never, not even in Leicester and Essex, wholly ful-
> filled her need of love. She exacted the forms of devotion, but she
> avoided the profound fact. In all this she was not far removed from that
> long-dead pair who had mated against such terrible odds to produce
> Elizabeth. Her father and her mother were not the libertine and light-
> o'-love which popular legend has made of them. Elizabeth's coldness
> was in part a legacy from them. (254)

Jenkins sounds a similar note, informed by mid-twentieth-century popular
psychology, when she diagnoses Elizabeth's "extreme susceptibility to male
attraction" as the result of "early impressions."

> In a creature of such intensity and power, the emotions connected with a
> vital instinct were, inevitably, of tremendous force. Held up in the arms
> of her imploring mother to her terrible father as he frowned down upon
> them: hearing that a sword had cut off her mother's head: that her
> young stepmother had been dragged shrieking down the gallery when
> she tried to reach the king to entreat his mercy—these experiences, it
> would appear, had built up a resistance that nothing, no passion, no
> entreaty, no tenderness, could conquer. In the fatally vulnerable years
> she had learned to connect the idea of sexual intercourse with terror and
> death; in the dark and low-lying region of the mind where reason cannot
> penetrate, she knew that if you give yourself to men, they cut your head
> off with a sword, an ax. The bloodstained key that frightens the girl in
> "Blue-Beard" is a symbol merely of the sexual act; in Elizabeth's case,

the symbol had a frightful actuality of its own. It was the executioner's steel blade, running with blood.

Consequently, says Jenkins, "she enjoyed being made love to [i.e., courted] with an abnormal avidity that was the penalty of a deranged instinct," but never "passed the point at which nature transforms the adoring suitor into the complacent lover" (100).

Characterizations such as these clearly inspired the novelists who read them. Not content with the documented romantic episodes in Elizabeth's life, they invented hypothetical ones. Irwin's *Elizabeth and the Prince of Spain* embellishes the historical role Philip played in getting Queen Mary to name her half-sister as her heir, by creating private scenes between Elizabeth and Philip which are overtly romantic. Kay takes a similar approach in *Legacy*, where the sexually charged relationship between Elizabeth and Philip is one of many carefully orchestrated strategies that lead Elizabeth to the crown. A coy Elizabeth "raised her eyes slowly to his face with an expression which could only flatter his taunted manhood, a look which promised an exquisite surrender." This scene takes place shortly after Queen Mary's long false pregnancy is finally revealed to be a tumor. Philip delicately suggests a marriage of convenience to his vassal, the Duke of Savoy, who "would not be a possessive husband." Elizabeth smiles and replies

> "You disappoint me, Philip. I had hoped for something better than a place in your harem."
>
> His breath caught in his throat. Was she telling him that in the event of Mary's death she would be prepared to give herself to him in marriage?
>
> "Dare I hope—" he began and faltered.
>
> She held out her hands to him and he lifted her to her feet; they stood staring into each other's watchful eyes.
>
> "When I am Queen of England, Philip," she said softly, "you will not find me ungrateful for your protection."
>
> The bargain was now quite plain to him. *Keep me and my inheritance safe from Mary and you shall have your reward!*

The scene ends with her calculating, equivocal promise: "Trust me, Philip," she said steadily, "trust my love for you—as I know I can trust yours." After he left, she rushed to her apartments "and scrubbed his kiss from her lips with a rough cloth" (206–07). This scene is pure invention, of course. By contrast, Alison Weir notes that there had been rumors during Mary's lifetime that Philip meant to marry Elizabeth, and that the Spanish Count de Feria claimed that she owed her throne to the king's influence; the claim, says Weir, "met with the contempt it deserved." In this matter, the queen "told him tartly, her gratitude was solely to her people" (24).[6]

Elizabeth's most sustained and extensively documented relationship was with Robert Dudley, Earl of Leicester. Kay represents them as lovers, but just as her Elizabeth manipulated Philip, so she knows that she must wield the controlling hand in her turbulent ongoing romance with Leicester. After an emotionally wrought scene early in her reign, Elizabeth reflects:

> Death waited in a lost corridor of her mind, waited for Robin in the glittering guise of her love. She knew now what she feared, what held her back from taking the very thing she desired. She could not trust herself with his life.
>
> For marriage would not content him. Men like Robin were never content, and men like Robin were all she would ever love, grasping, ambitious reflections of herself. Once he knew that the crown matrimonial would never be his, he would begin to plot and scheme behind her back, building up a court faction to force her hand. Robin was too like his father, neither men to be ruled by their wives. To emerge from that final conflict as the victor, it would be necessary to kill him. And she knew she was capable of doing it—it was as simple as that. . . .
>
> She had no choice but to let him go on hoping, hoping, till he saw that she had let him waste his life in a vain pursuit, and hated her for it; as she would hate herself. (267–68)

There is something nearly tragic about this realization; Kay attempts to make sense of Elizabeth and Leicester's lifelong relationship by endowing her subject with an acute recognition of the impasse in which she finds herself.

The complicated dynamics of William and Robert Cecil's roles in Elizabeth's life inspire some of the novelists' most powerful inventions. Robert Cecil, as represented by Garrett, Strachey, and other novelists, is a key character in the novels about the last decade of the reign, just as his father William Cecil plays a major role in fictional re-creations of the earlier years, starting before Elizabeth's accession. Kay's most original contribution to the Elizabeth I story is the role Cecil plays in the mysterious death of Amy Robsart. With the calculating deviousness of a Mafia boss, Cecil manipulates the Spanish ambassador into arranging Amy's "accidental" death in order to discredit Leicester, and thus insures that the queen will never marry him (270–71).

Years later, during her grief-stricken withdrawal after Leicester's death, Elizabeth has an extraordinary interchange with Cecil, now Lord Burghley. Employing violent language to shake her out of her suicidal despair, Burghley says,

> "I tell you this, my considered opinion, madam, the late Earl of Leicester was a worthless, grasping knave who used you for his own ends from the day he entered your service."

    She swayed to her feet with an immense effort and steadied herself
against the back of her chair.
    "Liar!" she breathed. "You white-haired snake, you lying, foul-
mouthed *clerk*!" (495)

As the scene swells to a shattering conclusion, she hits him and says malevo-
lently: "That was for him," she said slowly, "for him and the life you con-
demned him to all those years ago when you murdered his wife." He tries to
move away but she continues, "her harsh voice rasping in his ears . . . 'I lied
to you all those years ago, Cecil—did you never know it?—I betrayed your
precious trust. He was my lover from the very beginning. We had nothing to
fear, you see—I lost the Admiral's child when I was fourteen and Dr Bill told
me I could expect no more.'" Neither Elizabeth nor Cecil can escape the
roles in which the English monarchy has placed them. "You tell me I am not
free to die—so be it!" Elizabeth says. "I will play the Virgin Queen for you a
little longer." But in a final cruel stroke she adds: "You have served Dudley's
whore for thirty years and you will serve her to the end of your days. For just
as you refuse to release me, so shall I refuse to release you" (496).
    In a later invented scene, when Cecil is on his deathbed, Elizabeth tells
him that

    "It was said to hurt you, William, didn't you guess that? No man may
    strike me without receiving double the blow in return. Oh, my Spirit, do
    I seem like a woman who has known the joys of love?" . . .
    It was a small enough lie to buy the happiness of a dying man, a
    little worthwhile perjury which she would not regret. (533)

Moments like these in *Legacy* ally it with other new historical fiction-biographers' efforts to probe their subjects' inner lives to the very core.
Notwithstanding her indebtedness to the heroines of women-centered
romantic fiction, Kay's Elizabeth shares with Sherwood's Woolstonecraft or
Yourcenar's Hadrian, Wolf's Cassandra or Garrett's Raleigh the quality of
being intensely real—at once a modern woman and a character reconstructed
from the myriad documents that make up the historical record.

    Rosalind Miles's fiction-biography of Queen Elizabeth, *I, Elizabeth*,
goes considerably farther in the direction of psychological realism than any of
the novels discussed up to this point. Miles is a scholar whose work includes
The Problem of "Measure for Measure" and two critical-biographical studies of
Ben Jonson; she also writes frequently from a feminist perspective and had
written other novels before turning to the life of Elizabeth. Her foreword
acknowledges "an enormous debt of gratitude" to biographers, chroniclers,
and critics without naming any, and goes on to say that "there are as many

Elizabeths as there are people to write her story" (n.p.). This Elizabeth enters into an intimate relationship with the reader in a dual narrative, demarcated by alternating fonts, through which the aged queen of 1601, on the eve of Essex's execution, narrates her life and comments in italicized asides and interruptions on her own narrative. Like other novels that distinguish among different voices, *I Elizabeth* uses the alternating fonts to create the effect of a discontinuous text, a text composed at different times by a character who is not one coherent identity but a mingling of selves.

Miles's Elizabeth engages in another practice that recurs in the New Historical Fiction, that of addressing the reader directly, as if to fill in the other side of a dialogue. So, for example, she interrupts a conversation between the young Elizabeth and Kat Ashley about Thomas Seymour with:

> *I know what you would say. My Surrey, Seymour, Leicester, even my late last lord, my Essex—all tall and lithe, all bold and bright, all fair, red-gold, well-favoured; and all abundant with that special thing that women always seek—forgive plain speaking, I am no virgin-mouth of fifteen now—that thing that makes them men. . . .*
>
> *Were they all mirrors of my father, then, all those who cracked the glass of my indifference, all those I loved?* (134)

The two concurrent lines of narration distinguish *I, Elizabeth* from the seamless narrative of conventional historical fiction, with the italicized passages serving as a commentary that often undermines, ironizes, or qualifies the dominant voice.

Like other writers of New Historical Fiction, Miles approximates sixteenth-century cadences while simultaneously probing her subject's inner life through realistic fictional strategies. To achieve a semblance of period diction, she occasionally appropriates phrases from Shakespeare's plays, just as Burgess and Nye do, knowing that the reader will recognize them. Speaking of Essex in the 1601 prologue, Elizabeth says, "*In the beginning, though, he loved me—I was adored once*" (3). The phrase "I was adored once" uneasily links the aged queen with the comical Sir Andrew Aguecheek in *Twelfth Night*. Of Essex's impending execution, she reflects "*Now he goes to it, as we all must—we owe God a death*" (3). Later, when speaking of the execution of the poet Henry Howard, Earl of Surrey, whom Miles transforms into Elizabeth's first love, an embittered Elizabeth recasts her father as an evil Falstaff and Surrey as a young Hamlet:

> *And as for that old evil, that rotting hulk of venom, guts and bile, my father—that vicious tyrant, bloated bully and plain murderer, that killer whale who called himself king and thought himself a god, to doom or spare whoever he so willed—that man, that king, that father, that vile butcher who must pluck down the brightest and the best, the most beautiful of all, a*

poet, courtier, soldier, scholar, the rose of our age, the hope of the State, my love. . . . (124)

Some allusions are credited, for example: "*What is truth?*" *that jesting fellow Francis Bacon, that follower of his, used to demand, and for all his wit, never had an answer*" (4). This Elizabeth knows Bacon by name but not Shakespeare:

> *When sorrows come, said one of those rogue scribblers, those playwrights of the public stage, they come not single spies, but in battalions.*
> *With Amy dead and Robin gone from me, as foolish as a milkmaid once again, I thought nothing could befall that could be worse. But the same scribbler, the same pen-and-ink man I could swear, once also demanded, "Who is it that can say 'I am at the worst?'"* (315)

Elsewhere in *I, Elizabeth* the diction is more contemporary—and more cliché-ridden in the manner of historical romance. When the young Elizabeth's friendship with Robin Dudley turns to love we are subjected to a barrage of phrases like "My heart thundered his name; my blood whispered it. . . .," "My heart was singing. . . .," "My pulse was racing. . . .," "I felt my woman's power. . . ." (190–91). The private Elizabeth has her own recurring rhetorical strategies, foremost among them exclamations and rhetorical questions, the ellipsis, and repetition, all of which create the impression of uncensored thoughts. She can be brutally frank, as when she alludes to her Tudor great-grandfather, father of Henry VII, as "*that cunt-climbing Celt*" who "*popped himself between the sheets of the grieving widow and then married her,*" in an allusion that links him with *Hamlet*'s Claudius (255–56). The influence of late-twentieth-century feminism infiltrates the narrative as well; for example, an indignant, mocking Elizabeth, speaking of her advisers' insistence that she marry, sarcastically sums up their logic:

> *no woman could govern without a man to bear for her the cares of government.* Why, all men know that!
> And that my health required it—*for without coitus, never broken by a man, women have no passageway for their foul flux and bloody humours, and are always subject to greensickness, to the rash motions of an unruly womb and to a constant, ticking lust.* All men knew that too!
> *But above all,* they *required it—for being men, they never thought that I could live without one!* (276)

The Elizabeth of the italicized textual commentary often explodes with repressed rage, as in this passage about her cousin Lettice Knollys, whom Leicester married secretly in 1578; Lettice then married for a third time shortly after Leicester's death. The passage advances the historical narrative with another unmarked quote from *Hamlet* and in the process, reveals a particularly vindictive side of Miles's Elizabeth:

> *Yes, the funeral baked meats did coldly furnish forth the wedding feast! The lustful whore wed herself to a man young enough to be her son—indeed, he was the dearest friend of my lord her son. He was young Blount, Christopher Blount, who tilted with my lord of Essex and then fell under her spell. . . .*
> *I bled her of every farthing he ever owed me; I hunted her down like the bitch-wolf she was, and I had no mercy.* (486)

Much of this anger is fueled by the frustration experienced by a woman who was a

> *living legend, the wonder of the world . . . the paradigm of queens. For a woman still fallible—and yes, God help me, even more imprisoned in the flesh than ever, besides being mired in politics and frantic for ready cash—a living goddess was no easy thing to be.* (491)

Miles employs metacommentary here by enabling her Elizabeth to anticipate future historical and fictional constructions of her person and her reign, rather as Shakespeare's Cleopatra does toward the end of *Antony and Cleopatra*, when she dreads seeing "some squeaking Cleopatra boy my greatness / I'th' posture of a whore" in the public theaters (5.2.219–21).

There are disadvantages to first-person narration, particularly when the narrator is the novel's principal character, rather than a secondary one, like the boy actor who narrates the life of Marlowe in *A Dead Man in Deptford*. Without an external observer to describe the elegance, shrewdness, and sheer brilliance of Elizabeth's performance as queen, Miles's protagonist lacks the charismatic grandeur of other fictional Elizabeths. Too often, she come across as self-absorbed, self-indulgent, and obsessive in her repetitiveness, although these traits are sometimes redeemed by a wry awareness as the old Elizabeth looks back over her life, as in this commentary:

> *You see from this I thought that I held life then in the palm of my hand. I was the star of the Court, and I did not know that stars may have a fall. The whole world danced to my tune through days and days of pleasure and privilege, days devoid of care. But when life's drum beats at its highest, then the wisest virgin learns to hear another sound, the soft pulsing of the dance of death.* (194)

There is also a witty, irreverent side to Miles's Elizabeth; here, the casual use of mocking intertextual allusions that readers of Shakespeare and Marlowe would recognize ally her with Burgess's and Nye's characters:

Bastard again, then, was I?
So be it.
There are worse things.
Some great men have been bastards. Our Lord Jesus Christ was a bas-
tard and his mother no virgin, said that blaspheming playwright, you
remember him, the scribbling spy that my old spymaster Walsingham had
killed when his loose talk grew dangerous. . . .
And would he [Jesus] not cry with me in the words of the old Greek
comedy, "Now gods, stand up for bastards"? (202–03)

This last line, misattributed to "an old Greek comedy," is Edmund's in *King Lear*. Rather than attribute it anachronistically to Shakespeare, as Scott might have done, Miles slyly suggests that it originated in an earlier text.

In *The Secret Diary of Anne Boleyn*, Robin Maxwell takes the interplay between two voices farther than Miles, inasmuch as she uses the device to tell two stories simultaneously. The novel turns upon the by-now-familiar theme of the influence Anne's life had on her daughter's attitudes toward men and marriage. Newly crowned queen, Elizabeth believes that "she could do as she pleased" and so flirts dangerously with Robin Dudley, despite Kat Ashley's warnings (15). Twenty pages into the novel, an old woman named Matilda Sommerville brings her Anne Boleyn's secret diary, and tells her the story of her mother's final days. Just before her execution, Anne entrusted the diary to her attendant with these words:

"Take this," she said. "It is my life. Give it to my daughter, Elizabeth. Give it to her when she is grown, when she is queen. She will have need of it." (25)

The volume, begun in January 1522 and ending with a letter to her infant daughter written just before her death in May 1536, follows the format of a young girl's diary, with each entry addressed to "Diary" and concluding "Yours faithfully, Anne." The text is fragmentary and full of gaps, with months, sometimes years, between entries.

Elizabeth reads the diary entries in clandestine sessions that alternate with scenes (printed in a different font) in which she recalls familiar episodes from her earlier life, such as the Seymour affair, her imprisonment in the Tower, her childhood games with Robin Dudley, and so forth. She also embarks on a quest for more information about the mother she never knew, exploring the contents of a long-forgotten room containing Anne's material possessions and visiting her mother's chamber in the Tower, all the while immersing herself in Anne's version of the events that led to her death. Unlike other fictional Elizabeths, Maxwell's heroine wishes to marry Dudley, although William Cecil warns her that "if you are determined to pursue this dangerous course, I will be unable to continue in your service as Secretary" (219). Anne's story changes her mind, however, and by the end of the novel, in the aftermath of Amy Robsart Dudley's mysterious death, she recognizes "*the treachery of men*" and sends Dudley away (264). Sadder and wiser, she admits to herself that "love, for a woman, was to be feared."

> "Will I never marry?" Elizabeth said aloud, the words echoing in the marble chapel. Never marry? Never bear sons? Never birth a daughter? Hot tears sprang unexpectedly to Elizabeth's eyes. To never have a daughter, who would speak kindly of her, cherish the tokens of her life. . . .

Maxwell's invocation of the mother-daughter bond adopts the tone of contemporary fiction and nonfiction written for and about women. The monologue continues: "But no, she forced such sentimentality from her thoughts. What need had she of children? She would be rich with subjects who loved and adored her, who would long remember her glorious reign." And so, with "the strength of destiny at her back," the queen embraces her role in history, telling herself in the novel's final sentences that "I am my mother's daughter. And I shall make her proud" (280–81).

The conventions of women-centered fiction-biography clearly shape Maxwell's retelling of Anne Boleyn's story, for this is a revisionist account written to contest the politically motivated Tudor history that represents Anne as a wanton woman and adulteress. Maxwell also explores a potential "what-if" scenario: if Elizabeth had not read the diary, she might have married Dudley and history would have followed an entirely different path. Like other historical fictions that attempt to fill the dark spaces in history with explanations, *The Secret Diary of Anne Boleyn* sets out to make sense of Elizabeth's supposed refusal to marry; as Maxwell observes elsewhere in an author's note, "conjecture extrapolated from fact is, after all, the very heart of historical fiction (*Virgin* 243).[7]

The connection between Anne Boleyn's marriage and the events of 1560 receives a rather different treatment in another unusual historical fiction that purports to be a secret text. *My Lord the Fox: The Secret Document of Anthony Woodcott Concerning the Year 1560*, "recounted by" Robert York is an invented character's account of his activities as a secret agent for William Cecil. Dated April 1561, the narrative mingles excerpts from Woodcott's "day-book," his reports to Cecil, and other letters and documents interspersed with Woodcott's reflections on his double life. Cecil is the "Fox" who employs subterfuge to salvage his career as Elizabeth's adviser at a particularly dangerous moment in her reign, caused by her infatuation with Dudley:

the ship of State [had become] rudderless, and such was the power of the crown that unless a royal hand was on the tiller, no proper course was steered. . . . The ship wallowed in a swell, sails ill-set, destination uncertain, and the crew, the people of England, were on the brink of mutiny. (67)

Cecil sends Woodcott on fact-finding missions from June to October 1560 which require him to assume a variety of invented personae. The first of these missions yields valuable information confirming the rumors that Anne Boleyn's musician, Mark Smeaton, was Elizabeth's true father; the second is an intriguing rewriting of the Cumnor Hall episodes of *Kenilworth*, in which Woodcott, acting upon Cecil's instructions, sets up the naive and ambitious Richard Verney (*sic*) to murder Amy Robsart Dudley. The scheme is remarkable in its deviousness and is ultimately more convincing than either Scott's or Kay's theories concerning Varney's and Cecil's roles in Amy's death. York says in his author's note that he was inspired by Hugh Ross Williamson's *Historical Enigmas* and found support for his fictional re-creation of Amy's fall in Professor Ian Aird's theory regarding the fragility of her spine due to breast cancer (151). Woodcott's final service to Cecil in this skillfully constructed short novel involves a man named Buckland in Dudley's service, a young poet "greatly addicted to the theatre" with a "liking to drink and boast," a "likeable mountebank . . . [who] pretends somewhat to the Catholic faith" and serves as an envoy between Dudley and the Spanish Embassy (115, 117). In a final effort to discredit Dudley, Woodcott and an accomplice known only as "the Child" contrive to make it appear that Dudley, not Cecil, sought out the information regarding Elizabeth's parentage and was passing it through Buckland to the Spanish ambassador.

The queen makes an appearance in the final chapter of the novel. Like Cecil, she is shrewd in matters of espionage, and tests Woodcott's assumed persona as an uneducated fellow by accusing him in Latin of being a liar and a rogue and then, when he does not respond, continues speaking to Cecil in Latin about the document testifying to her illegitimacy. Summing up the incident, Woodcott remarks that

> my lord did not misjudge the Queen's cunning, rather he played upon it; for had she been any ordinary woman she would not have foreseen where his arrest would lead, but being extraordinary, she saw it well, and saw that he held her in the palm of his hand, and as far as it was in her to do so, she bowed to his will. . . .
>
> So, after the eternity was passed, in which those two strong wills met and recognised the other, Majesty and her servant face to face. . . . The Queen nodded and smiled a little smile; thus was the treaty ratified. . . .
>
> To this day I do not know whether or not she realised that I had understood all that was said; but I know her to have been sure in her

mind that I had not understood its meaning, because my head is still upon my shoulders. (146–47)

Just as York's male narrator depicts Anne Boleyn in a more negative light than Maxwell does, so his tale about Elizabeth's parentage is much less sympathetically recounted than Maxwell's second Queen Elizabeth novel, in which Elizabeth and Dudley produce an illegitimate son.

The Queen's Bastard is more interesting as speculative historical fiction than its precursor because it embellishes a little-known and probably—but not certainly—apocryphal event in Elizabeth Tudor's story. In her review of the rumors about Elizabeth's supposed pregnancies and illegitimate children that circulated "among hostile foreign Catholics" in the 1560s and 1570s, Carole Levin briefly describes an incident first recorded in the *Calendar of Letter and Papers Relating to English Affairs* in Spain.

> In 1587 a young Englishman in pilgrim's garb was arrested in the north of Spain on suspicion of being a spy. He was sent to Madrid where Philip II's English secretary, Sir Francis Englefield, examined him. The young man claimed to be Arthur Dudley, the illegitimate son of Robert Dudley and the queen. . . .
>
> "Arthur Dudley" gave Englefield a detailed account of his childhood in the household of Robert Southern, who had told the boy his real identity on his deathbed. Dudley described meetings he had had with important members of Elizabeth's government before he finally successfully fled the country in the mid-1580s to wander the continent in the company of disaffected English and Elizabeth's enemies. Arthur Dudley proposed to Englefield that Philip II take him under his protection and utilize him in the coming attack on England. (81–82)

Levin goes on to say that the basic premise of Dudley's story is "impossible," since Elizabeth had smallpox in 1562, and "this was not a cover for her having given birth to a child" (82).

Maxwell reports having read Levin's account and argues in her afterword that "[m]uch of the dating from that part of history is imprecise." She continues,

> If, in fact, Arthur Dudley was twenty-*six* at the time of his arrest in Spain, his year of birth would have been 1561, and during that year Elizabeth's summer progress is completely undocumented from the middle of the month of June till the end of October—a huge hole in history. (434–35)

This, then, is fiction that aspires to be revisionist history, and it is marketed as such by Simon and Schuster. The back jacket blurb celebrates Maxwell for having

defied stodgy academics who would have kept us from knowing that such
a character existed. Her plausible tale has allowed us to decide for ourselves if Arthur was, in fact, Elizabeth's and Leicester's illegitimate son.[8]

The Queen's Bastard opens, dramatically, with the line "*My Father is dead
and my Mother is Queen of England*" (3). Thus begins the retrospective journal
of Arthur Dudley, written on a long ship voyage to the New World after the
events of the novel have taken place. Using contrasting fonts, Maxwell juxtaposes the journal with the story of Elizabeth's pregnancy and secret child-
birth, after which Cecil and Kat Ashley spirit away the baby and substitute a
dead infant in its place, so that Elizabeth and Dudley are unaware that they
have a living child. Arthur's autobiographical journal occupies only four of
the novel's first hundred pages. At page 125 the two stories come together
briefly when the royal party pays a visit to Enfield to hunt, and the young
Arthur—who leads a Cinderella-like existence in the home of his adopted
family—meets Dudley and Elizabeth. From this point onward, Arthur's
story predominates. At age sixteen, the young hero mounts his beloved horse
Charger and "without a backward glance rode out of Enfield into the wide
world to seek . . . [his] fortune and find adventure" (192), after the fashion of
Joseph Fielding's *Tom Jones*. Maxwell makes gestures at period diction,
orthography, and capitalization in the journal sections, although not as
extensively as other New Historical Fiction writers such as John Barth in *The
Sot-Weed Factor* or Peter Ackroyd in *Hawksmoor*. Like his father, Arthur is an
accomplished horseman; like his mother, he is skilled at languages and playacting; like his grandmother, Anne Boleyn, he was born with a small sixth
finger on his left hand. Determined to be a soldier, he goes to the
Netherlands and serves as a spy during the Spanish wars so chillingly
described by Patricia Finney in *Firedrake's Eye*. The novel thus ranges beyond
the traditional confines of women-centered historical fiction as it takes the
reader into the experience of war, culminating in a re-creation of the Armada
invasion from both sides, as short chapters set in England alternate with
Arthur's account from his vantage point as spy on a Spanish galleon.

Having reopened the question of Elizabeth's offspring, Maxwell adheres
to the unspoken rule of historical fiction, that the course of history must
remain unchanged. Arthur disappears into the New World in search of his
beloved, Constanza, after telling Elizabeth that he craves adventure, not
political power. Elizabeth reluctantly lets him go, hoping that he may change
his mind. The novel thus answers the question, why did the queen refuse to
name a successor?, by constructing a hypothetical heir who, as it turns out,
never returned to claim his inheritance.

Some twenty years earlier Joseph W. Turner observed that "if a novelist
were to write about Queen Elizabeth, the reader would expect from the very
first that Elizabeth bore no legitimate children and that the crown was

passed on to James I" (343–44). In Turner's taxonomy, this sort of historical expectation underlies the distinction between the documented historical novel and the kind of historical fiction that contains invented characters. He hypothesizes a reader who "expects certain things to happen and will no doubt be surprised—perhaps even disappointed—if they do not," invoking a reader-response approach to historical fiction which "allows us to follow the way the implied reader adjusts his conception of history to the one the novelist is creating" (345).

Turner's notions of historical expectation don't take into account some of the wilder counterfactual fictional inventions perpetrated by postmodern novelists. Carlos Fuentes's *Terra Nostra*, for example, is an alternative history of Spain and Spanish America in which Philip II marries Elizabeth and brings her to live with him at the Escorial. In Nye's *The Late Mr. Shakespeare*, a chapter entitled "What if Queen Elizabeth was Shakespeare's mother?" spins a surrealistic fantasy in which John Shakespeare comes upon the thirty-year-old queen walking alone in the Forest of Arden. After some suggestive conversation, she strips off her clothes to bathe in a spring and commands him to join her, attracted by his impressively large "donkey."

> "O Mr Spermspear!" cries Queen Elizabeth. "O Mr Shakespunk! Mr Shakespunk! Mr Shakespunk! O Mr Fuckster, O make your donkey go in deeper, my gentleman!" . . .
> So John Shakespeare does.
> He does what the Queen commands him.
> He does Queen Elizabeth thoroughly all over again. . . .
> Mr John Shakespeare and Queen Elizabeth met thus and parted the same day. You will find their son's version of it in his play called *A Midsummer Night's Dream*.
> Nine months after the sweet encounter in the water, to that very day, to that very hour, so they say, the poet William Shakespeare came into this world. His mother, knowing a bastard prince might bring civil war . . . left him with John Shakespeare, who by that time was long married to Mary Arden. Mary Arden had a good heart, and she brought up the child as her own. (80)

This episode in Nye's mock biography reads as a parody of the sustained speculation Maxwell develops in her more conventional historical fiction.

Not surprisingly, Shakespeare's England is a natural subject for popular historical mystery series; for example, the popular Edward Marston novels revolve around the actor and amateur detective Nicholas Bracewell, a member of the Lord Westfield's Men. Recently, historical mystery series set

in other times and places have featured women amateur detectives who combine feminine intuition with shrewd problem-solving abilities, not to mention some low-key sex appeal. Some of these series are extensively researched
and designed to appeal to readers with a good working knowledge of history,
literature, and languages. Sharan Newman's Catherine LeVendeur leaves the
convent of Heloise in twelfth-century France and finds herself solving crimes
involving her extended family as she travels throughout Europe and
England; Glynis Tryon is the mystery-solving town librarian in Miriam
Grace Manfredo's Seneca Falls novels, set during the feminist and antislavery
movements of the 1850s; and Sister Fidelma, a highly educated late-seventh-
century Irish nun, stars in a series of novels by Peter Tremayne (the pen
name of the Irish historian Peter Berresford). The device of casting an historical figure, rather than an invented one, as the principal character in a
mystery series entails taking greater liberties with the documented past. An
ongoing series by Stephanie Barron casts Jane Austen, somewhat improba-
bly, as the sleuth of the country-home circuit.

Karen Harper takes a similar approach; she transforms the young
Elizabeth into an amateur detective in *The Poyson Garden, The Tidal Poole*,
and *The Twylight Tower* in her "Elizabeth I Mystery Series." Although predictable in their use of amateur detective conventions, the Elizabeth I mysteries are innovative inasmuch as they give Elizabeth an active role in
combatting the plots against her life, rather than representing her as the
essentially static object of a plot that is exposed and foiled by heroic males
(as, for example, in Pamela Bennetts's romantic *Envoy from Elizabeth*[9]).
Harper provides Elizabeth with a partly invented, partly historical inner
circle of confidants that includes William Cecil and Kat Ashley along with
Ned, a player adept at disguises, and Meg, a young herbalist who conve-
niently bears an uncanny resemblance to her mistress and can assume her
identity while Elizabeth engages in undercover sleuthing. The novels draw
heavily on the Shakespearean device of the girl disguised as a boy, freeing
Elizabeth from the constraints of her public role and enabling her to engage
in various adventures, including one in which she disguises herself as a boy
actor in a traveling acting company.

Patricia Finney's Elizabeth is the prospective victim of a complex plot in
Unicorn's Blood, a sequel to *Firedrake's Eye* (it is not clear whether these novels
constitute part of an ongoing series). *Unicorn's Blood* is set in 1586, when
Elizabeth is fraught with ambivalence about the execution of Mary Queen of
Scots, an episode other novelists have dramatized to great effect. The
middle-aged Elizabeth is beset with recurring nightmares in which she is
attacked by a unicorn. Assuming a learned reader, Finney's narrator remarks,

> For Pliny tells us that although the unicorn is full of rage and will stab
> lions through the heart with the horn on his head, still, if he be led to a
> virgin by strong men, he will lay his head upon her lap and be tamed. (2)

Finney's Elizabeth is high-handed and impatient with her ladies-in-waiting, whose ministrations are described in the novel's opening chapters in great detail. In the course of a lengthy account of the attiring process, with its elaborate layers of clothing, jewels, wig, and so on (a scene that has counterparts in many other historical novels), Finney evokes the court's obsession with gossip by imagining a daily routine that no other novelist, to my knowledge, has attempted:

> Parry did the office of the Stool, as well as overseeing the Queen's robes, and drew income from half a dozen separate sources for a daily bulletin on the state of the Queen's bowels. It was a wry joke between them.
>
> The Queen coughed and took the napkin handed to her. She stood and Parry came immediately to drop the lid and assess the results.
>
> "You may tell them that I am utterly constipated," the Queen told her tartly.
>
> "Again, Your Majesty?" Parry asked, amused.
>
> "Ay, again. Tell them I am stopped up with bile and may well take purge."
>
> Parry smiled and shook her head. "You are cruel, Madam."
>
> "By God, if they will not heed me, let them fear me." The Queen's bowels were as healthy as ever, but only she, Parry and the chamberer who did the emptying knew that. Meanwhile Parry would pass the word of an unsuccessful Stool and the councillors would tremble, the Gentlemen of the Privy Chamber walk softly and the cooks of the Privy Kitchen prepare further messes of prunes and dried rubarb, which she would send back untouched. It cheered her to think of the ripples of consternation spreading from her humble (though velvet-covered) Stool throughout the Court and thence perhaps even into London. (10)

This is a far cry from the Elizabeth of Irwin's or Kay's or Miles's fictions: she sleeps in her bed of state with a beautiful young lady-in-waiting in her bony arms; when her unicorn dream recurs she screams "like an Irish banshee" (44), she suffers from bad teeth, surrounds herself with lap dogs, not suitors, and her only reference to Leicester in the novel concerns his poor health. Elizabeth's closest confidante is her court dwarf, Thomasina, who is a tumbler possessed with a shrewd intelligence belied by her childlike appearance. Thomasina is based on a historical personage; according to Elizabeth Jenkins, "the little creature appears in the large picture at Penshurst of the queen dancing with Lord Leicester, and Dr. Dee in his diary noted that one of his visiters [*sic*] was 'the Queen's dwarf, Mrs. Tomasin'" (195).

Just as the reader learns a great deal about English Catholics and Jews from *Firedrake's Eye*, so *Unicorn's Blood* contains a compelling account of the fate that awaited nuns at the dissolution of the religious houses. Mary, the aged night soil woman from whose perspective parts of the novel are narrated, never chose to be a witch, nor made a pact with the Devil. In a way, the witchery chose her.

Consider the sorrows of a land without the Queen of Heaven. When King Henry's clerks and pursuivants destroyed the monasteries fifty years ago, all they did was cast into the world a number of men who knew no trade but writing and reading and singing. . . .

But when they destroyed the nunneries—ah, then they did a far different thing, for then they stole from women our very last redoubt from men. If a woman cannot be sanctified by Christ as a nun and if she further cannot marry or is not married—until she is too old, she is every man's prey, and when she has at last become old she is likewise prey. Then they call her a witch, the better to justify their cruelty. (85)

Mary's story is also narrated by the Virgin Mary, who seems to inhabit Mary's body in a curiously magic-realist fashion; she tells how Mary was given a small pension that was never paid and told to make her own way in the world as a midwife. Finney also constructs a backstory for the thirty-five-year-old Thomasina, an outsider who was mistreated by men before she came into the queen's service. Thomasina and Mary meet in the female underworld of the palace, "behind the outward show of magnificence" (88) in the laundry where the queen maintains a secret spy network of her own, unbeknownst to Walsingham and his agents. Mary and Thomasina are the two principal characters in this women-centered New Historical Fiction, but there are many others, all linked by the common experiences of womankind.

The invented male characters in *Unicorn's Blood* will be familiar to readers of *Firedrake's Eye*, set three years earlier: the Jewish cryptographer Simon Ames, his uncle the physician Dr. Nunez, and the soldier of fortune David Becket. Interestingly, they play a far less active role than the women, for while Becket languishes in prison Thomasina becomes the information-gatherer and rescuer, disguising herself and undertaking dangerous exploits to locate the Book of the Unicorn, which contains information regarding the queen's sexual history that could be used to blackmail her. The reader is kept in the dark about the contents of the book until the very end of the novel. With the recovery of the Book of the Unicorn, Elizabeth's secret remains hidden, and her elaborately constructed identity as Virgin Queen unchallenged.

Maxwell includes a comparable—and metafictional—moment in *The Queen's Bastard*, when Elizabeth tells Cecil in a sentence taken from archival material that "with God as my witness, that although I loved Lord Robert Dudley with my heart and soul, nothing improper ever did pass between us." This, clearly, is a barefaced lie, but Cecil realizes that

she knew that long after the men in this room were reduced to dust, history would record her words for all posterity as the truth. She, like her father Henry VIII, did hold herself, if not above God, then shoulder to shoulder with him, and she dared fearlessly to lie in his name. Her will, in any event, would be done, and in death she would be remembered as she desired—as good and virtuous, the Virgin Queen. (94–95)[10]

In both novels Elizabeth is the deliberate author of her own mythic identity, constructing her public image with cold-blooded artifice.

In a good summary of the historical novelist's method, Finney informs the reader in her foreword that

I have used history as skeleton and scaffolding, but I have freely jumped off into fantasy whenever I felt like it, turned speculation into fact and rank conjecture into assumption—although I have tried to keep within the boundaries of what might just be possible, given the evidence. (*Unicorn's Blood* n.p.)

She also provides an historical note at the end of the novel, which deals mostly with political events, but ends with speculations, similar to Maxwell's, that seek to fill the holes in the narrative we call history. Finney observes that Elizabeth's actions around the time she signed the warrant for Mary Queen of Scot's death were

so extraordinary, even for a highly strung woman under heavy pressure and in genuine fear of her life, that I began to wonder how she might have been maneuvered into executing her cousin-queen. A connection with the vague mutterings of scandal around her liaison with Thomas Seymour . . . became part of the answer—and so the plot of this book was born. (367)

Unicorn's Blood, like several other New Historical Fictions by women, participates in the reconstruction of an alternative women-centered culture of herbal lore, midwifery, and healing arts and the accusations of witchcraft that accompanied these skills in medieval and early modern England. Eva Figes's novel *The Seven Ages* traces seven generations of British women herbalists and healers from ancient to modern times; Judith Merkle Riley's *The Oracle Glass* tells the story of the seventeenth-century French "Affaire des Poisons," narrated by an invented character who can read futures in her glass and who belongs to a network of women poisoners, abortionists, and manufacturers and purveyors of potions of all kinds; and Kathryn Harrison's *Poison* contains a vivid description of a seventeenth-century midwife's contraceptive methods using stones and herbs. Like Finney's Mary, these women are marginalized figures, threatened by and threatening to the men who attempt to control their respective social orders.

Many of the novels I have discussed in this chapter place Elizabeth in the conventional role of protagonist, the character who remains at the center of the action throughout the novel. George Garrett's innovative writing strategies, as one might expect, convey Elizabeth's dominating presence in the age that bears her name without casting her as a protagonist in the usual sense. *Death of the Fox* is subtitled *A Novel of Elizabeth and Ralegh*—an odd choice, one might think, since the narrative begins, ends, and regularly circles back to the year 1618. Yet the queen, as Garrett depicts her, casts a long shadow across her successor's reign and is never far from his thoughts. Early in the novel, King James ruminates on her self-fashioning as he rides in a coach with the curtains drawn against the rabble:

> He blames the late Queen for this trouble with the rabble. For her own reasons that woman was ever on display. She permitted them, those who could press close enough, to offer gifts, to kneel and tender petitions. And she did not discourage the old belief that she might heal, cure them with a Sovereign Touch. Indeed, in her great age, in the last years, she seemed eager for these encounters. To what good purpose? The risks were grave. Perhaps it was all female vanity, which is boundless beyond measuring, deeper than the ocean and higher than clouds.
>
> No, the old Queen never doubted or denied the truth of her divinity, a truth so certain to her that she need not speak of it. Moved easy among her subjects, enjoying their love while it lasted. (54)

A younger Queen Elizabeth emerges from the monologue of the ghost-soldier, who tells the reader how Raleigh "caught her eye" and became one of her favorites. He speculates that she saw herself reflected in Raleigh: a soldier, he was "A man who had gambled his life for no reward many times. Just as she had. Just as she must" (294). The courtier-ghost offers up another portrait of the queen, just as he depicts another side of Raleigh: "She came [to the throne] all unprepared and thus, by paradox, was the one Tudor perfectly prepared to rule" (326). England was in debt and she was shrewd enough to realize that "she could not afford the most limited defensive wars" (327). And so she ruled frugally:

> —A most economical woman, our Queen. She knew prices to the penny and could have outbargained a fishwife. She could squeeze a gold half angel coin until the angel dropped his spear and fell like the groaning dragon at his feet. (328)

Eventually, the tale turns to Raleigh, who came to seek a place at court in the 1570s. The courtier-ghost recounts the events of the next twenty-five years, including Raleigh's secret marriage to Bess Throckmorton, but always with the queen in the foreground. Relishing his role as chronicler, he contrasts the queen's court with King James's in a few pages that look ahead to *The Succession*:

—The Court the Queen left behind her was an apple, red and ripe, polished to a high luster. Down came the King from Scotland, hungry as a wolf. Bit into that apple with joy. To taste no sweetness, only dust and rot and worms. (361)

Here as elsewhere in his Elizabethan trilogy, Garrett wears his scholar's robes lightly. An extraordinary sweep of history is casually related through the ghost-narrators' informal monologues without ever assuming the weightiness of a lecture. Richard Tillinghast remarks that "the novelist has in his imagination entered so deeply into his material that his intuitions allow him to make guesses that turn up facts." He recalls the passage in *Death of the Fox* in which the queen is described sitting naked in a private bathing chamber where the walls and ceiling are made of mirrors, so that "she would know and never forget the truth of herself." Evidently, it was only after reading the novel that "the curator of royal properties at Windsor Castle divined what the huge rectangular frames stored in an attic there had held—the mirrors having long since been broken. Thus the imagination marries the fact" (61–62).

The reader is granted similar glimpses of Elizabeth as she is perceived by her subjects in *The Succession*. The hundred-page "Player: 1602," the longest section of the novel, is an encounter between a player in the Lord Chamberlain's Men and an unnamed visitor who had come to the tiring house after a performance of *Troilus and Cressida* to meet him. After a leisurely interval the subject of the succession comes up:

. . . And behind all this, sir, is the great unspoken thing. What must not be said aloud, but must surely be understood as the secret cause behind so many actions of these days.

And what would that be, in your opinion?

. . . Well sire, it is the Queen's age and health. May she live and reign long. But it does not seem likely. It is given out that she is healthy as a horse. But there are other stories, too. . . .

As I take it, the younger gentlemen of Court (who will honor and serve whoever sits next on the throne) tend to favor the claims of King James of Scotland. Because he is a man and a practicing King who must have learned some lessons in Scotland. And because he is a stranger. One who can offer England a new beginning. Of course, every new reign is a new beginning, but a new reign by a foreigner is fresh enough so it can be every man for himself. And unlucky he who gets the hind tit of the sow. (399–400)

The conversation turns back to the player's life, which includes a sly gesture to the many theories about how Shakespeare left his father's glove-making business to enter the acting profession. Garrett employs his characteristic third-person narration of dialogue as the player tells his story:

> Tells how he did well as an apprentice at leatherworking. Might have gone far, might be a man of importance in the Guild, if he had not delivered a pair of boots to a player at an Inn in Southwark. If that player had not taken a liking to him at sight. (403)

Later, the player describes how he did some spying on Essex for Anthony Bacon and other unnamed patrons. Then, at the end of the evening, the two men return to the player's home to dig up incriminating papers concerning the Essex rebellion which are buried in his garden. The papers and ongoing conversation tell the story of Essex's desperate final days, including the famous episode in which Essex commissioned a performance of *Richard II*:

> *The players were troubled to remember their speeches. I could tell the play had not been well rehearsed. But more than half of the audience were from Essex House. Who cheered & laughed & applauded. All knowing how Essex has been called the new Bullingbrook & the Queen herself called (privately) "Richard the Second." And when came the celebrated (& now forbidden) scene, where Richard is deposed & gives up his crown, you would have thought it was some clownish comedy. Such roars of laughter & catcalls!* (440)

Surely Garrett expects the reader to know the other part of this story, the queen's remark, "I am Richard II. Know ye not that?"[11]

Garrett introduces the old Elizabeth of *The Succession* in the opening chapter, "Queen: March 1603." She has only a few days left (Elizabeth died on March 23, 1603) and knows that death, "the dark, patient, invisible Prince" will "be here, soon or late, and when it pleases him" (6). A corresponding framing chapter ends the novel, set a few months earlier at Christmastide 1602–1603. In an elegiac mood and with encyclopedic lavishness of detail, Garrett describes the Christmas revelry and feasting, the extravagance of candles "left burning night and day" (501) during a "holy, happy time" that keeps "the fear of war or the Plague . . . trouble, pain, sorrow and suffering" at bay (536). He also quotes from the lists of gifts Queen Elizabeth received each New Year's Day throughout her reign; these are documents of the kind historians use to reconstruct the material culture and customs of a time and place. This scene serves as a retrospective summing up of the major players in Elizabeth's long life, while brilliantly conveying her famous acquisitiveness and vanity:

Come January 1, Feast of the Circumcision (and, in the olden days in England, Feast of Fools), and it is time for the giving of gifts. No place is the getting and giving more important than at court. Where the Queen's clerks make a receipt of every gift that is made to the Queen. And likewise prepare a counterlist for the gilt plate which the Queen gives in return. Noting the exact weight of the plate in ounces and its market value, too, to the nearest halfpenny. . . .

Something or other she takes in her hands, bends and holds closer to the light to examine. Perhaps an exclamation of pleasure. Maybe a request for the clerk to read again the name of the giver. . . . Her request to the clerk to speak up more loudly. (*Nowadays you must raise your voice, but without seeming to, when you speak to the Queen*). And so someone begins a new year with good fortune. (512-513)

A list of gifts follows, each one triggering an excursion into the past that is also a catalogue of historical information:

Item: By the Duke of Norfolk. A purse of purple silk and gold filled with sundry coins of gold.
Her Howard cousin. The only Duke in England and the richest man in this kingdom. Lived at his palace of Kenninghall in Norfolk more grandly than any Prince. . . . Once dreamed, indeed aimed to rule this kingdom as husband to the Queen of Scots. Thus, by his own doing and before his thirty-fifth year, felt the cold edge of a heading ax. (513–14)

Garrett's signature sentence fragments produce a stream-of-consciousness effect, the illusion of a mind leaping quickly from thought to image, image to thought. As Kelly Cherry observes in "Meaning and Music in George Garrett's Fiction," the streams of sentence fragments give the impression of a "fugal interplay" among overlapping and echoing voices; drawn into this "sportive syntax," the reader becomes implicated in generating the text (17, 20).

Some of the letters which Garrett had originally planned to use as the basis for his novel occupy a sixty-page chapter about midway through *The Succession*, entitled "Mr. Secretary and the Letters: 1603." The chapter begins with a letter from Elizabeth to James, dated 4 October 1586, which Robert Cecil is reading in 1603. The letter is printed in its entirety.[12] As Cecil reads,

It is easy for him to summon up the King of Scots, poet and scholar, poring over the letter. Studying it so carefully. Wide brow wrinkled. His full lips (if paintings and drawings and the descriptions of others are to be taken as true) pouting with annoyance he is seldom able to disguise.

> What in the world is this woman trying to tell him? What is it that
> she is really saying? (298–99)

In her letters, Cecil observes wryly, Elizabeth dangles the succession before
James's eyes as a bait:

> It amuses Cecil that even in her official letters she could not resist
> a chance to apply her usual pressure. Urging him to act more vigorously
> against his Catholic subjects. Forever pushing him toward the exercise of
> justice. And thereby, as Cecil sees it, committing himself more openly to
> the Protestant cause. (324)

The queen's letters "almost always contain instruction of one kind or
another" as she teaches her cousin how to be a king (325). As suspense about
the succession grows, James initiates a correspondence with Cecil in 1601,
"with [a] quaint little code—30 for the King, 10 for Cecil, 3 for Lord Henry
Howard" (333). These letters, and Cecil's carefully worded responses, interspersed with a third-person narrative from Cecil's point of view, describe in
considerable historical detail the various participants in the scheming and
maneuvering that occurred during the last year or two of Elizabeth's reign.

The young Elizabeth of 1575 makes a brief appearance in *The Succession*
in the first of three chapters of reminiscences by Robert Carey in 1626.
Carey is a Boleyn cousin of Elizabeth's and a familiar figure to readers of
Finney's novels; he appears as the lover of Elizabeth's young attendant and
bedmate Bethany in *Unicorn's Blood* and as the amateur detective in the three
historical detective novels she wrote under the name of P. F. Chisolm.
Garrett's Carey (called the "Courtier") is an old man in 1626, whose memories are unpredictable but "always return to roost like pigeons in a dovecote"
to "that time of Queen Elizabeth" (153). The first of these chapters contains
an account of the Kenilworth revels based on the same sources Scott had
used. Carey's fragmented account resumes 120 pages later in *The Succession*
as a seven-page letter to a friend, and again near the end of the novel, when
he tells how, as soon as his sister Lady Scrope notified him of the queen's
death, he raced to Scotland ahead of Cecil's messengers to be the first to
bring James the news.

Lady Scrope was in the room when the queen died and so the historical
Carey was at one remove from an eyewitness account of this much-debated
final moment in the Elizabeth Tudor biography. Speaking of Cecil, Garrett's
Carey says

> —I am sure he feared also that the Queen would reject James in
> those last hours. Would name another in the presence of witnesses. He
> must later, later (at the time he sweated pearls) have thanked his stars
> that the Queen had lost the power of speech. Or, anyway, did not
> choose to speak again. . . .

—It was given out, afterward, that in the presence of the Archbishop and a few others, she was asked by Cecil to affirm that James of Scotland was her right worthy, chosen successor. And she was able to nod her head in affirmation. You can believe that if you want to. My own sister, who was in the chamber, doubts the truth of it. (478)

All of the Queen Elizabeth novels and many of the biographies tell the story of Elizabeth's final moments differently. In *Elizabeth and Essex* Strachey relates that:

Cecil and the other Councillors gathered round her; had she any instructions, the Secretary asked, in the matter of her successor? There was no answer. "The King of Scotland?" he hinted; and she made a sign—so it seemed to him—which showed agreement. (285)

Kay imagines a Cecil, kneeling at the queen's bedside, struck with "sudden terror" by the "gleam of hostility" in the dying queen's eyes and asking urgently:

"Your Majesty—the succession. Is it to be the King of Scotland?"
Nothing!
He got to his feet frantically and leaned over the bed, shielding her from view.
"Madam—if speech tires you, a sign will do. Is it to be Scotland?"
But there was no movement from the bed, only those dark, dreadfully knowing eyes staring up into his in their last moment of challenge.

Legacy then shifts to Elizabeth's point of view: "Let him go away and stew, he and the master to whom he had already transferred his allegiance; let them wait till she was ready." When the others ask him what she said, he knows he must brazen it out. "He fixed them with a haughty stare, as though daring any man among them to deny it" and said in a casual tone, "'By the Queen's own wish, my lords—who but her cousin of Scotland?'" (567–68)

There are still other accounts of Elizabeth's final moments. Camden, writing during James I's reign, ends his history with the queen declaring James her successor:

The Queen made Answer with a gasping Breath, *I said that my Throne was a Throne of Kings, that I would not have any mean person succeed me.* The Secretary asking her what she meant by those words; *I will* (said she) *that a King succeed me: and who should that be but my nearest Kinsman, the King of Scots?* (660–61)

According to the historian Alison Weir, Elizabeth was "beyond speech" when Nottingham, Egerton, and Cecil asked her to name her successor; however, "it was afterwards alleged [that] she used her hands and fingers to make the sign of a crown above her head, which they took to mean that she wanted King James to succeed her." Robert Carey, she adds, was "one of those kneeling in the bedchamber" when the Archbishop Whitgift came to pray with the queen later in the evening and she quotes from his description of the scene (483–84). In a widely read "authoritative" biography published in 1934, J. E. Neale tells us that "having performed her last royal duty by nominating James as her successor, [Elizabeth] centred her mind on Heavenly things. . . " but does not indicate how she performed the nomination. He notes without comment that on 20 March Robert Cecil sent a draft of a proclamation naming James King of England to the eagerly waiting heir (408). Did the queen know of the proclamation? History remains silent on this, as on so many other matters.

Elizabeth Tudor has been and will continue to be a natural subject for historical fiction, for all the reasons I have suggested, not the least of which is that she took on the characteristics of a fictional construct during her own lifetime. A number of scholars have remarked upon the way she and her advisers and admirers strategically invented a larger-than-life character whose forty-five year reign was a series of staged performances. Roy Strong's *The Cult of Elizabeth* is one of the most frequently cited studies of the imagery associated with the queen, imagery that was "deliberately and carefully composed" through tournaments, the summer progresses, Accession Day celebrations, portraiture, pageantry, and poetry (114–15). Christopher Haigh, not normally given to flights of rhetoric, sums up this and other aspects of Elizabeth's reign in an extended conceit that brings together court and theater in Elizabeth's and Shakespeare's England:

> Elizabeth brought real dramatic talent to the role of Virgin Queen and mother, and freed herself from some of the restrictions of her sex. But the production in which she starred ran for forty-five years, she had no understudy, and she had to appear in every show: it was a constant strain. Her performances were not flawless: she disliked her part in the early years, when she hoped to marry Dudley; she was bored with it in 1579, when she thought of marrying Alencon; and she could not quite carry it off in her last decade. . . .
>
> Her relationship with supporting actresses was always poor, she worked uneasily with young newcomers, and as an old trouper she was upstaged by the fiery talent of Essex. But hers was an award-winning performance, and what was missing in dramatic conception was more than made up for in sheer professional skill. (172)

Chapter 6

Rewriting Shakespeare
The Henriad with and without Falstaff

*C*hapters four and five have addressed some of the counterfactual scenarios, the "what ifs" posed by historical fiction: what if secular drama
evolved directly in response to acting companies' interventions in local
events? What if Queen Elizabeth bore a child, or was secretly married, or
was vulnerable to blackmail because of her sexual activities? Such speculations question traditional historical metanarratives. This chapter looks at
novels that pose alternative scenarios of a rather different order.
Shakespeare's renditions of English history have long been such familiar fix-
tures in British and North American culture that readers tend to be taken
aback by interpretations that dispute them. Even when based on detailed
research, such accounts—whether fictional, scholarly, or both—seem paradoxically less "real" than the plays' familiar portrayals of the English kings,
their allies, families, and enemies.

Many Shakespeare plays have inspired fictional appropriations and offshoots, some motivated by a desire to fill in gaps and resolve critical cruxes,
other ranging from the playful and irreverent to the bitterly satirical. Such
fictions often exploit the reader's resistance to tampering with the Bard's
words and characters, and in doing so send us back to the playtext with new
questions, new readings, new awareness of passages or clues passed over or
taken for granted.[1] A recent example of this kind of fictional rethinking of a
Shakespeare play is John Updike's *Gertrude and Claudius*. This extended

143

speculation about the events that led to King Hamlet's death belongs at once to the past of Shakespeare's sources and to the present of Updike's many novels and stories about male-female relationships.

Shakespeare's history plays lend themselves to this kind of revisioning because they are themselves historical fictions. Working from histories, chronicles, hearsay, and politically biased documents of various kinds, Shakespeare reimagined episodes in Western history from the death of Julius Caesar to the early reign of Henry VIII. Like nearly every subsequent writer in the genre, he took the liberty of adding fictitious characters to his cast of historically documented ones.

In the fifteen historical or quasi-historical Shakespeare plays derived primarily from Plutarch's *Lives of Noble Grecians and Romans* and Holinshed's *Chronicles*, no invented character is comparable to Falstaff. Falstaff appears or is mentioned in four plays, including *The Merry Wives of Windsor*, a wholly fictitious comedy written after *1 Henry IV* specifically as a showcase for further Falstaffian exploits. This chapter focuses on two historical novels of the 1970s inspired by the Henriad (*1 Henry IV, 2 Henry IV*, and *Henry V*). Falstaff is entirely absent from one novel; in the other, he is the narrator and principal subject of a mock memoir that runs to 450 pages. Edith Pargeter's *A Bloody Field by Shrewsbury* and Robert Nye's *Falstaff* employ entirely different historical fiction strategies, for each novel is descended from a discrete lineage of fiction writing with its own conventions and posture toward the hypothetical reader. However, both novelists presume upon the reader's familiarity with the plays and thus critique, interpret, and embellish the documented historical accounts from which Shakespeare and his contemporaries derived their understanding of the past.

In all of the editing and revisions that Shakespeare's work has been subjected to, there has never been a *1* or *2 Henry IV* without Falstaff. It goes without saying that Falstaff is intrinsic to these plays in the way that Bottom, for example, is intrinsic to *A Midsummer Night's Dream*; both display a comic genius that makes their roles star turns, and unlike their near relatives, the Porter or the Gravediggers, both have names and a recurring presence in their plays. Falstaff's popularity may well have prompted Shakespeare to write *2 Henry IV*, and there is a legend that *The Merry Wives of Windsor* was written expressly at the request of Queen Elizabeth, who wanted to see Falstaff in love. When Shakespeare's plays were subjected to the rules of decorum during the Restoration and eighteenth century, important characters such as Lear's Fool disappeared altogether and virtually all of the plays performed during those years were radically transformed so as to minimize bawdy and broadly comic elements. The Henry IV plays fared otherwise: John Russell Brown notes that as early as 1612, *2 Henry IV* seems to have been called *Sir John Falstaffe* when performed at court and in 1625 the plays were performed as *Falstaff, Part One* and *Part Two* (Brown 1). Pepys saw a production of

1 Henry IV in 1660; and the publication of a 'droll' or skit called T*he Bouncing Knight, or The Robber Robbed* in 1662 and again in 1672, with depictions of Falstaff and the Hostess on the frontispiece, suggests that the tavern scenes remained popular (Weil and Weil 42–43).

Falstaff continued to be a sought-after role in the eighteenth and nine-teenth centuries. After playing Hotspur for many years, Thomas Betterton began performing the part of Falstaff in 1700, and a printed edition of his adaptation of *2 Henry IV*, dated 1721, is entitled *The Sequel of Henry the Fourth; With the Humours of Sir John Falstaffe, and Justice Shallow.* In 1760 a sequel to *2 Henry IV* appeared, entitled *Falstaff's Wedding: A Comedy being a Sequel to the Second Part of the Play of King Henry the Fourth*, "written in imi-tation of Shakespeare" by a Mr. Kendrick, and dedicated to a Mr. Quin who had performed as Falstaff. In this play, as in Shakespeare's, the Falstaff scenes alternate with political ones involving King Henry, Lord Scroop, the Dukes of York and Exeter, and others; Falstaff marries Dame Ursula, his "old sweetheart" whose aunt "has left her four hundred marks a year" (Kendrick 41). Maurice Morgann's *Essay on the Dramatic Character of Sir John Falstaff*, published in 1777, was an early instance of a critical study devoted to a single Shakespearean character, to be followed by other "defenses" of Falstaff and rebuttals thereof (indeed, an entire section of the *Garland Annotated Bibliography*, about 150 entries, is devoted to Falstaff crit-icism). In 1829 a lawyer named Charles Short produced an adaptation of the *Henry IV* plays entitled *The Life and Humours of Falstaff*, consisting essen-tially of the Falstaff scenes, and ending with Falstaff's rejection at the end of part 2 and the scene from *Henry V* in which Mistress Quickly describes Falstaff's offstage death.

Orson Welles, of course, was to produce a more skillful—and more serious—compilation in 1966: the celebrated film *Chimes at Midnight*. The recent stage history of the plays has followed this precedent: when the *Henry IV* plays are cut for performance (either individually or as a combined text), the speeches of the historical characters are shortened or excised, while the Falstaff scenes are deemed essential not only to the structure and theatrical effect but also to the plays' themes. Falstaff is so engaging and irresistible a scoundrel that audiences await his appearances with great anticipation, so much so that a *Henry IV* without Falstaff would seem to be an impossibility, a wrongheaded undertaking.

So I assumed when I began reading Edith Pargeter's novel *A Bloody Field by Shrewsbury.* Pargeter, also known as Ellis Peters, is the author of a number of fine historical novels as well as the Brother Cadfael medieval mys-teries. Her novels belong to the type of historical fiction that is expertly and thoroughly researched, conventional in respect to plotting and characteriza-tion, unlike more experimental historical fiction, and distinguished by an extraordinary amount of well-integrated visual and topographical detail,

mostly drawn from the area around Shrewsbury and the Welsh border country, where Pargeter lived for most of her life. The *Brother of Gwynedd
Quartet* and *Heaven Tree Trilogy* have an epic sweep, building from one generation to the next after the fashion of other novel sequences. *A Bloody Field
by Shrewsbury* is unlike either the medieval mysteries or the quartet and trilogy inasmuch as it deals more directly with historical personages and events.
Furthermore, it corresponds almost exactly to the timeline of the Henry IV
plays, with most of its action centering on the events culminating in the confrontation at Shrewsbury and the battle itself. And like many New Historical
Fictions, it challenges the canonical (in this case, Shakespearean) version of
historical events in a way that is both historically convincing and clearly fictional. Regrettably, Pargeter provides no afterword or author's note listing
the historical resources she consulted, but a cursory reading of Peter Saccio's
chapter on the reign of Henry IV in the invaluable *Shakespeare's English Kings*
suggests that she consulted the standard histories of the period.

Pargeter chose Hotspur as the protagonist of her retelling of the Henry
IV story, and she crafts a romantic heroic figure from the material provided
by the historical record. Her most obvious departure from Shakespeare's
plays is to restore Hotspur to his rightful age, two years older than his cousin
Henry Bolingbroke, whose coronation in 1399 is the first event of the novel.
It is not immediately evident that Hotspur is going to emerge as the novel's
protagonist, however, since we observe the coronation from the point of view
of the twelve-year-old Hal, who had been living at Richard II's court when
the deposition occurred.

Indeed, after reading the first chapter of *A Bloody Field by Shrewsbury*,
the experienced reader of historical fiction might conclude that the novel will
chronicle the young Hal's coming of age and emergence as the hero of
Shrewsbury. Just as the Hal of *1 Henry IV* feels estranged from his own
father and has adopted Falstaff as an alternative father figure, so Pargeter's
Hal, we are told, feels very close to the childless King Richard who

> had kept the borrowed boy always about him, lavished gifts on him,
> ridden with him, played with him—when had his real father ever found
> time or inclination to play?—and prophesied great things of him, taking
> such delight in his wisdom and his prowess that the boy grew like a
> nursed sapling during the year Richard had charge of him. (8–9)

This is a very different Richard from Shakespeare's Richard II, as well as a
very different kind of relationship from the more ambiguous and manipulative
friendship with Falstaff that Shakespeare invents for his seemingly older,
more wary Hal. Pargeter's invention serves a couple of purposes: it helps
establish sympathy for the deposed Richard by recasting the contrast between
Richard and Bolinbroke from the perspective of a character with whom we
are encouraged to identify, and it also makes sense of the coolness between

Henry and his eldest son. Pargeter introduces a poignant conflict of loyalties into the depiction of the young man who suddenly finds himself elevated to the position of the Prince of Wales and expected by the adults around him to view his former mentor as an enemy. Richard, however, remains an offstage character and the close relationship Hal recalls is never elaborated upon. From the moment he arrives in London for the coronation, Hal puts his past behind him, and transfers his allegiance and admiration to Hotspur.

Thus the reader's first introduction to Hotspur is through Hal's eyes: as Hal looks around at the lords assembled for the coronation ceremony (a conventional device that enables Pargeter to introduce the major historical figures), his eye alights on Harry Percy. A lengthy physical description follows, culminating in this sentence: "And what filled the boy with a sudden ease and confidence, he [Hotspur] looked upon his work as a man looks who has no doubts at all" (12). Once again we can see the romantic novelist's strategies of characterization at work; having established a strong bond of sympathy between the reader and Hal, in a manner analogous to the way Shakespeare uses Hal's act 1, scene 2 soliloquy to create a sense of intimacy with *his* Hal, Pargeter then transfers that sympathy to Hotspur by means of Hal's intense admiration for the older man. Anticipating his installation as Prince of Wales, Hal fervently hopes that Hotspur will be chosen as the governor who would guide him until he attained "years of discretion" (13). According to Saccio, Hotspur was in fact assigned chief authority in Wales, where Hal progressed within a few years from being the nominal head of the governing council to becoming the king's lieutenant in Wales at age sixteen (47). Thus Hal and Hotspur had the opportunity to develop the close mentor/student relationship Pargeter elaborates on in *A Bloody Field*, though the historical Henry Percy resigned from the position in 1401 to pursue his political interests in northern England.

Commenting on Hal's apprenticeship for the kingship, Saccio remarks drily that

> If there is any truth behind the stories of his youthful profligacy in London that Shakespeare inherited from late Plantagenet and Tudor legend and used in *Henry IV*, Hal must have squeezed a great deal of self-indulgence into his winter trips to the capital. During campaign season he was otherwise occupied. (47)

The sober, self-controlled young Hal of Pargeter's novel is never granted a playful moment in the London taverns or elsewhere; his infrequent appearances in the novel nearly always take place in Chester, where he attends conscientiously to his role as Prince of Wales. In defiance of the legends, which, as Bullough points out, can be traced for the most part to a single source,[2] Pargeter deliberately excludes the young companions, friends, and festivities and trickery that give *1 Henry IV* its distinctive comic quality. Unlike novelists who employ metafictional strategies, Pargeter never mentions Shakespeare, but she is clearly contesting his representation of Hal. She uses strategies analogous to those of the postmodern historical fiction writers who employ counterfactual conjecture to speculate about possible alternate directions history might have taken. Nevertheless, Pargeter's Hal is not totally unlike Shakespeare's; indeed, her "what if?" reworking of his character builds on hints Shakespeare gives the reader in the soliloquy in which Hal reveals the calculated method behind his seeming idleness:

> Yet herein will I imitate the sun,
> Who doth permit the base contagious clouds
> To smother up his beauty from the world,
> That when he please again to be himself,
> Being wanted he may be more wond'red at
> ·
> So when this loose behavior I throw off
> And pay the debt I never promised,
> By how much better than my word I am,
> By so much shall I falsify men's hopes . . . (1.2.196–211)[3]

A Bloody Field by Shrewsbury retains and develops the serious themes Shakespeare explored in *1 Henry IV*. Pargeter writes at length about the political tensions between the Welsh and the English, focusing, like Shakespeare, on the character of Owen Glendower. Glendower is a Robin Hood-like guerilla leader in *A Bloody Field*, who communicates with Hotspur through the novel's principal invented characters: a courageous young Welsh widow named Julian, her father, a merchant and intelligence-gatherer, and the fearless go-between Iago Vaughan, who slips back and forth across the Welsh border with arms, money, and messages. These characters inhabit a subplot that alternates with the scenes at court or among the Northern rebels. They are in many ways typical character types from nineteenth- and early-twentieth-century historical fiction: heroic, dedicated to the cause of Welsh independence (not unlike their counterparts in other historical periods, such as French Resistance fighters or American Revolutionary War patriots), and connected to the principal historical figure through plot complications that keep them in the foreground until the novel's denouement. But because the reader attuned to Shakespeare's pro-English bias expects the Welsh to be dismissed as superstitious and undependable, Pargeter's representation serves as a critical rewriting of Shakespearean history.

As the Queen Elizabeth novels demonstrate, women historical novelists often find ways of insinuating women characters into the largely male history recorded by the male chroniclers, archivists, and historians.

Pargeter's reinvention of the events of 1399 to 1403 enlarges the role of Lady Percy beyond the scenes Shakespeare gave her and introduces an historical figure unmentioned by Shakespeare: Joan of Navarre, who married King Henry shortly before the battle of Shrewsbury. Both women are engagingly drawn-warm, sympathetic, and supportive wives to their careworn husbands. The most prominent female presence in the novel, however, is Julian, whose androgynous name prepares us for the Shakespearean role she will play during the battle, dressed as a boy, rather like Imogen in *Cymbeline*. Her poignant love for Hotspur, who senses her feelings but remains faithful to his wife, gives the novel a romantic cast. Hotspur's tragedy is her tragedy, but it is Hal's as well, for these two young people who meet only briefly in the novel are strangely linked by their devotion to a tragic hero who cannot avoid the inexorable pull of political events that leads to his death on the field of Shrewsbury.

Obviously, a densely written 378-page novel can include many things a 2,500-line play cannot. Pargeter's presentation of the events leading up to the Battle of Shrewsbury can be read as a companion piece to Shakespeare's play because it explains the political pressures in much greater detail. The incident of the Scottish prisoners with which *1 Henry IV* begins, for instance, receives extensive treatment in a 25-page chapter about one-third of the way through the novel. Counseled by the Scots renegade George Dunbar, who had quarreled with Douglas and allied himself with the Percys, Hotspur confronts the Scottish army at Homildon Hill in a strategic battle Pargeter describes at length. The account is reminiscent of a later, more famous Shakespearean battle, the defeat of the French at Agincourt: the disciplined English bowmen wait for the Scottish cavalry to come within range, and then shower arrows down upon them, causing heavy casualties (there is even a reference to "muddy spray" (152), an allusion, perhaps, to the famous mud at Agincourt). Hotspur, impatient with modern strategic warfare, plunges into the combat, "ploughing through the thickest of the struggle with bared sword" (153) and finally takes Douglas prisoner in an heroic confrontation.

Douglas becomes an honored guest in Hotspur's household (a common practice with prisoners of high rank) and a good friend to Hotspur and Lady Percy. When the order for the Scottish prisoners arrives from court some weeks later, there is no direct confrontation between the king and the Percys and no mention of Shakespeare's "popingay" messenger on the battlefield. The historical King Henry was hopelessly in debt to his nobles, and Pargeter's Hotspur fears that in return for the prisoners "he'll give us another bad tally, life-long, never to be redeemed" (166). But he is motivated by more than money. In contrast to his coldly pragmatic father, Northumberland, this very sympathetically drawn Hotspur is fiercely committed to ransoming Mortimer

for Lady Percy's sake (she is Mortimer's sister) and is just as determined to
keep faith with his new found companion, Archie Douglas.

There is an interesting moment in the Homildon chapter in which
Pargeter shifts narrative perspective. King Henry, who has suffered a humiliating military defeat in Wales while Hotspur was defeating the Scots, is
alone in his chamber, "burst[ing] with anger and chagrin, and something else
which he did not or would not recognise for pure hatred." His inner monologue dwells obsessively on Hotspur:

> Too happy Harry, the darling of fortune always, and always so sure of
> the love other men bore him. . . . How was it possible for any man who
> fell within the circle of his radiance to forgive Hotspur for being
> Hotspur? In and out of season he must give off these sparks of personal
> brightness, to dazzle as he had dazzled James of Lusignan, King of
> Cyprus . . . so overblessed a nature must bring a man either to a throne
> or a grave before ever he lived to be old. But I am no such creature, the
> king thought, burning in his own fury and grief, I cannot be thus con-
> stantly outdone and bear not grudge. . . . I will see him come to terms
> and kiss the hand that curbs him. (157–58)

King Henry goes on to reflect on his son Hal's "chill assessment of his
father's achievement and his friend's" (159). In his bitterness he resolves to
"make an adjustment" between himself and Hotspur, through the peremp-
tory letter demanding the Scottish prisoners without recompense, one of
several "outmoded rights" that, according to the Percys, he has revived for
his own profit (166). This embellishment of the historical record questions
the historicity of Shakespeare's corresponding scene; unlike the hot-tem-
pered, even arrogant, Hotspur of the play, Pargeter's Hotspur is justified in
his response.[4]

The interpersonal dynamic of *A Bloody Field* adapts Shakespeare's trian-
gular scheme though it positions the characters differently: the king desperately wants to win his son's approval and seeks to draw his allegiance away
from his rival Hotspur, while Hal remains distant and seemingly unmoved.
It would have been difficult to find a role for Falstaff in this arrangement,
though there is a counterpart to the choice Shakespeare's Hal must make
between the competing claims of princely responsibility and holiday.
Pargeter's Hal chooses his father and duty over the bonds of friendship, and
Hotspur never for a moment expects him to make any other choice. Indeed,
like a protective parent, he tries to keep Hal from the battle at Shrewsbury,
and the final meeting between them (over one hundred pages before the
novel's end) is a poignant moment. Hotspur's last words to the prince sound
a Shakespearean note, particularly in the metaphor of paying dues, which

echoes Hal's vow to "pay the debt I never promised" in the soliloquy quoted earlier:

> "For some of us, I doubt, will stand in great need of advocates before we come to our life's end. By your judgment," he said whole-heartedly, "I will gladly abide, and whatever dues you charge me with, I will pay with a good grace." (252)

Pargeter has Hal remember these words ten years later in the epilogue.

Hotspur's death is the climactic event in *A Bloody Field by Shrewsbury*, just as it is the climactic event of *1 Henry IV*. Saccio, following Bullough and others, observes that "an ambiguous sentence in Holinshed makes it possible to suppose that Hal killed Hotspur," although Hall, Holinshed's source, is not ambiguous on this score and modern historians assume that Hotspur was killed by an unknown combatant (Saccio 51; Bullough 4: 164). Pargeter makes use of this ambiguity to challenge Shakespeare's dramatization of the event, replacing it with an intensely tragic climax that is consistent with her portrayal of the two friends. The buildup to the battle begins with a psychologically convincing revision of Shakespeare's treatment of the parley in act 5, scenes 1 and 2. Pargeter's Worcester says this to Hotspur:

> Me, perhaps, being old, not of his own generation, not fore-fated to go through life stride for stride with him, at every day's beginning a challenge and a gall to him, at every day's end out-shining him, he might forgive. . . . But you—you, Harry, too close, too much praised, too dear to his boy, too gloriously his overmatch, you he cannot now leave live in this world. (332)

Hotspur assures him, "You chose rightly" (332); hence there is no duplicity or betrayal of the younger man by his uncle, an idea Shakespeare inherited from Holinshed and other chroniclers.[5] Pargeter intensifies the tragic conflict by posing Henry and Hotspur against one another in this way, with Hal as the unwitting object of affection for whom the two cousins compete.

Pargeter's battle scenes contain all of the vivid detail we expect from good historical fiction heightened by an ongoing, though never overt, dialogue with Shakespeare. For instance, she uses Shakespeare's "counterfeit" motif in a scene that has Douglas convinced he has killed the king, when in fact he has killed Sir John Calverley. Douglas, disgusted, dismisses the deception as "Dunbar's counsel," as "it was not in Henry's style" to hide in this way (342). In fact, Pargeter assigns to Dunbar an uncomic version of Falstaff's pragmatic antiheroic instinct for self-preservation. Later, Dunbar tries to urge King Henry away from the battlefield, but Henry and the wounded Hal both insist on plunging into the thick of the fighting. The chapter culminates in a strikingly cinematic moment: a single voice cries out

"Henry Percy, king!" and a chorus of others take up the cry, but all the shouting falls away behind Hotspur as he charges forward, then checks his horse abruptly when he sees Hal in his path. As he swings aside to avoid meeting his young friend in battle, Hotspur moves into the sightlines of a nameless archer perched high in a tree.

> The passage of the arrow was like the flight of a bird, a strong vibration of wings and a vehement alighting. It pierced dinted breastplate and fine mail hauberk under, and drove clean into the heart he had deliberately exposed to assault. The sword slipped almost silently out of his relaxing hand, while he still sat erect and immovable, turned away from the combat he would not accept upon any terms. Then slowly, as it seemed, he leaned backwards towards the crupper of his horse, stiffly and solidly as a tree falls, and heeling to the right, perhaps drawn by the mere remaining impulse of the weight of his fallen sword, crashed from his saddle at the prince's feet. (346)

The cry of "Henry Percy, king!" changes to "Henry Percy, slain!" and the camera, as it were, lingers on Prince Hal, not yet sixteen years old, struggling through the crowd "to get back to the fallen hero, weeping like a heartbroken child within the privacy of his helmet, blind and choked with blood and tears" (347).

The powerful Shrewsbury chapters conclude with Hal and Julian meeting by chance when each returns to the dark and deserted battlefield to seek out Hotspur's corpse. As they take up the body together, their shared grief heightens the tragic aura that surrounds Hotspur's death. Julian, in her boy's attire, refuses Hal's offer of a place in his service, and carrying Hotspur's sword as a talisman, walks westward toward Wales. True to the conventions of Shakespearean comedy and historical romance, Pargeter reunites Julian with the daring spy and go-between Iago Vaughan, leaving the reader with the knowledge that love and renewal will eventually come to the brave and devoted heroine.

Taking her cue from Shakespeare, Pargeter passes over the last ten years of Henry's reign and ends the novel with an epilogue dated March 1413. The twenty-five year old Hal who comes to his father's deathbed in the Jerusalem chamber at Westminster is "fully awake to his own powers, and well aware that for some years now the populace had looked to him as king rather than to his father" (375). Unlike his Shakespearean counterpart, who seems arrested in time, still passing idle days in the tavern with Falstaff, Mistress Quickly, and Doll Tearsheet shortly before his father's death, Pargeter's Hal has established his own court at Coldharbour and rules England capably during his father's recurrent bouts of ill health. The king's intermittent recoveries

> meant the prince's relegation to the background, a banishment jealously decreed and coldly accepted, where he amused himself after his own

imperious fashion, asking no man's leave, caring nothing for any man's disapprobation, but always ready to emerge again when the need arose. Need? Or opportunity? Do him justice, he had never shown any sign of impatience with the long duration of his apprenticeship. (376)

This passing reference to the prince's penchant for amusing himself with no care for "any man's disapprobation" may summon up images of the tavern scenes for readers familiar with the plays, though Pargeter very deliberately omits any mention of his companions.

The climax of the epilogue is the final conversation between father and son, which pales in certain respects beside Shakespeare's powerful scene in *2 Henry IV*. Pargeter's fictional strategy is to have the omniscient narrator describe the inner feelings of Henry and Hal: Shakespeare's dramatic strategy, of course, is to have them speak their thoughts. Consider Hal's monologue to the crown and his father's seemingly lifeless body:

> O polish'd perturbation! golden care!
> That keep'st the ports of slumber open wide
> To many a watchful night, sleep with it now!
> Yet not so sound, and half so deeply sweet
> As he whose brow with homely biggen bound
> Snores out the watch of night. O majesty!
> When thou dost pinch thy bearer, thou dost sit
> Like a rich armor worn in heat of day,
> That scalds with safety.
>
> . . . .
> My gracious lord! my father!
> This sleep is sound indeed, this is a sleep
> That from this golden rigol hath divorc'd
> So many English kings. Thy due from me
> Is tears and heavy sorrows of the blood,
> Which nature, love, and filial tenderness
> Shall, O dear father, pay thee plenteously.
> My due from thee is this imperial crown,
> Which as immediate from thy place and blood,
> Derives itself to me.
>
> (4.5.23–43)

Although the crown is present on a cushion between the two men in Pargeter's corresponding scene, it inspires no such passionate declarations. Rather, the king and his son speak warily to one another in short, clipped utterances. King Henry—who, it must be said, emerges as a more complex and interesting character than Shakespeare's king—reflects on his son and their relationship for the last time as follows:

He wasted his time, he knew, for he was speaking to a stern, decisive creature who found a choice everywhere, and took his course fearlessly and ruthlessly, rigid in honour but absolute of will, despising the feeble excuse that there could be any situation in which a man had no choice. . . . He knew well who the two men were who stood invisibly but implacably between his son and himself. And he know, even as his vision began to fail and his son's face to fade, that they were still there, watching him through hazel eyes that burned upon him like two green flames. (377)

The two men, of course, are Hotspur and Richard II. The pity and affection which Hal finally allows himself to feel for his dying father are "Hotspur's gift," he realizes as he remembers Hotspur's words from their parting before Shrewsbury. Shaken out of "his ten year frost" he is finally able to experience "the first spontaneous motion of warmth, and the last" toward his father (377). Perhaps because she does not want to compete with Shakespeare, Pargeter tells us that Hal "found some words of his own to say, unfamiliar, not even completely true . . . " (377), but we must imagine what they are. The scene—and the novel—end with Hal "gently cradling his father's hand" as the king ceases to breathe and, no longer a "stranger to humility," discovering the humility that would sustain him in his own kingship (377).

Any novelist who retraces the history Shakespeare dramatized can assume that the reader's familiarity with Shakespeare's treatment of characters and events will color and complicate the reading experience. Denise Giardina's *Good King Harry*, a fiction biography of Henry V, begins just before the events of Shakespeare's *Richard II*. Henry (called Harry, not Hal) is the narrator. The novel begins as he looks back on his life as he lies dying of a bloody flux, beginning with a childhood incident when he angered his father, an unsympathetically portrayed Bolingbroke, by refusing to joust. Harry is repelled by the violence of his age, preferring a life of study or a ramble in the Welsh hills to warfare and chivalry. Giardina's long and detailed novel invents a tragic romance between him and a Welsh girl named Merryn; otherwise, the characters are drawn from the historical record. The novel's one-dimensional Hotspur is a cruel governor to the Prince of Wales, who knows his young charge "had no taste for a fight." Harry views Hotspur as a man "determined "to break my spirit . . . that I might learn humility" (59). A very un-Shakespearean Falstaff is restored to his original name, Sir John Oldcastle; he is "a short sturdy man . . . [with] a neatly trimmed beard" who is only ten years older than the fourteen-year-old Harry when they meet. Though he shares Harry's distaste for killing and offers to introduce him to the women of Eastcheap, he has none of Falstaff's comic spirit.

In an interview that forms part of the reader's guide appended to the paperback reissue of *Good King Harry*, Giardina explains that Oldcastle is "an actual historical figure whose role in Henry's life was very much as I described." (In fact, Sir John Oldcastle was a Protestant hero and Lollard martyr.) She also says that in her portrayal of Henry V she was "looking for the human, the insecure, the person trying to do what was right but failing miserably" (n.p.) Hence her Henry awaits death knowing that the "God's work" he has done at Agincourt and elsewhere in France was in fact

> ever sin and the same sin from time immemorial. Nothing had come from it save the death of everyone and everything I had loved, and the everlasting fires of Hell would be gentle compared to the knowledge of it. (388)

In general, Giardina says, she used Shakespeare "as a mirror image; in other words, I tried to do a reversal of Shakespeare."

A more thoroughgoing "reversal of Shakespeare" occurs in James Goldman's *Myself as Witness*, an epistolary novel about King John. Shakespeare's play *King John* is clearly influenced by the Robin Hood legends and chronicle history in its portrayal of John as a treacherous and weak monarch overshadowed by the shrewd, witty Bastard, who emerges as the most appealing character in the play. *Myself as Witness* is based, as Goldman remarks in his note to the reader, on revisionary historical accounts that have reassessed the reign of King John; interestingly, his research for the novel caused him to revise his own earlier portrayal of King John in his play *The Lion in Winter* (v–vi). As depicted in the letters of the narrator, the scholar-priest Giraldus Cabriensis, the John of *Myself as Witness* turns out to be a surprisingly sympathetic character, in part because Giraldus's devotion to him shapes our response. Just as the omission of Falstaff enables Pargeter to side-step the legends and chronicle history that inspired the comic scenes in the Henry plays, so the omission of the Bastard helps to make Goldman's John a complex three-dimensional character. Like Hotspur in *A Bloody Field by Shrewsbury*, John is caught in the play of historical forces which eventually leads to a sorrowful death in the midst of a vividly described military action.

These novelists all employ a novelistic realism that gives their principal characters lives that are much more fully developed over time than their dramatic predecessors, whose personalities must necessarily be conveyed in a few brief scenes. Pargeter and Goldman go farther than Giardina in shifting our perspective by realigning the characters and by recovering or accentuating other historical figures (including the wives of the monarchs, John's Isabelle and Henry's Joan, who contribute to the element of romance so pervasive in much historical fiction). The realignment of characters entails a realignment of values as well, particularly in *A Bloody Field by Shrewsbury*. By eliminating Falstaff's dual role as comic anti-father and spokesman for pragmatic survival as opposed to noble self-sacrifice, Pargeter circumvents Shakespeare's contrast between characters who stand for duplicity and dishonor and those who display chivalric heroism. There is no place for a comically subversive scoundrel in Pargeter's created world, where even Glendower is an heroic freedom fighter, and where Hotspur's doomed nobility and Julian's unshakeable loyalty command our unqualified sympathy. As for Hal, the boy-prince who grows into King Henry V, Pargeter provides a satisfying counterpart to Shakespeare's father-son scene in *2 Henry IV*, but her Hal does not need to reject the embodiment of comic misrule and embrace Justice personified in order to prove himself. Rather, as a creation of twentieth-century novelistic psychology, he finds his antagonists within and rises above them to ascend the throne.

A Bloody Field by Shrewsbury* is descended from a popular tradition that begins with the novels of Sir Walter Scott, William Thackeray's *Henry Esmond*, and other nineteenth-century fiction, and continues through the novels of Mary Renault and into our own time. Robert Nye, on the other hand, writes the kind of nonlinear, satiric narrative, heavy with arcane information and seeming irrelevancies, that is reminiscent of Lawrence Sterne's *Tristram Shandy* or the works of James Joyce and Anthony Burgess. In his award-winning *Falstaff*, Nye employs a form that he uses again in *The Late Mr. Shakespeare*; his book is divided into one hundred short chapters, each numbered with a Roman numeral, dated like a diary entry, and nearly always marked by a sentence-long title that begins with "About . . ." or "How . . . ." In contrast to *A Bloody Field by Shrewsbury*, whose plot follows a traditional arc from Henry IV's coronation to his son's, Nye's often disconnected chapters seem to be the stream-of-consciousness ramblings of a self-indulgent writer. Falstaff's encyclopedic knowledge, his inability to resist the lure of an interruption or a digression, and his preoccupation with his own body invite comparison with sixteenth- and seventeenth-century texts like Robert Burton's *Anatomy of Melancholy*, Montaigne's *Essays*, or Pepys's *Diary*. While Pargeter employs a wise, perceptive, inconspicuous third-person omniscient narrator, periodically adopting the perspective of one character or another, Nye invents an outrageous speaker dictating his memoirs to a series of secretaries, whom he delights in insulting and shocking (rather like Frederick Buechner's irreverent Saint Godric in *Godric*).

To perpetuate the illusion of a spoken text, Nye's Falstaff also addresses the reader alternatively as "Sir," "Madam," or "Reader" (*The Late Mr. Shakespeare* also uses this narrative device), and occasionally interrupts himself to speak to Clio, the muse of history, whom he envisions as a strumpet, much like the women who people his sexual reminiscences. Along with other invented characters in the novel, these young women all have Shakespearean names, and it is startling, to say the least, to encounter a pet rat named

Desdemona and explicit sex scenes in which Ophelia and Miranda are lusty participants. The hodgepodge of Elizabethan lore, drawings and diagrams, lists, and menus mingles with verbal quibbles such as the meditation on honor in which Nye recasts the famous speech from *1 Henry IV* act 5, scene 1, lines 127–41 as a dialogue between Falstaff and Hal's brother, Thomas Duke of Clarence. During the course of this dialogue, Falstaff diverts himself by substituting "the richer and lovelier word ONION" for "honor" in his mind as Thomas talks on:

> Your ONION, now, is the emblem of chivalry—ONIONS are what chivalry achieves. . . . The ancient Romans knew all there is to know about ONIONS. . . . Jealous in ONIONS, sudden and quick in quarrel. . . . ONION, high ONION, and renown. . . . Have you not set my ONION at the stake? (241)

Falstaff continues in this vein, paraphrasing from Shakespeare's plays with wild abandon.

Falstaff also offers up metafictional commentaries on the text he is narrating, as, for instance, when he says, "[a]llow me to indulge myself in one of the little incidental pleasures of authorship. Namely, *forgetting* a character" (255). In a more interesting metafictional aside, Falstaff proclaims that

> My belly gives me licence to give imaginative body to what is essentially sparse, even skeletal material: memories, biographies, jokes, histories, conversations, letters, images, fragments. I make patterns of my fragments. This book is the pattern I am making. But I give you also the fragments . . . so that you, the reader, are free to put upon them *your* pattern, or simply to find within them or beyond them another pattern, other patterns, an infinite series of possibilities. (159–60)

This disclaimer of the author's authority is deliberately and satirically postmodern, as is the long paragraph that sets forth an analogue between Falstaff's "Acta," as he titles his memoirs, and the construction of Chartres Cathedral, which is followed by the wry comment:

> Does this old reprobate seek to justify his obscenities by comparing them to Chartres Cathedral? I hope that he does not. I hope you do not think I do. I mean only to suggest that there are truths and parallels and correspondences in the world, which masons who made Chartres knew about. . . . And that there are other truths and parallels and correspondences in a man's life . . . which I trust to place before you in *this* book.
> I juxtapose fact and fiction. . . .
> So when you allow me my mortar and bonding, my corbels and capping stones, my gablets and jambs and quoins . . . *will you permit me*

also my most necessary gargoyles? Only inferior masons suppose your gargoyle to be a detail. Sometimes the gargoyle is the point. (171)

Falstaff's verbal flourishes begin on the title page, which announces what is to follow at great length and in elegant script: "Being the *Acta domini Johannis Falstolfe*, or *Life and Valiant Deeds of Sir John Faustoff . . . ,*" complete with the names of the seven secretaries to whom he "told" his deeds, and crediting the transcribing and editing in modern spelling to Robert Nye. It is followed by an inscription familiar to Shakespeareans:

> TO. THE. ONLIE. BEGETTER. OF
> THESE. ENSUING. FICTIONS.
> MR. GILES GORDON

and so forth, in mimicry of the much-debated dedication of the sonnets. Just as Burgess does, Nye calls attention to erratic spelling; in his second chapter, he lists sixty-nine variants of the name Falstaff, adding, "[t]hey are all of them right, every one" (11). Falstaff claims to have a family tree "somewhat superior to the shrub Plantagenet" and traces his ancestry to a Fastolf in the *Domesday Book*, who fought at the Battle of Hastings (8). He is more immediately descended from the Fastolfs of Norfolk whose ancestral home was Caister Castle (12–13), where he is dictating his memoirs in the year 1459 (367). Nye is presumably thinking of the Sir John Fastolf who demonstrated his cowardice by fleeing before Rouen (Shakespeare included him in *1 Henry VI* 3.2.104ff).[6] Like his historical counterpart, who died of a fever at age eighty or more (Bullough 4:171), Nye's Falstaff lives on into Henry VI's reign. He is also present at the battle of Agincourt, which he describes in some detail, and where, unbeknownst to Henry V, he leads a rearguard action that consists of pelting the French with the baggage (374–75); this, of course, is a revision of a scene from *Henry V*, in which the French defy the law of arms by "kill[ing] the boys and the luggage," in Fluellen's words. (4.7.1)

Following *Tristram Shandy* and other purportedly autobiographical novels, Falstaff begins his memoir with a fanciful account of his birth and descriptions of his parents, overshadowed somewhat by a detailed menu of the baptismal feast. The chapter begins: "I was born at three o'clock in the afternoon, with a white head and something of a round belly" (14; cf. *2 Henry IV* 1.2.187–89). This is typical of the many unacknowledged quotations from the plays. Nye, like Burgess, expects the reader to recognize the quotations and allusions, most of which blend imperceptibly with Falstaff's eclectic diction.

Apart from a brief description of Falstaff's first encounter with Hal and his three brothers in chapter 26, there are few references to the events of the Henry IV plays until over halfway through the novel. In his more serious moments Nye gives the reader a fine description of fourteenth-century London and a powerful chapter on the Black Death filled with vivid detail, including a catalogue of the herbs Falstaff's mother burned to ward off infection (36). Such chapters are infrequent, however, for Falstaff's accounts of his early years consist mostly of sexual and martial adventures, drinking and carousing. Finally, at page 250, the novel arrives at the point corresponding to act 1, scene 2 of *1 Henry IV*. A one-page chapter that begins with what appears to be a quotation from the historical record describes Hal thus:

> *He was in the days of his youth a diligent follower of idle practices, much given to instruments of music, and one who, loosing the reins of modesty, though zealously serving Mars, yet fired with the torches of Venus herself, and, in the intervals of his brave deeds as a soldier, wont to occupy himself with the other extravagances that attend the days of undisciplined youth.*
>
> Worcester's translated that for me. It's from the *Gesta Henrici Quinti*. . . .[7]
>
> I throw in this bit of authentic History from a disinterested but well-instructed source, just to prepare you for the high jinks which must follow. Without it, you might not believe me.
>
> I put it in also to introduce HAL in the days when he *was* HAL.
>
> My diligent follower of idle practices.
>
> My undisciplined youth.
>
> My mad lad, sweet lad, more comparative, rascalliest, sweet young prince, mad wag, the young prince that misled me. (250)

Several of the subsequent chapters are expanded paraphrases of the Hal-Falstaff scenes in *1 Henry IV*, including a very funny sequence of three versions of "How the Battle of Gadshill was won," each more exaggerated than the last (259–64). These accounts serve as the occasion for some metahistorical observations that slyly undermine the notion that authentic history exists. Falstaff begins the next chapter with a disquisition on the unreliability of historians, who are not to be believed, since they can't accept the idea that "truth is various" (265).

Falstaff's cynicism about war as chronicled by historians runs through the novel; early on, for instance, he looks ahead to the Battle of Agincourt and comments to the reader:

> Agincourt, as you shall come to learn from one who fought there, was not the clearcut nonsense imagined by a generation of armchair soldiers since. It was random, bizarre, bloody, absurd. It was a parcel of chaos imperfectly given shape by its survivors, who looked back on the events of the day, counted the dead, and said: 'We won this: you lost that. I'm still alive—so I am victor.' (68)

There is an interesting convergence between Falstaff's debunking of the heroism associated with war and much Shakespeare criticism of the last two or three decades, which displaces the heroic Henry of Agincourt in preference for a much darker reading of the play as a critique of political opportunism.

As the old Falstaff looks back on the events of 1403, both his affection for and resentment of Hal color his narrative. In the chapters that correspond to the second tavern scene (2.4) Nye appropriates much of Shakespeare's language, but because the scene is recast from Falstaff's point of view we lose the multiple perspectives of drama. Nevertheless, it is impossible to read *this* account without thinking of the original, which gives it a satiric edge. Falstaff, in reviewing his behavior in the tavern scene, insists that his boldfaced lies were intended to *"put an end to the joke without him losing face"*:

> Was it for me to kill the heir-apparent?
> Was it for me to destroy the lad's confidence?
> Of course not. And I ran the faster away (in good order) the better not to kill him, or to tamper with his confidence. For, as you know, Madam, I am a man of instinct, and here I was, a lion, in the presence of a true prince. (267)

Does Nye's Falstaff believe this? Does he expect us to? With only his voice telling the tale, it is difficult to know.

The following chapter culminates, just as act 2, scene 4 does, with Falstaff's heartfelt speech "If sack and sugar be a fault, God help the wicked . . . Banish plump Jack, and banish all the world." As the sheriff knocks on the door and confusion ensues,

> there was a moment when Hal and I stayed looking at each other, kept on gazing steadily at each other, and that eagle in his eyes was suddenly as cold as death, and I was the only person in the Boar's Head tavern who heard him say, the future King of England, Henry the 5th:
> *I do. I will.* (272–73)

This, I have always felt, is the most arresting moment in the play, and Nye does it justice, in a description that sounds almost like an extended, un-Shakespeare-like stage direction. Equally poignant are the hypnotic rhythms of his treatment of the actual banishment at the end of *2 Henry IV:*

> 'God save your grace!' I cried. 'King Hal! My royal Hal!'
> For a terrible moment, it crossed my mind that he was not even going to draw rein. He was mounted on a great black horse, which struck horribly at the rush-strewn cobbles already an inch deep in snow, and as I say it seemed for a second that he had every intention of letting that horse trot on, and buffet me, and strike me down, and ride right over me.

But no. Black gloves moved on those reins, and shortened them. He stopped.

'God save you, my sweet boy!' I cried.

King Henry the 5th did not look at me. He turned round in his saddle and addressed Gascoigne.

'My Lord Chief Justice,' he said, 'speak to that vain man.' . . .

I snatched at the King's foot.

'My King!' I cried. 'My Jove!'

The King, that Jove, quite deliberately moved his boot through the stirrup so that the spur dug into my hand. . . .

I said, 'Harry.'

I said, 'I speak to you, my heart.'

King Henry the 5th lowered his gaze. He consented to look at me. He saw.

What did those cold eyes see? What did those King's eyes find before them in the London Street?

A fat man.

Standing.

Bleeding.

In the snow.

The King's lips moved. King Henry the 5th spoke:

'I know you not, old man,' he said. 'Fall to your prayers.' (327–28)

Nye adapts Henry's twenty-five line speech in *2 Henry IV*, making Henry a harsher, more one-dimensional character than Shakespeare's young king. Falstaff's bleeding hand adds pathos to the scene, as does the narrative style, but the somber mood does not last long; two pages later, the irrepressible Falstaff is his old self again, chronicling his marriage to Millicent, mother of Stephen Scrope, who is one of his secretaries.

Postmodern historical fictions are often disrupted by narrative interventions that provide a counterpoint to and sometimes undermine the authority of the primary narrative persona. Stephen Scrope performs this role in *Falstaff*, inserting "Notes" into his stepfather's "Acta" seven times in the latter part of the novel. The notes are suffused with Scrope's hatred for Falstaff, an understandable emotion, considering the contemptuous remarks Falstaff makes about his stepson to the other scribes. The first of these notes, chapter 78 begins thus:

Scrope writes this.

N.B.: Not him saying 'Scrope writes this.'

He is saying something else altogether. He is boasting about some pilgrimage he claims to have made to the Holy Land with his man 'Bardolph.'

Lies!
I do no write that.
I do not write lies.
I do not write Fastolf.
These dolls, these pawns, these puppets—they do what he tells them. They write what he tells them. Worcester & Hanson & Nanton & Bussard and even (may God forgive him) Friar John Brackley.
They write him.
I write me.
I write Scrope. (337)

Scrope vows to "kill" Falstaff's lies, since he cannot kill Falstaff himself, and ends his chapter calling Falstaff "the devil himself" and "King Liar" (338), in a startling pun on "King Lear."

The second note explains how Falstaff did not, in fact, die of a broken heart not long afterward as described by Mistress Quickly in *Henry V*, in what seems to be a continuation of the outburst on lies. Scrope reports that he met Falstaff on the road after hearing of his death, only to find that his stepfather "had staged some kind of death to escape from his creditors." He goes on to say that "I would cut off my hand rather than let it write down a word of his filth," and that Falstaff is a "made-up man" (how true!), a monster who "uses words I never heard on any living tongue." One of these words, ironically, is "potatoes": "What are these 'potatoes'? I never heard this word. Does it represent some infernal magic?" After another diatribe on the submissiveness of the other secretaries, he insists: "*There are no such things in this world as potatoes*" (350–51). In chapter 96, an inventory of Caister Castle, one of several inventories in the novel, Scrope also expresses his disbelief in the existence of Falstaff's favorite drink, sack. "(What is 'Sack'? It is like his 'potatoes.' It doesn't exist)" (422). Evidently Scrope has led a sheltered life. Through this bit of verbal folly, Nye calls into question the accuracy of recorded histories; who knows how often a chronicler who hasn't heard of something simply refuses to believe it exists?

Scrope's sixth document, "The Last Will & Testament of Sir John Fastolf" (chapter 98), has a footnote indicating that the original draft, in the hand of Worcester (one of the compliant scribes) has been revised by Scrope, who is responsible for the added passages in brackets and the words that are crossed out. So, for instance, Scrope changes "executors" to "executor," preceded by the word "sole," and adds phrases like "at the discretion of my executor, my well-loved stepson and good-doer Stephen Scrope" (441), thus changing the will significantly. He also erases Falstaff's speaking voice at times by substituting "Helen" for "Nell," "Dorothy" for "Doll," and "great King . . . his Majesty King Henry the 5th" for "sweet prince . . . my royal Hal" (443). Just as so many of the Shakespeare and Marlowe novels contain a mocking commentary on biographical speculation, so this doctored will serves as a reminder of the intense scrutiny Shakespeare's will has received at the hands of scholars.

The penultimate chapter offers still a third perspective on Falstaff, for it consists of the old man's notes for his dying confession to Friar Brackley. In these fragments he confesses to the many lies with which he filled his "Acta": "Lies about my whole life. But try & explain: some *true* lies?" He goes on to say: "Father, I am a vain man, and conceited, and all through these memoirs I have sought, however curiously, the admiration of my secretaries and whoever should one day cast his eye upon them" (447). This disclaimer is in some ways analogous to Chaucer's retraction at the end of *The Canterbury Tales*, asking the reader for forgiveness and retracting his sinful books and translations and his lecherous lays. As he acknowledges his faults and asks for penance and absolution, Nye's Falstaff proclaims his "Acta" to be an invention motivated by his "unconquerable pride" (447). By withholding this confession until the very end, Nye engages in the postmodern strategy of disorienting the reader, who has come to believe in Falstaff as a character who deceives himself with his exaggerations.

And so the mock autobiography of a fictional character who only exists for a few scattered days throughout four of Shakespeare's plays turns out not to be a biography at all, but a monstrous imposition, a 450-page riff on the propensity for exaggeration, invention, and wishful thinking which has made Falstaff such an appealing and appalling character. There is no place for this Falstaff in Pargeter's fictional world, just as there is no place for Pargeter's doomed, heroic Hotspur in Nye's. Different as the two novels are, it is noteworthy that neither gives Prince Hal a particularly large or interesting role. In this respect, Pargeter and Nye seem to agree; the prince and his historical predecessor have less to offer the historical novelist than other characters, real and invented, who participated in the events Shakespeare chronicled in the Henriad.

A Bloody Field by Shrewsbury and *Falstaff* tell still another story about the genre of historical fiction in the last quarter of the twentieth century. Both Pargeter and Nye continued to write through the 1980s and 1990s. Pargeter devoted herself to the Brother Caedfel mysteries, which sold widely and became the basis for a popular public television series; they may well have inspired other historical mystery series with nuns, physicians, and scholars as amateur detectives. Although she wrote over forty novels, she never revisited Shakespearean history in the way that *A Bloody Field by Shrewsbury* does. Nye continues to write in a number of genres.[8] His novels of Shakespeare's England include *The Voyage of the "Destiny," The Late Mr. Shakespeare* (discussed in chapter 2), and *Mrs. Shakespeare: The Complete Works*, which first appeared in 1993 and was reissued in 2000, no doubt as a result of the success of *The Late Mr. Shakespeare*. The similarities among the narrating voices of Pickleherring, Falstaff, and Anne Hathaway suggest that Nye, rather like Pargeter, developed an effective fictional strategy and returned to it. As is the case in other fictional genres, the allure of the successful formula proved irresistible. With very few exceptions, serious historical fiction does not sell on the scale of popular formula fiction, but this may change, as the authors of the New Historical Fiction become increasingly adept at appealing to our fascination with the past.

Chapter 7

Teaching Shakespeare's England through Historical Fiction

*T*he previous chapters have demonstrated, I hope, that writers of historical fiction are inspired to construct and furnish past worlds by a desire to participate in the ongoing revision of what we call "history." Similarly, the reader's desire to recover and learn about other times and other places has contributed to the popularity of this frequently overlooked genre. Where but in a historical novel could one read so pleasantly and concisely of the transnational economy behind the British tea-drinking ritual, as in this virtuoso sentence by A. S. Byatt?

> This too was a miracle, that gold-skinned persons in China and bronze-skinned persons in India should gather leaves which should come across the seas safely in white-winged ships, encased in lead, encased in wood, surviving storms and whirlwinds, sailing on under hot sun and cold moon, and come here, and be poured from bone-china, made from fine clay, moulded by clever fingers, in the Pottery Towns, baked in kilns, glazed with slippery shiny clay, baked again, painted with rosebuds by artist-hands holding fine, fine brushes, delicately turning the potter's wheel and implanting, with a kiss of sable-hairs, floating buds on an azure ground, or a dead white ground, and that sugar should be fetched

from where black men and women slaved and died terribly to make these delicate flowers that melted on the tongue. . . . (*Angels and Insects* 333)

There is clearly a political message contained within the elaborate detail of this reverie experienced by a nineteenth-century British woman pouring tea; although the woman may not be aware of it, the reader is.

Susan Suleiman's discussion of the *roman a these*, or ideological novel, proposes a classification of genres based on where a given genre falls on the continuum between the practical or didactic function and the aesthetic. Suleiman was drawn to the ideological novel because of the dialectic or tension between "message" and "spectacle," "communication" and "poetry" (19–22).[1] The same dialectic, surely, is present in historical fiction. Whether or not the novelist will admit to such an intent, an historical novel "teaches" history, and does so with more attention to the values, superstitions, workaday life, pastimes, and material culture of a particular time and place than most textbooks do. How then can historical fiction serve as an alternative or supplement to textbooks and other pedagogical resources for those of us who try to teach the past to students whose lives are rooted very much in the present?

Teachers of Shakespeare face the special challenge of helping students negotiate what one high school teacher calls "the ubiquitous language barrier" between Shakespeare's time and ours (Simmons 281). Unfamiliar language is the most immediate manifestation of Shakespeare's "otherness," an otherness that remains part of the experience of the plays no matter how they are taught. The many annotated editions on the market make a concerted effort to render Shakespeare accessible; they provide general introductions, appendices, and extensive marginal notes translating difficult or obsolete words and phrases and explaining topical allusions, puns and slang, and so forth. But these editions require a disjunctive method of reading, for the notes are of little use unless the reader constantly moves back and forth between text and gloss, sorting out the useful information from the superfluous. Student readers often become increasingly self-conscious about what they cannot understand without assistance and find it hard to maintain continuity within a dialogue or scene. Not surprisingly, the annotations often frustrate them by providing explanations that assume knowledge they do not have.

Consider, for example, the prophecy delivered by Lear's Fool, an admittedly difficult speech, and the footnotes provided by the *Riverside Shakespeare*, one of the most frequently used student editions in college Shakespeare courses.

> When priests are more in word than matter;
> When brewers mar their malt with water;

When nobles are their tailors' tutors;
No heretics burn'd but wenches' suitors;
Then shall the realm of Albion
Come to great confusion.
When every case in law is right;
No squire in debt, nor no poor knight;
When slanders do not live in tongues;
Nor cutpurses come not to throngs;
When usurers tell their gold i' th' field,
And bawds and whores do churches build;
Then comes the time, who lives to see't,
That going shall be us'd with feet. (3.2.81–94)

The Riverside editors chose to quote William Warburton's eighteenth-century gloss of the speech as "a satirical description of the present manners as future" followed by "future manners which the corruption of the present would prevent from ever happening," culminating in the explanation that "the whole is a parody of a pseudo-Chaucerian 'Merlin's prophecy'" (Evans 1275). The student reader, however, may be more intent on decoding words like "Albion," "bawd," or "cutpurse," or phrases like "come not to throngs," or the meanings of the word "tell" in the phrase "tell their gold," none of which are addressed in the marginal notes. To move from the level of language to historical context, students would also benefit from knowing about the burning of heretics, the tensions between Protestant preachers and Catholic priests, and the spending habits of squires and knights.

Teachers do their best to help students through speeches like this one, but there is never enough time to anticipate and answer all of the questions that might arise. A response to this dilemma presented itself to me when I was teaching a course on historical fiction set in medieval and early modern England. In the end-of-term written evaluations, some of my undergraduate students commented that they now felt ready to "tackle" Shakespeare after the experience of reading hundreds and hundreds of pages of fiction that had immersed them in the history, the culture, the language and idioms of the past. As one student observed, "You wouldn't have to look down at the footnotes for the meaning of a word like 'codpiece.'" It occurred to me that if I were to begin a course devoted to Shakespeare with a well-chosen historical novel, I could draw my students into the period and acclimate them to aspects of its language, geography, clothing, character types, and eminent historical figures before we embarked on an annotated Shakespeare play.

Accordingly, I decided to begin my Shakespeare course the following semester by assigning Finney's *Firedrake's Eye*. Without seeming to do so, *Firedrake's Eye* could convey in advance some of the "information" an annotated edition is designed to provide—but in a more effective and enjoyable way, because it would offer a less piecemeal, more vivid and visually evocative exposure to Shakespeare's world. Finney does a particularly good job of helping readers come to terms with the otherness of the past by providing a glossary of Elizabethan terms and thieves' cant, an alphabetical "cast list" that distinguishes historical from fictional characters and gives brief identifications, and a remarkably informative three-page historical note. Unlike footnotes, these resources can be consulted at any point in the reading process.

The strategy of using modern fiction in literary history courses isn't new; for example, courses on the Victorian period have been known to include such works as Graham Swift's *Waterlands*, John Fowles's *The French Lieutenant's Woman*, and A. S. Byatt's *Possession*. In each case, the historical fiction helps construct a world by gradually and repetitively immersing the reader in conversational styles, thought patterns, landscapes, and that residue of miscellaneous details and allusions that constitute the culture of a particular time and place. A good film can accomplish some of this, but in a much more visual way, without giving students the same opportunity to build vocabulary and see idiomatic language in written form.

Knowing that I would have time for only one novel in a thirteen-week Shakespeare course, I selected *Firedrake's Eye* partly because it is a fast-moving, well-written, sophisticated novel, partly because it is especially good at creating a sense of what it was like to live in Elizabethan London, and partly because of the connection between the novel's narrator and Edgar's "Poor Tom" disguise in *King Lear*. I hoped that my students would emerge from their reading with the same vivid sense of Shakespeare's England that one of the students in the historical fiction course described on her final essay:

> To my delicate sensibilities, the descriptions of everyday physical discomfort and (lack of) hygiene were most memorable and helpful in forging a realistic picture of life in Elizabethan times with its sights, smells and feelings. Descriptions of unwashed, flea-bitten bodies and greasy clothing, and of cold damp weather (I could go on) made for an incredibly authentic, almost smellable and touchable world in *Firedrake's Eye*.

She added: "I've become fairly well-versed in some Elizabethan language at this point: for instance, I've no problem with words like 'jakes,' or 'stews' or 'hinds.'"

Reading this essay, I thought of act 2, scene 1 of *1 Henry IV*, a scene most students find difficult because of the unfamiliar colloquialisms the carriers use to complain about "the most villainous house in all London road for fleas," where one gets "stung like a tench" since "they allow us ne'er a jordan, and then we leak in your chimney, and your chamber lye breeds fleas like a loach." While a reader of *Firedrake's Eye* might not know all of these words ("tench" and "loach" are used only once in the Shakespeare canon) the gist of the passage would be more accessible after a few weeks' immersion in Finney's "almost smellable and touchable world." *Firedrake's Eye* also help students make sense of other, less pungent details in Shakespeare's plays; for example, Becket's friend Eliza provides him with clean linen sold to her by thieves who, like the conscripts in *1 Henry IV*, find linen on every hedge.

Like many novelists who set their fictions in Shakespeare's lifetime, Finney incorporates Shakespearean elements and themes in *Firedrake's Eye* without explicitly mentioning Shakespeare. Using the Throgmorton Plot as her starting point, she evokes the horror the Elizabethans felt at the prospect of a deposed monarch and foreign invasion, the heroic valor of loyal subjects who risked their lives to protect the queen, and the way villainous ambition and religious controversy divide families and lead to plotting, betrayals, and changes of identity. All of this would have been utterly familiar to original audiences of *1 Henry IV* or *King Lear*, as would the character type of the Bedlam beggar. Finney's Tom explains how he came to be an inmate in Bedlam, from which "hell" he escaped with Becket's assistance:

> I was a gentleman once and heir to lands and some wealth and good kin, as indeed was Becket also though not heir to any lands being a younger son. . . . Yet I could find no ease for the pain in those thoughts, so took a nail and scratched my arms with it, to let out the pain and the fumes in my blood. (212)

Compare this with Edgar's soliloquy in *King Lear*, in which he describes Bedlam beggars "who, with roaring voices, / Strike in their numb'd and mortified arms / Pins, wooden pricks, nails, sprigs of rosemary . . . " (2.3. 14–16). Shakespeare's description of self-mutilation is more vivid, but it doesn't explain *why* the insane mortify themselves. Finney does, and instructs her readers on the differences between older and younger sons in the process, but without calling attention to the fact, as a note would do. Some twenty pages later in *Firedrake's Eye*, Poor Tom describes himself as "a scrawny jumping bundle of sticks wrapped in tawny velvet, a creature with his hair and beard in elflocks and blood streaking his tattered arms and hands where he had scratched them with a nail" (231). The image of the arms scratched with a nail is reiterated, since it is the most striking detail in the portrait of the madman, but now other elements are added, again adapting Shakespeare's language (see *King Lear*: "My face I'll grime with filth . . . elf all my hair in knots . . ." [2.3. 9–10]). Shakespeare's Poor Tom is not, of course, a character in the same sense that the Fool or Cordelia are. Finney alludes to both the disguise motif in *King Lear* and to the practices of beggars and thieves in Elizabethan London when she has Simon Ames ask Tom if his madness is counterfeited, if he is "one of those who coneycatch by feigning lunacy." Tom replies, "I am not mad, it is the world and men like you that are mad and blind both, being

unable to see Tom's angels . . ." (32). These angels (like the devils that
oppose them, morality play style) are visible to Tom and help him detect and
oppose the evil around him. The visionary madness Tom exhibits thus bears
the same relationship to the world's madness and blindness as the Fool's folly
bears to Lear's folly.

In one of Tom's most powerful descriptive passages in *Firedrake's
Eye*, Finney sums up the uncertainties and treacheries of Elizabethan
court life, the subject of Raleigh's poem "The Lie" and so many other
texts of the period:

> But the Court . . . Her Majesty has built it into a reflection of her-
> self, a brilliantly coloured, never-still maze, cast around and about and
> set by the ear by this whim and that, this faction and that, but somehow
> keeping a steady purpose and a steady beat about the bejewelled small
> woman at the heart of it, Queen Elizabeth.
>
> I served her before strangeness overcame me, like hundreds of other
> young men, and I was none so bad at dancing and my new tawny velvet
> suit matched well with my chestnut hair. Twice she smiled upon me and
> gave me her hand to kiss and cast the glamour of her beauty on me. But
> it was not that which sent me mad, for all the sonnets I wrote protesting
> that it was, only the falsity of the Court itself. It was lie built upon lie
> but powdered and prinked to seem like a greater truth, artfully conceived
> by the Queen to entertain restless men. It seemed all to be a dream, with
> its lurid clash of silks and velvets and jewels and ruffs all in ceaseless
> motion through the stench of shit and piss, until it was so bad the
> Queen went upon her progress while her palaces were cleaned. It was a
> dream full of Arcadian poetry, but with no firm ground underfoot, as if
> the floor were of marchpane and sugar plate and wet comfits, and so I
> lost my footing and fell through. (60–61)

This description of the court resists and subverts the romanticizing of
"Merrie England" so commonplace in many old historical fictions; indeed,
it paints a darker picture of Elizabeth's court than any of the historical fictions discussed in chapter 5. The passage also taught me something I had
never realized before, after years of reading about the sixteenth and seventeenth centuries—that one practical purpose of the queen's progresses, or
extended trips around the country, was to allow for an annual cleaning of
her London residences.

The elaborate plot of *Firedrake's Eye* is driven by the ballad, "Tom
O'Bedlam's Song," which Finney reprints in its entirety at the beginning of
the novel and then uses in very ingenious ways as a source of clues. A pedlar
and ballad singer, inspired perhaps by Autolycus in *The Winter's Tale*, is a
recurring shadowy presence, demonstrating to the reader how effectively ballads served as a source of information and a form of communication in the

sixteenth century. Falstaff's threat to Hal when left horseless during the rob-
bery scene—"And I have not ballads made of you all and sung to filthy tunes,
let a cup of sack be my poison" (*1 Henry IV*, 2.2.44–46)—makes more sense
after reading *Firedrake's Eye*.

The difficult syntax of Falstaff's characteristically Shakespearean sentence would also make more sense to students steeped in Finney's adaptations of Elizabethan locutions. "I cannot think it is the French we need to
fear," a member of Walsingham's staff tells Simon Ames as they close in on
Throgmorton (54), in an utterance reminiscent of Hotspur's line "It cannot
choose but be a noble plot" (*1 Henry IV*, 1.3.279). This same character says
scornfully of Becket, "No doubt of it but the man is an English scholar, all
sword and buckler play and none of your Italian pig-stickers," to which Ames
replies, "he gives not a fig for styles English, Italian or Spanish . . ." (55–56).
The placement of the words "not" and "but" in these examples is a source of
confusion for students reading Falstaff's and Hotspur's lines for the first
time, as is the word "your" in the phrases "your chimney" and "your cham-
ber-lye" quoted earlier from *1 Henry IV*. Eventually first readers of Shakespeare will become accustomed to such usages, just as they will become
familiar with expressions like "give not a fig." But the challenge of sorting
out the characters, following the plot, adjusting to the stage directions (and
lack thereof), figuring out who is speaking to whom, mentally rearranging
poetic word inversions, and consulting the notes, all at once, can make the
reading process far less enjoyable than we, as teachers, would like it to be.
While the experience of reading an historical fiction like *Firedrake's Eye* would
hardly resolve all of these difficulties, it provides a 250-page mix of modern
narrative strategies and modified Elizabethan syntax and vocabulary, along
with a wealth of description, upon which to build once the class moves on to
1 Henry IV and *King Lear*.

In a Shakespeare course such as the one I have been describing one
could certainly experiment with novels other than *Firedrake's Eye*. *Nicholas
Cooke: Actor, Soldier, Physician, Priest* by Stephanie Cowell, for example,
seems deliberately designed to teach students about Shakespeare's career and
surroundings by including in Nicholas's first-person narrative much of what
many teachers try to incorporate into their "background lectures." In the
space of thirty pages at the beginning of the novel, we get an effective one-
sentence account of the Reformation and the repression of Catholicism, followed almost immediately by a glimpse of the classical education boys
received in the 1590s contrasted with the life of a boy apprentice, an account
of a troupe of traveling players performing *Tamburlaine*, descriptions of the
booksellers at St. Paul's and of the boy actors at Blackfriars performing
Endymion. All of this is told from the perspective of the thirteen-year-old
protagonist-narrator, who leaves his home in Canterbury and goes to
London early in the novel. Nicholas becomes the protégé of Marlowe, called

Morley, and then of Shakespeare, called Shagspere (in each case the spelling change "allow[s] his depiction as a person and not as a literary deity," the author explains in her historical notes) [438]). The novel takes Nicholas from his boyhood to an apprenticeship with John Heminges as a boy actor with the Lord Chamberlain's Men and onward through twenty-odd years of adventures and career changes, in the process introducing readers to many of the major events of Shakespeare's lifetime. For instance, Cowell's vivid descriptions of the plague, which claims the life of Nicholas's son and spurs his interest in medicine, would give students a different perspective, I suspect, on the frequently invoked curse, "A plague upon _____."

While Cowell's characterization of Shagspere (influenced, she says in an interview in *Shakespeare Newsletter*, by her correspondence with A. L. Rowse) may raise eyebrows among scholars who no longer draw inferences from the infamous bequest of the second-best bed or put much stock in other traditional biographical constructions, the novel's strengths as a panoramic portrait of Elizabethan London and the Irish Wars outweigh its deficiencies. Easier to read and follow than *Firedrake's Eye* (although considerably longer), it offers students an introduction to Elizabethan diction; as Cowell remarks in the interview, after talking about the years of research that went into writing the novel, "the cadences of the language are very much with me, between reading the Book of Common Prayer and Shakespeare and all those things . . . I wanted to get the feeling of Elizabethan speech, and yet on the other hand, I wanted people to know what I was talking about" (29).

Nicholas Cooke's story continues in *The Physician of London*, the second part of a projected trilogy, according to the title page. Cowell deals with less familiar aspects of Shakespeare's England in this novel, as Nicholas embarks on a project to design a successful microscope and meets William Harvey, who invites him to join a society for scientific thought, an invented precursor of the Royal Society. Nicholas also becomes involved in the complex political events that lead to the English Civil War as the novel traverses the period from 1617 to 1645 in the course of its four hundred pages. The principal historical character, Thomas Wentworth, Lord Strafford, becomes a close friend to Nicholas, and his execution in 1641 is the novel's climactic event. Cowell ends with detailed historical notes acknowledging "an enormous simplification of the politics of the period" and providing character profiles (404). This novel might work well in a history course on the social, political, and cultural history of seventeenth-century England.

Many of the novels I have discussed in the preceding chapters lend themselves to the kind of "world-building" I try to achieve in my teaching. For my course on historical fiction about medieval and early modern England, I have assigned *Nothing Like the Sun, Kenilworth, Elizabeth and Essex, Orlando, The Tree of Knowledge*, the Garrett novels, Robert Bolt's play about Sir Thomas More, *A Man for All Seasons*, and a fine young adult novel about Eleanor of Aquitaine by E. L. Konigsburg called *A Proud Taste for Scarlet and Miniver*. I like to start the course with Frederick Buechner's *Godric* and an exercise that asks students to read about the twelfth-century Saint Godric in two classic compilations of lives of the saints (by Alban Butler and Sabine Baring-Gould) and then answer a series of questions about the way Buechner's novel expands upon and differs from each account.

Godric is a parody of a conventional saint's life, a spirited uncensored autobiography that undermines the "life" which Reginald of Durham is attempting to compose (the historical Reginald's account is a main source of information about Saint Godric). The episodes in Godric's life are not presented chronologically, since the old man's irreverent ramblings jump from one adventure to another. Moreover, Godric is not always a cooperative subject for hagiography, as in the opening paragraphs of a chapter entitled "How Godric kept Saint Giles's door and went to school":

> "How old were you when Elric died?" asks Reginald.
> "Buck, buck, begawk," I cackle. I flap my arms like wings. "If years were eggs, by then I'd laid some forty-odd."
> Reginald shuts his eyes to work his sum. He counts out on his fingers. "So Henry the First was king," he says. How pleased he is to know.
> "Cockadoodledoo!" I crow. "The wisest thing that old cock ever did was clap Ralph Flambard in the Tower. I've heard it from his own lips how he got away. He made his jailers drunk, then took a rope his friends had sent him in a cask of wine and swung down from his window like a mitred ape. They say his mother was a one-eyed witch."

When Reginald momentarily forgets an event Godric had recounted some days earlier, the old man mocks him and, by extension, the saint's life genre: "'You dunce! You *monk*!' I cry. 'Is your life of Godric then so dull and dry you've dozed through it yourself?'"(128–29). This kind of satirical metafictional commentary on the source text and the process of composition is, as I have shown elsewhere, a recurrent feature of the New Historical Fiction.

The *Godric* exercise establishes a methodology for the students' final papers, comparing the fictional treatments of a major or minor figure in one or more of the novels with biographers' accounts. When asked to describe how the course has helped them to read more perceptively and critically (a question on my department's course evaluation form), some students responded with remarks like "I have learned to be a skeptic when it comes to history, not to take printed word as fact," or "It has helped me to understand another aspect of the constructedness of one's beliefs," or "It has taught me that history is subject to tremendous interpretation," or "I question apparent facts when I read a work that seems factual." Both assignments, I feel, help

students to begin asking the kinds of questions Brenda Marshall poses in
Teaching the Postmodern: "*who* presents *what* history, and *who* reads and
interprets it, toward *what* purpose?" (153)

After teaching the undergraduate historical fiction course and using
Firedrake's Eye in my Shakespeare course I developed a graduate course called
"The New Historical Fiction," designed to pass on my ideas to current and
future high school and college teachers (the course has also attracted some
fiction writers, including a returning student who had supported herself by
writing historical "bodice rippers" for several years). This course begins with
The Name of the Rose along with Eco's *Postscript* and proceeds through the
centuries. I have assigned *Morality Play*, Winterson's *The Passion*, Kurzweil's
A Case of Curiosities, and a number of other novels that exhibit various characteristics of the New Historical Fiction. Some of my students have written
publishable seminar papers about contemporary historical fictions that, in
most cases, have not yet attracted critical attention.

At the other end of the educational spectrum, I have taught a freshman
Shakespeare course coordinated with small sections devoted to issues of identity and diversity in which the instructors assigned a young adult novel that
was explicitly didactic in intent. Published by the Jewish Publication Society,
Pamela Melnikoff's *Plots and Players* invents three Jewish children who meet
Shakespeare during the Lopez incident in 1594. The children become friends
with Lopez, the queen's Jewish physician, and try unsuccessfully to save him
from being executed (many other historical novels set in the 1590s include or
refer to the Lopez incident). Shakespeare is writing *The Merchant of Venice* at
the time, and near the end of the novel young Robin Fernandez asks him,
"But why must the Jew be a villain? Why can't he be the hero?" A wise and
practical Shakespeare replies, "No audience would accept such a thing. . . .
The time has not yet come." The conversation continues:

> "Then if we can't be heroes, why can't we at least be human beings?
> *You* know we don't hate Christians, or poison wells, or gloat over our
> money-bags. You know we're just people like any other, except that we
> live in fear of our lives. Such inventions do us nothing but harm. You
> won't let us be giants, but why do we have to be horned beasts?"
> There was a long silence. Then Will Shakespeare, with his eyes cast
> down, replied, "You are right, I cannot deny it." (153)

Like so many other historical novels, this one addresses a question for which
there is no definitive answer; Shakespeare scholars have argued for centuries
about Shylock's character. Melnikoff's Shakespeare creates a Shylock who at
first glance "could have been the twin brother to Marlowe's Barabas" with his
flowing beard and yellow cap, yet when he begins to speak he becomes a
"real person with real grievances" because of Robin's intervention (158).

The Spanish Inquisition, which caused Jews like Robin's family to resettle in England and practice their religion secretly, has inspired some remarkable historical fiction. Not all the victims of persecution were Jewish, as recent novels such as Kathryn Harrison's *Poison* and Sebastiano Vassalli's *The Chimera* attest. I can envision a course that teaches the Inquisition through historical fiction just as I can envision a course on the First World War in which students read Sébastien Japrisot's *A Very Long Engagement* or Sebastian Faulks's *Birdsong*. A course on the history of science could include John Banville's *Kepler* or *Copernicus* and Andrea Barrett's collection of stories *Ship Fever*. If I were teaching American history I might juxtapose a New Historical Fiction like Charles Frazier's *Cold Mountain* with an old one like Stephen Crane's *The Red Badge of Courage*, or design a course with New York City as its focus that began with Michael Pye's *The Drowning Room* and included Peter Quinn's stunning recreation of the Irish race riots of the Civil War era, *Banished Children of Eve*, along with Steven Millhauser's Pulitzer Prize-winning *Martin Dressler*, Caleb Carr's thriller *The Alienist*, and Mark Helperin's magic-realist *Winter's Tale*. For a completely different perspective on the French Revolution from Dickens's *A Tale of Two Cities*, how about having students read Madison Smartt Bell's *All Souls' Rising* in order to understand the impact the revolution had beyond Europe? To give students a sense of what it was like to live in the Middle Ages, why not assign Ann Baer's *Down the Common: A Year in the Life of a Medieval Woman*, which takes the reader month by month through the daily activities of a small English village? A list like this could go on and on.

After all these pages of quotations and citations, I find myself rereading the notebook in which I charted the development of my thinking about the way New Historical Fiction constructs the past. After reading two very strange historical novels, *The Prophet of Compostela* and *Lempriere's Dictionary*, I wrote this note to myself:

> The New Historical Fiction tells you things you didn't know or couldn't possibly learn from a conventional history book—the underside of history—those aspects of the past that otherwise evade notice. It helps you think about the world in ways that are different from the kind of reflection you would otherwise be capable of.

In another effort to define the genre, I noted that:

> A characteristic of the New Historical Fiction is that it at once critiques and imaginatively participates in the historian's method of solving a problem through the gathering and making sense of evidence.

A chance reading of a newspaper essay written by the American novelist Don DeLillo caused me to copy this arresting passage into my notebook:

> The novelist does not want to tell you things you already know about the great, the brave, the powerless and the cruel. Fiction slips into the skin of historical figures. It gives them sweaty palms and head colds and urine-stained underwear and lines to speak in private and the terror of restless nights. (DeLillo 63)

And finally, one last observation about what constructing the past entails:

> Inventing the lives of real people always involves an element of speculation, of answering questions posed by the gaps in the record. The fact that sources resist interpretation by assuming that we know more than we possibly can constitutes an obstacle to be overcome for the historian; for the novelist, it offers an opportunity for creative intervention.

Notes

Chapter 1. Introduction: Historical Fiction Old and New

1. This phrase was introduced by Louis Montrose in 1986. For a discussion of the subsequent use and significance thereof, see Brook Thomas, *The New Historicism and Other Old-fashioned Topics*, p. 7. *The Name of the Rose* was published in Italy in 1980, and was translated into English in 1983. The *Postscript* was published separately in 1984 by Harcourt Brace; the version included in the 1994 paperback reprint of the novel does not contain the illustrations.

2. Weaver's account "In Other Words: A Translator's Journal," is presented as excerpts from his journal over a period of a year.

3. I learned from *Baedeker's Great Britain* that the cathedral was built between 1220 and 1280, with the decorated tower and spire over the crossing, the tallest in England, added between 1330 and 1370 by Robert of Farleigh. The building's marble piers support a weight of 6400 tons (240).

4. These quotations are taken from two essays, in *Tropics of Discourse*: "The Fictions of Factual Representation" (121–34) and "The Historical Text as Literary Artifact" (81–100), originally published in 1976 and 1974 respectively.

5. This is quoted by Jay Parini from Mario Vargas Llosa's essay, "The Truth of Lies" in "Delving Into the World of Dreams by Blending Fact and Fiction." Parini has written three historical novels, most recently *Benjamin's Crossing*, about the cultural critic Walter Benjamin. Parini begins his essay by speaking of the way he works in "a curious, alluring space between fact and fiction."

6. Stanley Fish's controversial Op-Ed piece in the *New York Times* argues for a wholesale rejection of biographies precisely because of the way the "explanatory structures" serve to "call attention to the stretch and strain of conceptual bridges" and "transitions that creak and analyses that you don't believe for a minute," all because "cause and effect are the biographer's very stock in trade, and contingency is what no self-respecting biographer can allow to stand. . . ." (A7).

7. A 1964 annotated bibliography of historical fiction lists hundreds of novels, organized chronologically, geographically, and by author, many of which are no long readily available. Here are just a few examples of novels by women that deal with

sixteenth- and seventeenth-century Britain: Jane Oliver, *The Lion and the Rose* (1958), an "unusual version of the Mary Queen of Scots story"; Anne Powers, *The Gallant Years* (1946), about "Rivalry of native chiefs in Ireland, and invasion by the English"; Hilda Price, *No Way Back* (1953), on the English Civil War; Evelyn Read, *My Lady Suffolk* (1963), on "Protestantism in England during the Reign of Tudors"; Eve Stephens, *All the Queen's Men* (1960), on Tudor England; Sally Watson, *Mistress Malapert* (1955), on Shakespeare and the Globe Theatre; Alice Herwood, *So Merciful a Queen, so Cruel a Woman* (1958), the story of Lady Jane Grey; and Eleanor Hibbard, *The Spanish Bridegroom* (1956), on Philip of Spain. For more examples, see Hanna Logasa, 65–77.

8. Matthews's essay contains a good example of the way nineteenth-century critics defined the historical novel: "A tale of the past is not necessarily a true historical novel: it is a true historical novel only when the historical events are woven into the texture of the story" (20).

9. Turner divides historical fiction into three kinds: "those that invent a past, those that disguise a documented past, and those that re-create a documented past" (335).

10. See, for example Faye Kellerman's *The Quality of Mercy: A Novel of Intrigue in Elizabethan England*. This mass market novel, which depicts a young Shakespeare in love with the daughter of Queen Elizabeth's physician Roderigo Lopez, is a colorful romance novel that ends with the composition of *The Merchant of Venice*, much as *Plots and Players* does (see chapter 7).

11. A very interesting feminist historical fiction dramatizing this approach to the past is Judith Merkle Riley's *The Serpent Garden* (1996), in which a young woman miniaturist named Susanna Dalet gains access to the major political figures in early sixteenth- and seventeenth-century England and France through her portrait painting. Invented modern catalogue descriptions interspersed through the novel attribute Susanna's miniatures to anonymous painters or male contemporaries, a reminder, among other things, that women artists often have no place in the historical record. A fiction-biography like *Artemisia* fills in the historical gaps using an actual historical figure; Riley, by contrast, imagines the women artists whose names have been lost.

Chapter 2. Of Narrators; or How the Teller Tells the Tale

1. At the very beginning of her career as an historical novelist Finney had written a novel about the mythic Irish warrior Cuchulain, in a style reminiscent of Renault's historical novels. *A Shadow of Gulls* (1977) was followed a year later by a sequel, *The Crow Goddess* (1978), which paid closer attention to the women of second-century Ireland and Britain. Finney subsequently wrote historical detective fiction set in Elizabethan England under the pseudonym P. F. Chisholm, employing a more conventional style than she had used for *Firedrake's Eye*.

2. See Schoenbaum, *William Shakespeare*, 112. See also Schoenbaum, *Shakespeare's Lives*, p. 105, in which Schoenbaum explains that the story originated with Sir William Davenant, who told Betterton, who told Rowe, who told Pope; eventually, it came to the attention of Johnson, who included it in *The Lives of the Poets of Great Britain and Ireland* and again in his edition of Shakespeare.

Chapter 3. Historical Novelists at Work:
George Garrett and Anthony Burgess

1. Burgess, a Joyce scholar among his other accomplishments, credits Stephen Dedalus in the Scylla and Charybdis chapter of *Ulysses* with this theory about Richard. There are a number of echoes of this chapter in *Nothing Like the Sun*, particularly the speculations about Shakespeare's wife Anne, whom Joyce calls "poor Penelope in Stratford," of whom there is "no mention . . . during the thirtyfour years between the day she married him and the day she buried him" (*Ulysses* 202). Stephen wonders why William was attracted to the names Richard and Edmund, saying "you will say those names were already in the chronicles. . . . Why did he take them rather than others? Richard, a whoreson crookback, misbegotten, makes love to a widowed Ann (what's in a name?) and wins her, a whoreson merry widow. Richard the conqueror, third brother, came after William the conquered" (211).

2. Williams quotes at length from the letter (254, 255, 256, 265). The "busy week" is the one in which Tounson wrote the November 9 letter, not the week culminating in Raleigh's execution on October 29.

3. A play entitled *Kit Marlowe* by David Grimm (1999; unpublished) combines these two roles; Thomas Walsingham is at once the friend and protector of the flagrantly homosexual and Faustus-like Kit and a reluctant lover whose arranged marriage is about to occur during the action of the play. The play was performed at the Public Theatre in New York in October-November 2000.

4. Menton goes on to say that the New Historical Novel's narrators often question their own discourse through parenthetical phrases and words like "perhaps" (23).

5. Wallace's biography of Sir Walter Raleigh contains an appendix listing no fewer than seventy-three variant spellings of Raleigh's name as it appeared in contemporary documents, and Raleigh himself used several of them (319).

6. The letter can be found in volume four of Henry James's *Letters*, ed. Leon Edel (Cambridge: Harvard University Press, 1984), 208. John Updike also quotes from it in a review essay on Thomas Mallon's *Henry and Clara*, in the *New Yorker*. James felt that the historical novel is "almost impossible" because "You have to *think* with your modern apparatus a man, a woman—or rather fifty—whose own thinking was intensely otherwise conditioned, you have to simplify back by an amazing *tour de force*—and even then it's all humbug" (Updike 102).

Chapter 4. Barry Unsworth's *Morality Play* and the Origins of English Secular Drama

1. Wickham notes that "[b]oth the habit of storytelling and a readiness to receive and respond to stories are well-nigh indispensable forerunners of the successful development of an organized, scripted drama . . ." (*Early English Stages* 126). For another account of the relationship between the sermon and the early drama, see Martha Tuck Rozett, *The Doctrine of Election and the Emergence of Elizabethan Tragedy.*

2. Creeth argues against a conventional evolutionary interpretation of the emergence of Shakespearean tragedy, theorizing instead that there was a "sudden and brilliant resolution midway in [Shakespeare's] career of the problem unresolved by Tudor playwrights of how to make literary tragedy out of the idea of the temptation plays like *The Castell of Perseverance* and *Wisdom Who Is Christ*" (8–9). He believes that Shakespeare "reiterates the patterns of archetypal English moral drama" in his tragedies and that the earliest surviving plays represent states, or kinds of plays that were widely performed up to the sixteenth century (10).

3. Interestingly, the same analogy appears in Lacey and Danziger's discussion of the hand signals used in medieval monasteries. Reading *Monasteriales Indicia*, with its 127 signs, they observe, "one gets the impression that mealtimes in a Benedictine refectory were rather like a gathering of baseball coaches, all furiously beckoning, squeezing their ear lobes, meaningfully rubbing their fingers up and down the sides of their noses, and smoothing their hands over their stomachs" as they signaled to one another to pass the wine or the salt (106).

4. There is an example of this in Bulwer's discussion of an incident in *Coriolanus*, in which a gesture in North's *Plutarch* became a stage direction in Shakespeare's play, at the pivotal moment in the play when Coriolanus cries out "Oh, Mother! what have you done to me?" and "*Holds her by the hand silent*" according to the First Folio. Joseph notes that Poussin painted Coriolanus holding his mother's hand in the manner described by Bulwer, which suggests that the actors used the gestures Bulwer describes (60-61).

5. Greenhall uses the passage from *Rubens and His Circle* as the frontispiece to his novel, and cites Duchartre, along with several other sources, in an author's note at the end.

Chapter 5. Fictional Queen Elizabeths and Women-Centered Historical Fiction

1. Quoted by Susan Frye in *Elizabeth I: The Competition for Representation*, 106. Frye gives the source as Historical Manuscripts Commission; *Report on the Manuscripts of Lord De L'Isle and Dudley Preserved at Penshurst Place*, and notes that an attempt to erase the words "and her faire neck" had been made by an earlier editor.

2. This theory has been current since the earliest written documents about Elizabeth; most notably, Ben Jonson famously wrote that the Queen had a membrane that made her incapable of sexual intercourse, though nevertheless "for her delight she tryed many" and contemplated having it cut when she was negotiating a marriage with Alencon. For this and other rumors see Carole Levin, "*The Heart and Stomach of a King*": *Elizabeth I and the Politics of Sex and Power*, 86.

3. In *World Historical Fiction: An Annotated Guide to Novels for Adults and Young Adults*, Lynda G. Adamson lists novels chronologically by subject with a brief description of the subject. The period 1492 to 1649 contains many novels about Elizabeth, including several about her relationships with Leicester and Essex, as well as novels about Anne Boleyn, Mary Queen of Scots, Frances Howard, Catherine Howard, Katherine Parr, Lady Jane Grey, Margaret Tudor (sister of Henry VIII), Bess Throckmorton (wife of Sir Walter Raleigh), and several novels proposing different theories about the death of Amy Robsart. There is also a Web site bibliography which I consulted in March 2000 devoted exclusively to novels about Elizabeth: http://www/bangor/ac.uk/hip01c/novels.htm.

4. *Elizabeth and the Prince of Spain* was also reprinted in 1969. According to the book jacket, Irwin wrote eleven other novels, mostly historical, including one on Mary Queen of Scots.

5. For the text of Ashley's February 1549 testimony, see *Elizabeth I: Collected Works*, edited by Leah Marcus, Janel Mueller, and Mary Beth Rose, 280.

6. Weir includes an exhaustive bibliography of over three hundred entries but no endnotes, so we cannot trace this conversation to its source.

7. This author's note appears at the end of Robin Maxwell's third Queen Elizabeth novel, *Virgin: Prelude to the Throne* (Arcade 2001), a prequel to *The Secret Diary of Anne Boleyn*. A more conventional novel than either of the earlier ones, *Virgin* dramatizes the Seymour affair, employing the steamy sexual language of "bodice ripper" romances. In the author's note, Maxwell addresses the kinds of questions she received from readers of her earlier novels and reviews selected historians' treatments of the ambiguities and contradictions in the historical record. The "guiding inspiration" behind her inventions, she concludes, "has been Elizabeth and Dudley's deep and abiding love for one another" (242).

8. There is certainly precedent for Maxwell's reconstruction of the past: historical fictions about lost heirs to the throne are at least as old as William Thackeray's *Henry Esmond* (1852). (This novel, in the form of a memoir, deals in part with the disappearance of Queen Anne's brother, the "Pretender," James III, who was taken up by the Catholic cause in the early eighteenth century). Anne Meeker's *The Queen's Rings: The True Romance of Elizabeth, Queen of England*, proposes Francis Bacon as the son of Elizabeth and Dudley, based on a decoding of passages from *The Advancement of Learning* by a cipher expert named Colonel George Fabyan. Meeker's Elizabeth and Dudley marry secretly when she is six months pregnant. In January 1561 a son is born, and Elizabeth is prepared to kill him "for his own sake" when Anne Bacon asks for him as "a little brother for Anthony." The decoded passages

include Bacon's claim that "I, therefore, being the first borne sonne of this union should sit upon the throne . . . "; these appear in a detailed appendix that includes Bacon's own instructions for reading the ciphers (277, 271) and facsimiles of the relevant pages in the 1605 edition of *The Advancement of Learning*.

9. In *Envoy from Elizabeth* Pamela Bennetts places an invented secret Spanish agent among the queen's inner circle; he plots to assassinate her at the outself of the Armada invasion. Three swashbuckling adventurers who lead double lives as country gentlemen infiltrate Philip's court and learn the assassin's identity.

10. In an interesting discussion about Elizabeth's much-debated chastity Milton Waldman, in *Elizabeth and Leicester*, quotes the line as reported by an unnamed source: "that though she loved, and always had loved, Lord Robert, as God was her witness, nothing improper had ever passed between them." Waldman observes wryly that "if the hypothesis of her chastity be true, her revision into a prodigy of innocence and his [Leicester's] into a monument of marble constancy [are] guises not easily reconcilable with their own natures" (61–62).

11. In *England of Elizabeth*, A. L. Rowse gives a fuller-than-usual account of the incident, adapted from the source-text, a memoir by the antiquarian William Lambarde. Not long after the Essex conspiracy, Lambarde brought Elizabeth a Latin catalogue of the documents reposing in the Tower.

She then politely asked the meaning of such terms as *oblata, litterae clausae*, and *litterae patentes*, giving the old scholar the opportunity to expound what she perhaps understood, and assuring him "that she would be a scholar in her age and thought it no scorn to learn during life, being of the mind of the philosopher who in his last years began with the Greek alphabet." Then, casting her eye down the list of reigns of the kings, "her Majesty fell upon the reign of King Richard II saying, 'I am Richard II. Know ye not that?'" Lambarde answered: "Such a wicked imagination was determined and attempted by a most unkind gentleman, the most adorned creature that ever your Majesty made." 37–38.

12. The original letter is included Marcus, et. al. (286–87); it is one among several similarly opaque letters Elizabeth wrote to James in 1586.

Chapter Six. Rewriting Shakespeare: The Henriad with and without Falstaff

1. For further discussion of Shakespeare appropriations, revisions, and offshoots, see Martha Tuck Rozett, *Talking Back to Shakespeare*.

2. Bullough notes that

"The Chronicles, from Thomas Walsingham to Stow, described at least six legendary incidents relating to his misbehaviour, most of them going back directly or indirectly to stories told by the 4th Earl of Ormonde and included by the English translator of Titus Livius's *Life of Henry V*: (1) the robbing of the

Receivers; (2) the riot in Eastcheat; (3) the striking of the Lord Chief Justice and the committal of the Prince to prison; (4) the Prince's coming to court strangely dressed and carrying a dagger; (5) the Prince's visit to his dying father during which he took away the Crown; (6) his dismissal of his former companions after the Coronation. (4: 159-60)

3. Unless otherwise noted, all quotations from Shakespeare's plays are taken from *The Riverside Shakespeare*, ed. G. Blakemore Evans et al.

4. Holinshed's account of the episode relates that the Percy faction "were greeved, bicause the king demanded of the earle and his sonne such Scotish prisoners as were taken at Homeldon and Nesbit," to which the Percys replied that the prisoners were "their owne proper prisoners, and their peculiar preis . . ." (Bullough 4: 184).

5. Saccio notes that Worcester's treachery was a tradition that Shakespeare inherited, and quotes Holinshed as follows: Worcester's aim "was ever (as some write) to procure malice and set things in a broil" (50).

6. According to Saccio,

Fastolfe was a notable veteran, at various times governor or captain of conquered French cities, whose deeds are approvingly mentioned in the chronicles. One episode marred his career: his retreat from Patay after the capture of Talbot could be interpreted as cowardice. Bedford (not Talbot, as in the play) temporarily stripped him of his Garter while the matter was investigated. He was exonerated of cowardice and the Garter restored, but the one incident, exaggerated in the chronicles, caught Shakespeare's attention. . . . (112)

7. Although he does not include this passage, Bullough quotes from the *Gesta Henrici Quinti*, citing the 1850 edition by B. Williams.

8. Nye is described as a poet, journalist, and critic on the jacket cover of *The Late Mr. Shakespeare* and has written, among other things, fantasy novels and a retelling of *Beowulf*.

Chapter Seven. Teaching Shakespeare's England through Historical Fiction

1. Suleiman cites Roman Jakobson on the distinction between the poetic and the communicative functions of fiction.

Works Cited

Ackroyd, Peter. *Chatterton.* New York: Grove Press, 1987.

——. *English Music.* New York: Knopf. 1992.

——. *Hawksmoor.* New York: Harper, 1985.

Adamson, Lynda G. *World Historical Fiction: An Annotated Guide to Novels for Adults and Young Adults.* Phoenix, AZ: Oryx Press, 1999.

Anthony, Katherine. *Queen Elizabeth.* New York: Knopf, 1929.

Aridjis, Homer. *1492.* New York: Penguin Plume, 1985.

——. *The Lord of the Last Days.* Trans. Betty Ferber. New York: William Morrow, 1994.

Axelrod, Alan. *Elizabeth I CEO: Strategic Lessons from the Leader Who Built an Empire.* Paramus, NJ: Prentice Hall, 2000.

Baedeker's Great Britain. Englewood Cliffs, NJ: Prentice Hall, n.d.

Baer, Ann. *Down the Common: A Year in the Life of a Medieval Woman.* New York: M. Evans and Co., 1997.

Baldick, Chris. *The Concise Oxford Dictionary of Literary Terms.* Oxford: Oxford UP, 1990.

Banks, Russell. "Creating a Morally Coherent Universe." *New York Times Book Review* 1 Aug. 1993: 27.

Banville, John. *Doctor Copernicus.* 1976. Reprint, New York: Random House, 1993.

——. *Kepler.* New York: Vintage, 1981.

Barrett, Andrea. *Ship Fever.* New York: W. W. Norton, 1996.

Barth, John. "Historical Fiction, Fictitious History, and Chesapeake Bay Blue Crabs, or About Aboutness." *The Friday Book: Essays and Other Nonfictions.* New York: G. P. Putnam, 1984.

———. *The Sot-Weed Factor.* 1960 Rev. ed. New York: Doubleday, 1967.

Begiebing, Robert. *The Adventures of Allegra Fullerton.* Hanover, NH: UP of New England, 1999.

———. *The Strange Death of Mistress Coffin.* Chapel Hill: Algonquin Books, 1996.

Bell, Madison Smartt. *All Souls' Rising.* New York: Penguin, 1995.

Belsey, Catherine. *Critical Practice.* London: Routledge, 1980.

Bennetts, Pamela. *Envoy from Elizabeth.* New York: St. Martin's Press, 1973.

Bermann, Sandra. Introduction. *On the Historical Novel.* By Alessandro Manzoni. Lincoln: U of Nebraska P, 1984.

Bernbaum, Ernest. "The Views of the Great Critics on the Historical Novel." *PMLA* 41 (June 1926): 424–441.

Betterton, Thomas. Adapt. *The Sequel of Henry the Fourth; With the Humours of Sir John Falstaffe, and Justice Shallow.* 1721. Facsimile reprint, London: Cornmarket Press, 1969.

Bevington, David. *From Mankind to Marlowe: Growth and Structure in the Popular Drama of Tudor England.* Cambridge: Harvard UP, 1962.

Bolt, Robert. *A Man for All Seasons.* New York: Random House, 1960.

Bricklebank, Peter. Untitled. *The New York Times Book Review.* 15 Oct. 2000: 23.

Brown, John Russell. Introduction. *The Life and Humours of Falstaff.* By Charles Short. 1829. Facsimile reprint, London: Cornmarket Press, 1971.

Bucknell, Peter A. *Entertainment and Ritual 600–1600.* London: Stainer and Bell, 1979.

Buechner, Frederick. *Godric.* San Francisxo: Harper Collins, 1980.

Bullough, Geoffrey. *Later English History Plays.* London: Routledge and Kegan Paul; New York: Columbia UP, 1962. Vol. 4 of *Narrative and Dramatic Sources of Shakespeare.*

Burgess, Anthony. *A Dead Man in Deptford.* New York: Carroll and Graf, 1993.

———. "Genesis and Headache." *Afterwords: Novelists on Their Novels.* Ed. Thomas McCormack. New York: Harper and Row, 1969.

———. *Nothing Like the Sun.* New York: W. W. Norton, 1964.

————. *Shakespeare.* 1970. Chicago: Ivan R. Dee Elephant, 1994.

Byatt, A. S. *Angels and Insects.* New York: Random, 1992.

————. *The Biographer's Tale.* New York: Knopf, 2000.

————. *On Histories and Stories: Selected Essays.* Cambridge: Harvard UP, 2001.

————. *Possession: A Romance.* NY: Random House, 1990.

Camden, William. *The History of the Most Renowned and Victorious Princess Elizabeth Late Queen of England.* 1688. Reprint, New York: AMS Press, 1970.

Carr, Caleb. *The Alienist.* New York: Random House, 1994.

Chamberlin, Frederick. *The Private Character of Queen Elizabeth.* London: John Lane and The Bodly Head, 1922.

Cherry, Kelly. "Meaning and Music in George Garrett's Fiction." *To Come Up Grinning: A Tribute to George Garrett.* Ed. Paul Ruffin and Stuart Wright. Huntsville, TX: Texas Review Press, 1989.

Chevalier, Tracy. *Girl with a Pearl Earring.* New York: Penguin Putnam, 2001.

Coletta, Christina della. *Plotting the Past: Metamorphoses of Historical Narrative in Modern Italian Fiction.* West Lafayette, IN: Purdue UP, 1996.

Connell, Evan S. *The Alchymist's Journal.* San Francisco: North Point Press, 1991

Cook, Judith. *The Slicing Edge of Death: Who Killed Christopher Marlowe?* New York: St. Martin's, 1993.

Cowell, Stephanie. "New Shakespearean Novel." An interview by Thomas A. Pendleton. *The Shakespeare Newsletter* 43. 2, No. 217 (Summer 1993: 1, 28–29.

————. Nicholas Cooke: *Actor, Soldier, Physician, Priest.* New York: W. W. Norton, 1993.

————. *The Physician of London.* New York: W. W. Norton, 1995.

————. *The Players: A Novel of the Young Shakespeare.* New York: W. W. Norton, 1997.

Craik, T. W. The Tudor Interlude: Stage, Costume, and Acting. Leicester: Leicester UP, 1958.

Creeth, Edmund. *Mankynde in Shakespeare.* Athens, GA: U of Georgia P, 1976.

de Bernieres, Louis. *Corelli's Mandolin.* New York: Vintage, 1994.

DeLillo, Don. "The Power of History." *New York Times Magazine* 7 Sept. 1997: 60–63.

Demos, John. "In Search of Reasons for Historians to Read Novels. . . ." AHA Forum on Histories and Historical Fiction. *American Historical Review* 103.5 (1998): 1526–29.

Dillard, R. H. W. "The Elizabethan Novels: *The Succession.*" *George Garrett: The Elizabethan Trilogy.* Ed. Brook Horvath and Irving Malin. Huntsville, TX: Texas Review Press, 1998.

Ducharte, Pierre Louis. *The Italian Comedy.* 1929. Trans. Randolph T. Weaver. New York: Dover, 1966.

Eco, Umberto. *The Island of the Day Before.* Trans. William Weaver. New York: Harcourt Brace, 1994.

———. *The Name of the Rose.* Trans. William Weaver, 1980. New York: Harcourt Brace, 1994.

———. *Six Walks in the Fictional Woods.* Cambridge: Harvard UP, 1994.

Engler, Bernd. "The Dismemberment of Clio: Fictionality, Narrativity, and the Construction of Reality in Historiographic Metafiction." *Historiographic Metafiction in Modern American and Canadian Literature.* Ed. Bernd Engler and Kurt Muller. Paderborn, Germany: Ferdinand Schoningh, 1994. 13–33.

Evans, G. Blakemore, et. al. *The Riverside Shakespeare.* Boston: Houghton Mifflin, 1974.

Faulks, Sebastian. *Birdsong.* New York: Random House, 1993.

Feuchtwanger, Lion. *The House of Desdemona or The Laurels and Limitations of Historical Fiction.* Trans. Harold A. Basilius. Detroit: Wayne State UP, 1963.

Figes, Eva. *The Seven Ages.* New York: Ballantine, 1986.

———. *The Tree of Knowledge.* New York: Ballantine, 1990.

Finney, Patricia. *Firedrake's Eye.* New York: St. Martin's, 1992.

———. *Unicorn's Blood.* New York: Picador, 1998.

Fish, Stanley. "Just Published: Minutiae without Meaning." *New York Times* 7 Sept. 1999: A7.

Fitzgerald, Penelope. *The Blue Flower.* Boston: Houghton Mifflin, 1995.

Fleishman, Avrom. *The English Historical Novel: Walter Scott to Virginia Woolf.* Baltimore: Johns Hopkins Press, 1971.

Fludernik, Monika. "History and Metafiction: Experientiality, Causality, and Myth." *Historiographic Metafiction in Modern American and Canadian Literature.* Ed. Bernd Engler and Kurt Muller. Paderborn, Germany: Ferdinand Schoningh, 1994, 81–101.

Ford, Ford Maddox. *The Fifth Queen.* 1908. Introd. A. S. Byatt. Reprint, New York: Penguin, 1999.

Forster, Margaret. "This Is Sort of Your Life, Mary Wollstonecraft." *New York Times Book Review* 11 Jul. 1993: 21.

Fowler, Alistair. *Kinds of Literature: An Introduction to the Theory of Genres and Modes.* Cambridge MA: Harvard, 1982.

Frazier, Charles. *Cold Mountain.* New York: Atlantic Monthly Press, 1997.

Frye, Susan. *Elizabeth I: The Competition for Representation.* New York: Oxford UP, 1993.

Fuentes, Carlos. *Terra Nostra.* New York: Farrar, 1975.

Garrett, George. *Death of the Fox: A Novel of Elizabeth and Ralegh.* 1971. Reprint, New York: William Morrow, n.d.

———. "Dreaming with Adam: Notes on Imaginary History." *The Sorrows of Fat City: A Selection of Literary Essays and Reviews.* Columbia, SC: U of South Carolina P, 1992. 19–35.

———. *Entered from the Sun.* New York: Doubleday, 1990.

———. "The Historical Novel Today: Two Instances." *The Sewanee Review* 104.3 (Summer 1996): 456–60.

———. *The Succession: A Novel of Elizabeth and James.* New York: Harcourt Brace Jovanovich, 1983.

Gass, William. "The Neglect of *The Fifth Queen*." *The Presence of Ford Maddox Ford.* Ed. Sandra J. Stang. Philadelphia: U of Pennsylvania P, 1981.

Giardina, Denise. *Good King Harry.* New York: Harper & Row, 1984. New York: Ballantine, 1999.

Gira, Catherine, and Adele Seeff. *Henry IV Parts 1 and 2: An Annotated Bibliography*. New York: Garland Publishing, 1994.

Glover, Douglas. *The Life and Times of Captain N*. New York: Knopf, 1993.

Golding, William. *The Spire*. New York: Harcourt Brace, 1964.

Goldman, James. *Myself as Witness*. New York: Random House, 1979.

Graham, Alice Walworth. *The Summer Queen: A Novel About the Last Plantagenets*. Garden City, NY: Doubleday, 1973.

Green, Peter. *The Laughter of Aphrodite: A Novel about Sappho and Lesbos*. 1965. Berkley: U of California P, 1993.

Greenhall, Ken. *Lenoir*. Cambridge, MA: Zoland Books, 1998.

Grimm, David. *Kit Marlowe*. Unpublished play, 1999.

Haasse, Hella S. *In a Dark Wood Wandering*. 1949. Trans. Edith Kaplan. Reprint, Chicago: Academy Chicago Publishers, 1991.

———. *The Scarlet City: A Novel of Sixteenth Century Italy*. 1954. Trans. Edith Kaplan. Reprint, Chicago: Academy Chicago Publishers, 1991.

———. *Threshold of Fire: A Novel of Fifth Century Rome*. 1954. Reprint, Chicago: Academy Chicago Publishers, 1993.

Haigh, Christopher. *Elizabeth I*. London: Longman, 1988.

Happé, Peter, ed. *Medieval English Drama*. London: Macmillan, 1984.

Harbage, Alfred, and Samuel Schoenbaum. *Annals of English Drama 975–1700*. London: Methuen, 1964.

Harper, Karen. *The Poyson Garden*. New York: Delacorte Press, 1999.

———. *The Tidal Poole*. New York: Delacorte Press, 2000.

———. *The Twilight Tower*. New York: Delacorte Press, 2001.

Harrison, Kathryn. *Poison*. New York: Random House, 1995.

Helperin, Mark. *Winter's Tale*. New York: Simon and Schuster, 1983.

Holman, Sheri. *The Dress Lodger*. New York: Atlantic Monthly Press, 2000.

———. *A Stolen Tongue*. New York: Atlantic Monthly Press, 1997.

Holmes, Frederick M. *The Historical Imagination: Postmodernism and the Treatment of the Past in Contemporary British Fiction*. Victoria: U of Victoria English Literary Studies, 1997.

Houle, Peter J. *The English Morality and Related Drama: A Biographical Survey.* Hamden, CT: Archon, 1972.

Humphrey, Richard. *The Historical Novel as Philosophy of History.* London: U of London; Bithell Series of Dissertations, 1986.

Hutcheon, Linda. *A Poetics of Postmodernism: History, Theory, Fiction.* New York and London: Routledge, 1988.

Irwin, Margaret. *Elizabeth and the Prince of Spain.* London: Chatto and Windus, 1953. Reprint, Allison and Busby, Ltd., 1999.

———. *Elizabeth, Captive Princess.* New York: Harcourt Brace, 1948. Allison and Busby, Ltd., 1999.

———. *That Great Lucifer: A Portrait of Sir Walter Ralegh.* London: Chatto and Windus, 1960.

———. *Young Bess.* New York: Harcourt Brace, 1945. Reprint, London: Allison and Busby, Ltd., 1999.

Jacobs, Naomi. *The Character of Truth: Historical Figures in Contemporary Fiction.* Carbondale: Southern Illinois UP, 1990.

Japrisot, Sébastien. *A Very Long Engagement.* 1991. Trans. Linda Coverdale. New York: Plume, 1994.

Jenkins, Elizabeth. *Elizabeth the Great.* New York: Coward-McCann, 1958.

Joseph, B. L. *Elizabethan Acting.* London: Oxford UP, 1964.

Joyce, James. *Ulysses.* 1914. New York: Random House, 1961.

Kay, Susan. *Legacy.* New York: Crown, 1985.

Kearns, Cleo McNelly. "Dubious Pleasures: Dorothy Dunnett and the Historical Novel." *Critical Quarterly* 32.1 (Spring 1990): 36–43.

Kellerman, Faye. *The Quality of Mercy: A Novel of Intrigue in Elizabethan England.* New York: Fawcett, 1989.

Kendrick, Mr. *Falstaff's Wedding: A Comedy being A Sequel to the Second Part of the Play of King Henry the Fourth.* 1760. Facsimile reprint, London: Cornmarket Press, 1969.

Konigsburg, E. L. *A Proud Taste for Scarlet and Miniver.* New York: Dell, 1973.

Kurzweil, Allen. *A Case of Curiosities.* New York: Ballantine Books, 1992.

Lacey, Robert, and Danny Danziger. *The Year 1000: What Life Was Like at the Turn of the First Millennium: An Englishman's World*. Boston: Little, Brown, 1999.

Lapierre, Alexandra. *Artemisia: A Novel*. Trans. Liz Heron. New York: Grove Press, 1998.

Lascelles, Mary. *The Story-Teller Retrieves the Past: Historical Fiction and Fictitious History in the Art of Scott, Stevenson, Kipling, and Some Others*. Oxford: Clarendon, 1980.

Levin, Carole. *"The Heart and Stomach of a King": Elizabeth I and the Politics of Sex and Power*. Philadelphia: U of Pennsylvania P, 1994.

Logasa, Hanna. *Historical Fiction*. 8th rev. enl. ed. Philadelphia: McKinley Publishing, 1964. Vol. 1 of *McKinley Bibliographies*.

Lukacs, Georg. *The Historical Novel*. 1955. Trans. Hannah Mitchell and Stanley Mitchell. Lincoln: U of Nebraska P, 1983.

Lytle, Andrew Nelson. "The Image as Guide to Meaning in the Historical Novel." *The Sewanee Review* 61 (1953).

Maitre, Doreen. *Literature and Possible Worlds*. London: Middlesex Polytechnic Press, 1983.

Malin, Irving. "Hermetic Fox-Hunting." *George Garrett: The Elizabethan Trilogy*. Ed. Brooke Horvath and Irving Malin. Huntsville, TX: Texas Review Press, 1998.

Manzoni, Alessandro. *On the Historical Novel*. Trans. Sandra Bermann. Lincoln: U of Nebraska P, 1984.

Marcus, Leah, Janel Mueller and Mary Beth Rose, eds. *Elizabeth I: Collected Works*. Chicago: U of Chicago P, 2000.

Marshall, Brenda. *Teaching the Postmodern: Fiction and Theory*. New York: Routledge, 1992.

Matthews, Brander. "The Historical Novel." *The Historical Novel and Other Essays*. 1901. Freeport, NY: Books for Libraries Press, 1968.

Maxwell, Robin. *The Queen's Bastard*. New York: Simon and Schuster, 1999.

———. *The Secret Diary of Anne Boleyn*. New York: Simon and Schuster, 1997.

———. *Virgin: Prelude to the Throne*. New York: Arcade, 2001.

Maza, Sara. "Stories in History: Cultural Narratives in Recent Works in European History." *American Historical Review* 101.5 (1996): 1493–1515.

McHale, Brian. *Postmodern Fiction*. New York and London: Methuen, 1987.

Meeker, Anne. *The Queen's Rings: The True Romance of Elizabeth, Queen of England*. Chicago: Daniel Ryerson, Inc., 1936.

Melnikoff, Pamela. *Plots and Players*. Philadelphia: Jewish Publication Society, 1988.

Menton, Seymour. *Latin America's New Historical Novel*. Austin: U of Texas P, 1993.

Miles, Rosalind. *I, Elizabeth*. New York: Doubleday, 1994.

Miller, Andrew. *Ingenious Pain*. New York: Harcourt Brace, 1997.

Millhauser, Steven. *Martin Dressler: The Tale of an American Dreamer*. New York: Vintage, 1997.

Morgan, Cynthia. *Court of Shadows*. New York: Ballantine, 1992.

Mortimer, John. *Will Shakespeare: The Untold Story*. New York: Delacorte Press, 1977.

Mumby, Frank A. *The Girlhood of Queen Elizabeth: A Narrative in Contemporary Letters*. Intro. R. S. Rait. London: Constable and Co., 1909.

Neale, J. E. *Queen Elizabeth I*. 1934. Garden City, NY: Doubleday, 1957.

Nicholl, Charles. *The Reckoning: The Murder of Christopher Marlowe*. New York: Harcourt Brace, 1992.

Nietzsche, Friedrich. *The Use and Abuse of History*. 1876. Trans. Adrian Collins. New York: Macmillan, 1957.

Norfolk, Thomas. *Lempriere's Dictionary*. New York: Harmony Books, 1991.

Nye, Robert. *Falstaff*. Boston: Little Brown, 1976.

————. *The Late Mr. Shakespeare*. London: Chatto and Windus, 1998. New York: Arcade Publishing, 1999.

————. *The Voyage of the "Destiny."* New York: G. P. Putnam, 1982.

Onega, Susan. "British Historiographic Metafiction in the 1980s." *British Postmodern Fiction*. Ed. Theo D'haen and Hans Berteus. Amsterdam: Rodopi, 1993.

Orel, Harold. *The Historical Novel from Scott to Sabatini: Changing Attitudes toward a Literary Genre, 1814–1920*. New York: St. Martin's, 1995.

Pargeter, Edith. *A Bloody Field by Shrewsbury*. 1972. Reprint, London: Headline Book Publishing, 1989.

———. *The Heaven Tree Trilogy*. New York: Warner Books, 1993. Reprint of *The Heaven Tree*. 1960. *The Green Branch*. 1962. *The Scarlet Seed*. 1963.

Parini, Jay. "Delving into the World of Dreams by Blending Fact and Fiction." *The Chronicle of Higher Education*. 27 Feb. 1998: B4–5.

Pears, Iain. *An Instance of the Fingerpost*. New York: Riverhead Books, 1998.

Penman, Sharon Kay. *The Sunne in Splendour*. New York: Ballantine, 1982.

Peters, Ellis, and Ray Morgan. *Shropshire*. New York: Time Warner, 1992.

Plowden, Alison. *The Young Elizabeth*. New York: Stein and Day, 1971.

Porter, Dale H. "The Gold in Fort Knox: Historical Fiction in the Court of Historiography." *Soundings* 76.2–3 (1993): 315–49.

Potter, Robert. *The English Morality Play: Origins, History and Influence of a Dramatic Tradition*. London: Routledge and Kegan Paul, 1975.

Pye, Michael. *The Drowning Room*. London: Penguin, 1995.

Quinn, Peter. *Banished Children of Eve*. New York: Penguin, 1995.

Renault, Mary. "Notes on *The King Must Die*." *Afterwords: Novelists on Their Novels*. Ed. Thomas McCormack. New York: Harper and Row, 1969.

Riley, Judith Merkle. *The Oracle Glass*. New York: Random House, 1984.

———. *The Serpent Garden*. New York: Viking, 1996.

Rowse, A. L. *The England of Elizabeth: The Structure of Society*. New York: Macmillan, 1951.

———. *Sir Walter Ralegh: His Family and Private Life*. NY: Harper, 1962.

Rozett, Martha Tuck. *The Doctrine of Election and the Emergence of Elizabethan Tragedy*. Princeton: Princeton UP, 1984.

———. *Talking Back to Shakespeare*. Newark, DE: U of Delaware P, 1994. Urbana, IL: NCTE, 1995.

Saccio, Peter. *Shakespeare's English Kings: History, Chronicle and Drama*. New York: Oxford UP, 1977.

Schama, Simon. *Dead Certainties (Unwarranted Speculations)*. New York: Knopf, 1991.

Schell, Edgar T., and J. D. Schucter. *English Morality Plays and Moral Interludes*. New York: Holt, Rinehart and Winston, 1969.

Schoenbaum, Samuel. *Shakespeare's Lives*. Oxford: Clarendon Press, 1970.

———. *William Shakespeare: A Documentary Life*. New York: Oxford UP, 1975.

Scott, Sir Walter. *Kenilworth*. 1821 New York: Airmont, 1969.

Seton, Anya. *Katherine*. Boston: Houghton Mifflin, 1954.

Shakespeare, William. *The Riverside Shakespeare*. Ed. G. Blakemore Evans, et. al. Boston: Houghton Mifflin, 1974.

Shaw, Harry E. *The Forms of Historical Fiction: Sir Walter Scott and His Successors*. Ithaca: Cornell UP, 1983.

Sherwood, Frances. *Vindication*. New York: Farrar, 1993.

Short, Charles. *The Life and Humours of Falstaff*. 1829. Facsimile reprint, London: Cornmarket Press, 1971.

Simmons, John S. "*Measure for Measure*: Links to Our Time." *Teaching Shakespeare Today. Practical Approaches and Productive Strategies*. Eds. James E. Davis and Ronald E. Salamone. Urbana, IL: NCTE, 1993.

Sontag, Susan. *The Volcano Lover*. New York: Farrar, 1992.

Southern, Richard. *The Staging of Plays before Shakespeare*. New York: Theatre Art Books, 1973.

Spears, Monroe K. "George Garrett and the Historical Novel." *To Come Up Grinning: A Tribute to George Garrett*. Ed. Paul Ruffin and Stuart Wright. Huntsville, TX: Texas Review Press, 1989: 61–72.

Steffler, John. *The Afterlife of George Cartwright*. New York: H. Holt, 1993.

Strachey, Lytton. *Elizabeth and Essex: A Tragic History*. 1928. New York: Harcourt Brace, n.d.

Strong, Roy. *The Cult of Elizabeth: Elizabethan Portraiture and Pageantry*. London: Thames and Hudson, 1977.

Suleiman, Susan. *Authoritarian Fictions: The Ideological Novel as a Literary Genre*. New York: Columbia UP, 1983.

Suskind, Patrick. *Perfume*. Trans. John E. Woods. New York: Washington Square Press–Simon and Schuster, 1985.

Sutcliff, Rosemary. *The Shining Company*. New York: Farrar, 1990.

Szczypiorski, Andrzej. *Mass for Arras*. New York: Grove Press, 1993.

Talbot, Margaret. "Inside Publishing." *Lingua Franca* (Nov./Dec. 1992).

Tarr, Judith. *Pillar of Fire.* New York: Tor Books, 1995.

Tey, Josephine. *The Daughter of Time.* 1951. New York: Washington Square Press, 1977.

Tillinghast, Richard. "The Fox, Gloriana, Kit Marlow, and Sundry." *George Garrett: The Elizabethan Trilogy.* Ed. Brooke Horvath and Irving Malin. Huntsville, TX: Texas Review Press, 1998.

Tremain, Rose. *Restoration.* New York: Penguin, 1989.

Thomas, Brook. *The New Historicism and Other Old-fashioned Topics.* Princeton: Princeton UP, 1991.

Thorpe, Adam. *Ulverton.* New York: Farrar, 1992.

Turner, Joseph W. "The Kinds of Historical Fiction: An Essay in Definition and Methodology." *Genre* 12 (1979): 333–55.

———. Letters to the author. 11 Sept., 19 Sept., 3 Oct. 1999.

Unsworth, Barry. *Morality Play.* New York: Norton, 1995.

———. *Sacred Hunger.* New York: W. W. Norton, 1992.

Updike, John. *Gertrude and Claudius.* New York: Knopf, 2000.

———. "Thomas Mallon's *Henry and Clara.*" *New Yorker* 5 Sept. 1994: 102–105.

Vassalli, Sebastian. *The Chimera.* New York: Scribner, 1990.

Vidal, Gore. "Reel History." *New Yorker* 10 Nov. 1997: 115.

Vincenot, Henri. *The Prophet of Compostela.* Trans. E. E. Rehmus. Rochester, VT: Inner Traditions International, 1996.

Vreeland, Susan. *Girl in Hyacinth Blue.* New York: Penguin, 1999.

Waldman, Milton. *Elizabeth and Leicester.* Boston: Houghton Mifflin, 1945.

Wallace, Willard M. *Sir Walter Raleigh.* Princeton: Princeton UP, 1959.

Walsh, Jill Paton. *Knowledge of Angels.* Boston: Houghton Mifflin, 1994.

Warner, Sylvia Townsend. *The Corner That Held Them.* 1948. Reprinted in *Four in Hand.* New York: W. W. Norton, 1986.

Warren, Wini. "The Search for Copernicus in History and Fiction." *Soundings*. Spec. issue on History and Historical Fiction (Summer-Fall 1973): 383–406.

Waugh, Patricia. *Metafiction: The Theory and Practice of Self-Conscious Fiction*. London: Methuen, 1984.

Weaver, William. "In Other Words: A Translator's Journal." *New York Times Book Review* 19 Nov. 1995: 16–20.

Weil, Herbert, and Judith Weil, eds. *The First Part of King Henry IV*. New Cambridge edition. Cambridge: Cambridge UP, 1997.

Weir, Alison. *The Life of Elizabeth I*. New York: Ballantine, 1998.

Wesseling, Elisabeth. *Writing History as a Prophet: Postmodern Innovation of the Historical Novel*. Amsterdam and Philadelphia: John Benjamins, 1991.

Whalen, Tom. "Eavesdropping in the Dark: The Opening(s) of George Garrett's *Entered from the Sun*." *To Come Up Grinning: A Tribute to George Garrett*. Ed. Paul Ruffin and Stuart Wright. Huntsville, TX: Texas Review Press, 1989: 90–98.

White, Hayden. *Tropics of Discourse: Essays in Cultural Criticism*. Baltimore: Johns Hopkins UP, 1978.

Wickham, Glynne. *Early English Stages 1300–1660*. London: Routledge and Kegan Paul, 1981. Vol 3 of *Plays and Their Makers to 1576*.

———. *The Medieval Theatre*. 3rd ed. Cambridge: Cambridge UP, 1987.

Williams, Norman Lloyd. *Sir Walter Raleigh*. London: Eyre and Spottiswoode, 1962.

Winterson, Jeanette. *The Passion*. New York: Vintage, 1987.

———. *Sexing the Cherry*. New York: Vintage, 1989.

Wolf, Christa. *Cassandra: A Novel and Four Essays*. Trans. Jan Van Heurck. New York: Farrar, 1984.

Woolf, Virginia. *Orlando: A Biography*. 1928. Reprint, New York: Harcourt Brace and Jovanovich, n.d.

York, Robert. *My Lord the Fox: The Secret Documents of Anthony Woodcott Concerning the Year 1560*. London: Constable, 1984.

Yourcenar, Marguerite. *The Abyss.* 1968. Trans. Grace Frick. Reprint, New York: Farrar, 1976.

————. *Memoirs of Hadrian.* New York: Farrar, 1954.

————. "Reflections on the Composition of *Memoirs of Hadrian.*" In *Memoirs of Hadrian.* New York: Penguin, 1986.

————. "Tone and Language in the Historical Novel." *That Mighty Sculptor, Time.* Trans. Walter Kaiser. New York: Farrar, 1992.

Index

DATE DUE